PENGUIN BOOKS

100 Samurai Companies

100 Samurai Companies

JAPAN'S TOP 100 GROWTH OTC COMPANIES

Henry Scott-Stokes

PENGUIN BOOKS

PENGUIN BOOKS

Published by the Penguin Group
Penguin Books Ltd, 27 Wrights Lane, London w8 5TZ, England
Penguin Putnam Inc., 375 Hudson Street, New York, New York 10014, USA
Penguin Books Australia Ltd, Ringwood, Victoria, Australia
Penguin Books Canada Ltd, 10 Alcorn Avenue, Toronto, Ontario, Canada M4V 3B2
Penguin Books (NZ) Ltd, Private Bag 102902, NSMC, Auckland, New Zealand

Penguin Books Ltd, Registered Offices: Harmondsworth, Middlesex, England

First published 1999
1 3 5 7 9 10 8 6 4 2

Copyright © Japan Investment Journal, 1999

For more information contact:
Japan Investment Journal (Nikkan Toshi Shimbun)
3–5, Shinkawa 1-Chome
Chuo-ku
Tokyo 104-0033
Japan

Tel.: +813 3297 2411
Fax.: +813 3297 2428
website: http://www.invest.co.jp

Set in 7.75/10.5 pt PostScript Monotype Sabon
Typeset by Rowland Phototypesetting Ltd, Bury St Edmunds, Suffolk
Printed in England by Clays Ltd, St Ives plc

Contents

Introduction

Small Japanese companies are not an obvious priority interest at this time of recession, verging on crisis, in Japan. Many big firms – banks, construction companies, retail chain giants – are in dire straits, their balance sheets loaded with debt following 8 years of Japan's longest recession since the 1930s. Surely it is the large firms that one should worry about? A further succession of corporate and bank failures could shatter world confidence. Japan has the second largest economy in the world, still; this country is the major creditor nation. A crisis in Japan could undermine confidence in the US economy in two seconds flat. Imagine Wall Street in the sudden absence of Japanese funds, Tokyo brokers, say, holding their breath.

All of the above may be correct. Yet should one turn a blind eye to all hopeful indications, as the Western financial press does? Perhaps not. There are, for example, signs of vitality in the 'small cap' company sector in Japan. Some 856 companies were registered on the Jasdaq (Japan Securities Dealers Association) lists at the end of 1998, as compared with only 196 at the end of 1988 (*see* Chart One). There has been a rush of small firms going public.

But what about the big companies, it may be reiterated? If they go bankrupt, the smaller companies will crash in tens of thousands. Bankruptcies are already at record levels for the last 40 years, as is unemployment among high school and university graduates. These ills may be traced to the collapse of asset values at the end of Japan's financial Bubble of the late 1980s. Japan has never recovered from that enormous reversal of fortunes . . . Yet if the country is to recover, it may be said, new blood has to come into the system. New firms, new bosses and new technology have to prevail. Our attention turned accordingly to the Jasdaq, not the only over-the-counter market in Japan – there are local markets in Osaka, Nagoya and elsewhere – but much the largest of these institutions.

Half a dozen different points of interest have driven forward this project – *100 Samurai Companies* – carried out by a team organized by *Nikkan*

Toshi Shimbun, a Tokyo afternoon daily owned by Claremont Capital Holding (chairman Yoshihiko Kokura):

1. Some remarkable little companies – in terms of technology brought to bear – chose to register themselves on the Jasdaq of late, such companies as Accès, an Osaka-based computer systems developer, first on our list for alphabetical reasons; Trend Micro, an anti-computer-virus company; Hikari Tsushin, a telecom firm rapidly spreading through the country; and Fancl, a non-additive cosmetics company. These and other companies constitute perhaps the most exciting crop of little firms, for all that most of them are still truly *small*, to appear since the late 1940s, that singular era in Japanese corporate history that gave birth to Sony, Honda, Pioneer, Omron, Sanyo Electric and others. For decades there has been a dearth of exciting newcomers. Now all of a sudden there are dozens of them to be seen.

2. An over-the-counter market, it should be explained, serves as a preliminary to the real thing, a stock market with major listing requirements. A company that comes to register on the Jasdaq, to make an 'initial public offering', or IPO, a first offering of its stock to the public, faces much less formidable criteria, especially in recent years, than one applying to go onto the much more prestigious Tokyo Stock Exchange. Jasdaq is a testing ground for companies wanting to go onto greater things. Relaxation of the criteria for registering there is generally credited with having brought about a brief leap in trading on the Jasdaq (*see* Chart Two) and in the value of IPOs in the late 1990s (*see* Chart Three).

3. Jasdaq, it is commonly remarked, is not much more than a pale version of the world's most publicized OTC market, the Nasdaq in New York, a home to Microsoft, Intel and other giants of our time. For years, that has been true, Japanese brokers agree. The Nasdaq took off in the early 1990s, but the Jasdaq totally failed to follow. The Jasdaq index stood at a 10-year low (*see* Chart Two again) at the end of 1998, while the Nasdaq had leaped by over 40% in that year alone. Yet Japanese analysts believe that the Jasdaq was close to a lowest possible level in late 1998; they say that trading in the last quarter of 1998, which saw some spectacular rises in a few stocks, mirroring New York, suggests that the Jasdaq can pick up an American flavour. 'The Japanese like to follow a well-beaten path in investment,' said a veteran broker.

4. Foreign analysts and fund managers are mostly sceptical of such thinking, or they were up to early 1999. Foreign investors, say

Japanese experts, have never been more active than in recent months in Jasdaq stocks (*see* Chart Four). Foreign buying accounted for 29% of purchases in 1998, and 23% of sales, with purchases thereby exceeding sales; by contrast, the largest group of investors were Japanese individuals who accounted for 48% of sales as against 41% of purchases, with the balance on the sellers' side. Sooner or later foreign trading on the Jasdaq is likely to exceed that of private investors here, observers say. Yet the scepticism of foreign investors remains widespread. Jasdaq stocks are too little traded for a foreign fund manager to be able to build up a position in a stock. Accounts are far from transparent. Selling out a position can prove impossible, without sacrifices in the form of lower prices. The bedrock of doubt among foreign investors is firmly implanted among the best performers among foreign fund managers over years. Yet the trading figures suggest that, sooner or later, foreign investors will dominate the Jasdaq, just as they have taken over as the driving force on the (somewhat moribund) Tokyo stock market as a whole.

5. It is not easy to rebut such criticisms as that company accounting standards are inadequate. However, some Jasdaq companies are aware of the general shortcomings and are taking action to improve reporting standards on their own account. Yahoo! Japan is one case that comes to mind: the company, still very small in size, has insisted on reporting quarterly, instead of making earnings forecasts that, as President Masahiro Inoue noted in an interview, 'could simply be wrong, or at best misleading – no one knows in advance what earnings will be, so it is much better to come out with those quarterly figures in timely fashion, as in the US'. Another company that has opted for higher standards than those usual on the Jasdaq is Sawako, a Nagoya-area systems builder; its President, Junichi Ohira, decided to join the Nasdaq, thereby committing himself to full reporting. It can be maintained that these efforts are so exceptional as to merit little attention. Yahoo! Japan's quarterly accounts stand out as unusual; simply the way they are printed looks strident and un-Japanese to some local eyes. Sawako is actually the first Jasdaq company to join the Nasdaq in a quarter of a century. However, Japanese analysts believe that companies like these two point the way to the future. 'Foreign investors are going to be the big force on the Jasdaq sooner or later,' said an analyst, 'that being the case, those firms that hold to high accounting standards will get the attention of those crucial investors.'

6. The task, once we had settled on the Jasdaq as a target, then became

to select a given number of promising companies. We chose 100 as a round number. How to select 100 firms? On the whole, we preferred to rest our choice on historical performance – selecting companies whose sales and current profits rose by 5% or more consecutively in three successive years to 1998; by this means we gathered 70 firms. It remained to include a certain number of highly prospective firms, with record earnings prospects; by this means – details are explained in an appendix that lists the 100 firms and identifies which criteria were used to select them – another 28 firms were identified. A round figure of 100 was obtained by adding in two relief players, with exceptional records. The analyst who made the first 98 selections, it may be mentioned, played no part in the reporting, and received no access to the company entries which follow. No one apart from our core team saw our work.

7. The resulting grab-bag of Jasdaq firms is open to criticism in that it includes many small, and some tiny, service companies – a number of catering establishments – that investors, including foreign investors, may never take much interest in. However, we believe we obtained a cross-section of some of the liveliest new and up-and-coming companies in all of Japan by the methods used. Having a cross-section seemed to us no bad thing given the way the economy is growing. But what a cross-section! These days the old manufacturing industries – steel, shipbuilding, heavy chemicals – are totally out of it. What the Japanese economist Tadashi Nakamae has called 'the old economy' is no more. Not one of those 'old' companies from heavy or manufacturing industry showed up in our collection of 100. Their performances did not qualify them. Instead, we found ourselves with a collection of service-based firms: in computer software, in retail and wholesale, in Internet marketing, in anything but the industries that made Japan's name 40 years ago. One auto-industry-related company featured in our original selection, and begged permission to withdraw, pleading a sudden deterioration in its numbers!

8. Not that we expect the future to be easy for many Jasdaq members. About half the current 856 members are, to judge by their accounts, on the verge of trouble if not deeply into it already. We learned that the Jasdaq authorities, however, are bent on a strategy of weeding out – de-selecting is the term used – firms that show signs of flagging. At the same time the officials say that they are pleased by the response from the broking community to Jasdaq-sponsored requests for a much more comprehensive effort at so-called 'book-building', i.e. preparing for public issues in advance, by seeking out potential

investors and establishing possible prices – rather than simply throwing issues on the market, only to see values collapse within a matter of weeks of the original issue, an all-too-common practice, pursued by brokers eager to make quick fees, in recent years.

Most observers of Japan still expect Disastersville to continue. To be sure, the outlook for the next 4 to 5 years is at best uncertain. It is a time when prophets – there are a few such economists in Japan – come into their own. One such is Mr. Tadashi Nakamae, quoted below from an article published by the *FT* on 31 December 1998, just as we were concluding our reporting for this work. He wrote:

I believe that Japan's future hinges upon whether this new (service-based) economy will be able to grow fast enough over the next 10 years to provide new jobs for 20 million Japanese – roughly one-third of the present working population. The engine for growth in the new economy will be small service-providing companies, typically with a workforce of around 10 people. Every year, if Japan's new economy is to absorb the 2 million unemployed released from the old economy, a net 200,000 such companies will need to be created.

So! Japan has to become a California of the 1980s, as in the days of the Reagan-era 'supply-side revolution'? Impossible! Yet what is the alternative? The fact is that Big Bangs – to use the term originating from Britain's financial deregulation in the 1980s – are transforming all the crucial areas in Japan, not only the financial industry, but the media, wholesale/retail industries and telecoms. Everything. To expect Japan to become another Golden State may be too much. But to imagine that things can stay put where they are is hard too. None of our 100 companies got where they are by standing still. None would have qualified on that basis. Most, in fact, were created by one man in the course of the last 30 years, starting from scratch. Among them might there be a new Sony? It is not too much to hope for, however far-fetched the idea may seem in today's downtrodden Japan.

January 20, 1999

A few words are in order on the text that follows. The ages of chief executives are given as of December 31, 1998. The payroll numbers for companies are last available totals, obtained from the firms by us, mostly for late summer 1998. All financial numbers are non-consolidated. Earnings estimates with a single star are from Toyo Keizai Shinposha, acknowledged with thanks. Lists of shareholders are of the same date as the number of shareholders. Thanks are hereby rendered to the team which worked on this reference book, namely Dennis Yang, who controlled the flow of operations and attended interviews; Kazno Kurosawa, who tabled and checked numbers on computer, Mayumi Kubota who did additional reporting; and Akio Suzuki and Shuzo Hanzawa, senior members of the Nikkon Toshi Shimbun staff.

Chart One

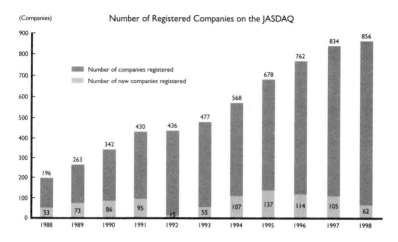

(Companies)   Number of Registered Companies on the JASDAQ

Number of companies registered
Number of new companies registered

Source: JASDA

Chart Two

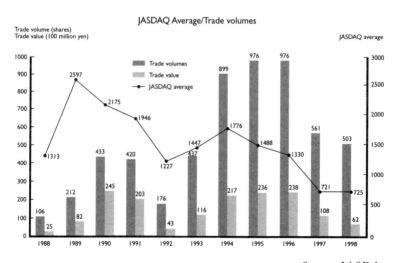

Trade volume (shares)
Trade value (100 million yen)

JASDAQ Average/Trade volumes

JASDAQ average

Trade volumes
Trade value
JASDAQ average

Source: JASDA

Chart Three

JASDAQ Companies' Equity Finance

(100 million yen)

- ▨ Capital increase through public offering
- ▨ Private placement of new shares, capital increase through third-party allocation
- —●— Convertible bond (domestic)
- ··▲·· Convertible bond (overseas)

6,000

5,000

4,000

3,000

2,000

1,000

0

	1988	1989	1990	1991	1992	1993	1994	1995	1996	1997	1998

Values shown: 816, 455, 155, 407, 104, 3,338, 4,317, 1,391, 1,015, 175, 0, 3,277, 1,374, 628, 300, 691, 490, 248, 104, 2,127, 1,336, 725, 63, 3,569, 1,544, 1,625, 112, 3,520, 721, 385, 26, 5,111, 1,755, 815, 676, 120, 1,990, 437, 142, 200, 418, 160, 1,179

Source: JASDA

Chart Four

Shareholders by Investors on the JASDAQ

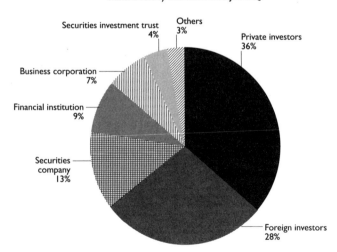

- Securities investment trust 4%
- Others 3%
- Private investors 36%
- Business corporation 7%
- Financial institution 9%
- Securities company 13%
- Foreign investors 28%

Source: JASDA

100 Samurai Companies

Accès

(Estd. 1994, listed 1998, stock code no. 4700)
Company address: 3-5-1 Bakuro-machi, Chuo-Ku, Osaka 541-0059
Tel: 81-6-6282-1600 Fax: 81-6-6282-1730

A system integrator, claimed to be independent, working with IBM Japan in conjunction with corporate clients in the Kansai. Owner/founder and President, Tsugio Murakami, 50, owns 46% of the stock. 119 employees.

Product/Sales breakdown: Accès has made an explosive debut in the recession. While others languished, this company went from a standing start in 1994 to ¥2 billion sales in its 1996/7 year and over ¥3 billion in the year to March '98. Gross margins were estimated at over 20% in the current and subsequent years, 1998/9 and 1999/2000. The company attributes 100% of its turnover to "systems integration". Murakami-san offers no breakdown.

Rivals/Competitors: The company says that it is "difficult" to name any particular rival, but NTT Information Systems, a division of NTT, comes to mind.

History/Strategy: Murakami-san, with a background of employment at Toshiba, NCR Japan and Lake, a consumer finance company (an unusual career), made it his strategy from the outset to line up with big corporate clients (see the stockholders' list on the opposite page). "Our accumulated expertise is concentrated in our proprietary integrated CASE tool 'Planet', developed by Object-Oriented approach," says the company.

Management: Accès is an extremely unusual case of a company, run and owned by one man, zooming to prominence in a short period.

Outlook/Hot News: When Accès was launched by underwriters Nomura and Nikko in July 1998, it caught the public eye. Other instances come to mind – Trend Micro, Yahoo! Japan – of firms that made recent debuts with extraordinary numbers. Accès is in that league and furthermore was created by a Japanese entrepreneur (while Trend Micro and Yahoo! Japan are foreign-owned). This case suggests that deregulation is having an impact on the software development industry. A Big Bang is going on in software development, as in finance and the media. Will Accès' brilliant results continue – with a 20% margin on sales? With clients and shareholders like Sumitomo Bank, Nippon Life and Meiji Life – and its ties with IBM – owner Mr. Murakami has strong support in the Kansai. Accès is "a powerful high-spirited contender in the fast-paced field of system development", says the company. Not that all is for the best. 1998/9 earnings forecasts look like being not met, to judge by first half results. Could this be a sign that competitors are coming to life?

Tsugio Murakami / President

Stocks (¥50,000 par value)

Shares Issued (Jul. 30, '98)	4,960 shares
No. of Shareholders (Sep. 30, '98)	41

Major Holders	(%)
Tsugio Murakami	46.0
Nomura Securities	6.0
Meiji Life Ins.	2.9
IBM Japan	2.9
JAFCO	2.1
Employees' Stockholding	1.8
Sumitomo Bank	1.4
Foreign Owners	0.5

Earnings

Period	Sales	Operating Profit	Current Profit	Net Profit	Earnings Per Share	Dividend Per Share
Mar 96	1,644	204	233	160	N/A	10,000.00
Mar 97	1,979	317	315	207	70,545.5	12,500.00
Mar 98	3,063	506	502	342	105,112.9	12,500.00
**Mar 99	4,140	900	850	500	125,000.0	12,500.00
*Mar 00	4,600	1,000	1,000	590	147,500.0	12,500.00
Mid-Term						
Sep 98	1,957	304	225	158	39,003.7	0
*Sep 99	2,100	350	350	180	45,000.0	0

*Estimates; **Company estimates. Per share values in ¥, all other amounts in millions of ¥.*

Balance sheet summary	1995	1996	1997	1998
Current assets	337	801	1,142	1,337
Fixed assets	156	252	761	1,071
Total assets	493	1,053	1,904	2,409
Current liabilities	390	781	686	750
Fixed liabilities	35	25	183	200
Total liabilities	426	806	870	950
Capital Stock	20	50	370	450
Shareholders' equity	67	247	1,034	1,458
Total liabilities and equity	493	1,053	1,904	2,409

Note: All amounts in millions of ¥. Balance sheet, end March..

Akatsuki Printing

(Estd. 1948, listed 1963, stock code no. 7918)
Company address: 1-44-4, Sekiguchi, Bunkyo-ku, Tokyo 112-0014
Tel: 81-3-3268-3155 Fax: 81-3-3267-8777

A small printing house, based in Tokyo. 168 employees, family-owned. President is Seiji Adachi, 45.

Product/Sales breakdown: The company prints periodicals – including *Shukan Manga Goraku*, a comic – and has long worked with Kadokawa Shoten, a leading book publisher set up after World War Two. Publication-related printing accounts for 52% of turnover, other printing for 8%. Other business accounts for the remaining 40% of revenues.

Rivals/Competitors: Little Akatsuki is dwarfed by the industry leaders. Records show that in the last full business year Dai-Nippon Printing recorded revenues of ¥1.16 trillion; and Toppan Printing (also a Tokyo Stock Exchange first section firm) ¥966 billion. To survive, Akatsuki has borrowed against its property holdings – borrowing from leading city banks; long-term debt extending up to 2006 totals ¥1.3 billion, according to Bloomberg.

History/Strategy: If earnings forecasts are right (see facing page) little Akatsuki will not claw its way back very far up to March 2000, the end of its next business year. Interest charges, even at current low rates, cut deep into operating profits on a potentially much expanded revenue stream. The credit squeeze – banks have been doing their utmost to call in loans to their clients, pressing customers to repay ahead of schedule – has, no doubt, made life interesting for Akatsuki President Adachi.

Management: Ideally, Adachi-san will succeed in paying back some of those loans from the banks (Asahi Bank, Sumitomo Bank) in advance, given that interest rates may rise.

Outlook/Hot News: Akatsuki Printing is the smallest of the 14 printing companies listed in Japan. Printing is an industry that has taken knocks in the recession. Yet Akatsuki's case shows that the "logic" of the market – allowing only giants such as Toppan Printing to survive – does not necessarily prevail. The company's long-standing relationship with Kadokawa Shoten (the self-described "Mega Software Publisher") was a factor in Akatsuki's survival (Kadokawa boasted sales of ¥80.4 billion in its year to March '98, and net income of ¥4.8 billion; like Akatsuki it has its roots in post-World War Two Tokyo). Another consideration, perhaps, has been that, when hard pressed, people will work for very little. Management has been effective of late, to judge by results, i.e. rising revenues. The key to the improvement has been diversification. An *Asian Wall Street Journal* article of January 3, 1999 alluded to Akatsuki Printing as a franchisee of Sazaby, the upmarket fashion and fancy goods house, also a Jasdaq firm. With some 40% of its revenues coming from non-printing sources, it looks as if even the "weakest" can survive. The prospect is for Akatsuki to diversify out of printing increasingly.

Seiji Adachi / President

Stocks (¥50 par value, 1,000 shares min. trade)

Shares Issued (Nov. 1, '98)   7,525,000 shares
No. of Shareholders (Sep. 30, '98)   511

Major Holders	(%)
Tadashi Yokokawa	46.5
Norio Yokokawa	18.6
Shigenori Kitamura	5.1
Shiki Corp.	2.1
T F Consults	1.3
Seiji Adachi	1.3

Foreign Owners   3.3

Earnings

Period	Sales	Operating Profit	Current Profit	Net Profit	Earnings Per Share	Dividend Per Share
Mar 96	2,818	84	53	54	13.7	0
Mar 97	3,561	143	83	79	16.9	0
Mar 98	5,303	224	90	87	17.3	0
*Mar 99	6,990	340	180	40	5.3	0
*Mar 00	8,000	400	250	130	17.3	0
Mid-Term						
Sep 97	2,394	63	23	21	4.3	0
*Sep 98	3,240	74	1	180	23.9	0

*Estimates. Per share values in ¥, all other amounts in millions of ¥.

Balance sheet summary	1994	1995	1996	1997	1998
Current assets	663	1,302	2,055	3,749	4,889
Fixed assets	814	1,094	1,326	2,317	4,033
Total assets	1,478	2,404	3,474	6,388	9,511
Current liabilities	1,025	977	1,527	2,290	4,664
Fixed liabilities	678	641	1,107	1,128	1,790
Total liabilities	1,703	1,619	2,634	3,418	6,454
Capital Stock	100	580	580	1,605	1,605
Shareholders' equity	−225	785	840	2,970	3,057
Total liabilities and equity	1,478	2,404	3,474	6,388	9,511

Note: All amounts in millions of ¥. Balance sheet, end March.

Altech

(Estd. 1981, listed 1996, stock code no. 4641)
Company address: 1-16-18, Nishi-Hashimoto, Sagamihara City, Kanagawa Pref. 229-1131
Tel: 81-42-774-3333 Fax: 81-42-774-5420

An engineering company, active in FA (factory automation). Works for others. Run by President Minoru Nakamura, 62. He has 1,330 employees.

Product/Sales breakdown: The company despatches its engineers to work with others on a temporary basis, as on-the-job helpers (59% of all revenues); or it does the jobs others want done in-house (the remaining 41% of revenues).

Rivals/Competitors: There are two rivals: Meitec, a larger company, employing 4,000 people, based near Nagoya; and Hitec, a Kyoto company. Their work is similar to Altech's, though their strategies are somewhat different (see below).

History/Strategy: To get to Altech Corp. from Tokyo you have to drive half way to Mount Fuji, eventually arriving at a modest head office. A girl asks you to take off your shoes and put on a pair of brown slippers . . . This is the provinces, not Tokyo any more . . . In such a setting the personality of the founder – his character, his decisions, his goals and vision – counts for a lot. President Nakamura, a stocky, smiling-faced engineer, constantly refers to "the owner". That person, Chairman Toshio Matsui, was absent the day we called; but on the wall of the sitting room was a large oil painting of a Himalayan peak. The owner has a first love: mountains. Hence the name of the company in Japanese: "Alps". Unusually, the company has two names: "Alps" within Japan, "Altech" outside (another company, Alps Electric, uses the "Alps" name overseas).

Management: The meishi (cards) used by Nakamura-san carry a company motto in English on one side: "The human makes future – The specialist of designing machines & electrical equipments". That is what they do at this fairly large company: design machines (and systems) for others. Often one-off jobs. What distinguishes Altech from its two rivals – Meitec and Hitec – is that Altech has its own factory, set up in 1990. "Since we have a factory, a workplace of our own, we can test new ideas, technology . . . and produce (a result) in a very short time," says Nakamura. The rivals lack their own factories.

Outlook/Hot News: Altech carries no borrowing on its balance sheet. It has a flow of orders, a busy workforce . . . what is wanting? Matsui-san, spending half the year in the Himalayas, is accustomed to delegation. Sooner or later, he has to make arrangements for the succession. That thought must be on his mind. But he is in no hurry. One doesn't hasten in the provinces, only those people in Tokyo do . . . Meanwhile, the firm is taking on 200 or so fresh graduates a year. Banzai!

Minoru Nakamura / President

Stocks (No-par value, 1,000 shares min. trade)

Shares Issued (Jun. 30, '98)	4,696,882 shares
No. of Shareholders (Jun. 30, '98)	814

Major Holders	(%)
Toshio Matsui	25.3
Matsui Management Laboratory	11.1
Employees' Stockholding	4.7
Sumitomo Trust	2.9
Bank of Yokohama	2.3

Foreign Owners	6.2

Earnings

Period	Sales	Operating Profit	Current Profit	Net Profit	Earnings Per Share	Dividend Per Share
Dec 95	5,052	414	392	170	56.2	7.50
Dec 96	5,762	457	420	260	81.6	15.00
Dec 97	7,180	469	517	260	65.6	20.00
**Dec 98	8,100	540	570	250	53.2	15.00
**Dec 99	9,000	580	600	280	54.2	10.00
Mid-Term						
Jun 98	3,994	249	269	92	19.6	0
**Jun 99	4,200	270	280	130	25.2	0

**Company estimates. Per share values in ¥, all other amounts in millions of ¥.

Balance sheet summary	1993	1994	1995	1996	1997
Current assets	939	1,177	1,182	1,722	2,863
Fixed assets	2,071	1,986	1,999	2,213	2,746
Total assets	3,010	3,163	3,182	3,936	5,610
Current liabilities	1,005	1,244	1,229	870	1,006
Fixed liabilities	710	5,834	416	48	54
Total liabilities	1,715	1,778	1,645	919	1,061
Capital Stock	528	528	528	832	1,502
Shareholders' equity	1,295	1,384	1,536	3,016	4,548
Total liabilities and equity	3,010	3,163	3,182	3,936	5,610

Note: All amounts in millions of ¥. Balance sheet, end December.

AM Japan

(Estd. 1957, listed 1963, stock code no. 8047)
Company address: 5-3, Koji-machi, Chiyoda-ku, Tokyo 102-0083
Tel: 81-3-3230-4611 Fax: 81-3-3262-9784

A used-car dealer, based in an upmarket part of Tokyo. Taken over by JAC in 1996. 142 employees. President is Yoshihiro Fujimaru, 59.

Product/Sales breakdown: Revenues shot up (from a low level) after the takeover by JAC (that name derives from "Japan Assessment Centre"), an up-and-coming name in the used-car trade that is spreading itself rapidly, using franchises. The best guess is that JAC, eager to see some results, pumped across some of its own business into AM Japan, thereby transforming what was a loss-making rump active in a variety of marketing fields (including printing machinery) into a nationwide used-car dealer network-in-the-making.

Rivals/Competitors: Aucnet, also a Jasdaq company, is the other big name in the used-car trade. Aucnet had "operating revenues" of ¥9.17 billion in the year to December '97. AM Japan, under JAC's direction, has set its sights on overtaking Aucnet or has already done so, assuming numbers are correct.

History/Strategy: JAC (President Noboru Watanabe, 44) aspires to joining the Jasdaq itself, the company's website proclaims. The company, clearly in the driving seat, has coined the slogan "Dreaming dreams & always doing something New (is what life is all about)". Buying control of

AM Japan was "a good move, but only a start", according to the website again. What's missing at JAC is "good employees – so we must recruit 200 a year, bringing in 'young power', to strengthen the company". JAC has built itself up, it turns out, by offering "free surveys" of their cars to owners who come into its "assessment centres".

Management: The turbulent scene over at AM Japan has brought some swift changes in both management and ownership. The shareholder roster now includes Hikari Tsushin, owning 3.5% of the stock.

Outlook/Hot News: Years ago, there was *no* market in second-hand autos in Japan (the cars were dumped in S.E. Asia, not to put too fine a point on it). The Japanese no more bought used cars than they bought, say, old shirts. Today, in recession times, when so many people are worth so much less, the second-hand car market is booming. AM Japan ("Nihon AM" in Japanese) and Aucnet are prominent among the dealer networks emerging in what promises to be a fast-paced business. The fittest will survive. AM Japan, buttressed by JAC, has announced a high target for sales – ¥1 trillion a year, as compared with ¥10 billion in the last full year to March '98. That's a wished-for 100-fold increase in business – wait a moment now!

Yoshihiro Fujimaru / President

Stocks (¥50 par value, 1,000 shares min. trade)

Shares Issued (Nov. 1, '98)	4,253,000 shares
No. of Shareholders (Sep. 30, '98)	321

Major Holders	(%)
JAC	50.5
Ikebata Ltd.	9.6
Shigeru Watanabe	7.5
Hikari Tsushin	3.5
Katsunori Kouto	2.4
Bunka Shutter	1.4
Foreign Owners	1.1

Earnings

Period	Sales	Operating Profit	Current Profit	Net Profit	Earnings Per Share	Dividend Per Share
Jul 96	3,140	−37	−28	−30	−9.5	0
Mar 97	2,723	9	13	11	3.6	0
Mar 98	10,064	525	533	275	73.2	5.00
*Mar 99	17,000	N/A	1,150	600	141.1	5.00
Mid-Term						
Sep 98	7,783	411	438	234	55.2	0

*Estimates. Per share values in ¥, all other amounts in millions of ¥.

Balance sheet summary	1994	1995	1996	1997	1998
Current assets	1,591	1,570	1,530	1,956	3,804
Fixed assets	152	151	148	153	515
Total assets	1,744	1,721	1,679	2,110	4,319
Current liabilities	769	770	792	1,226	2,805
Fixed liabilities	331	334	317	301	225
Total liabilities	1,101	1,105	1,109	1,528	3,031
Capital Stock	162	162	162	162	368
Shareholders' equity	642	616	570	581	1,288
Total liabilities and equity	1,744	1,721	1,679	2,110	4,319

Note: All amounts in millions of ¥. Balance sheet, end March, except 1994–6, end July.

Anrakutei

(Estd. 1978, listed 1997, stock code 7562)
Company address: 2-3-5, Kamiochiai, Yono City, Saitama Pref. 338-0001
Tel: 81-48-859-0555 Fax: 81-48-859-0560

A Korean barbecue chain. A very rapidly expanding business, mainly in the Tokyo area, but based in Saitama, outside the centre. Under chief executive Tokiki Yanagi, 54, the company is opening large-scale, brightly-lit Korean restaurants one after another, with low prices.

Product/Sales breakdown: The main activity is running restaurants (222 by Sept '98) and serving sizzling barbecue and beer. This accounts for 94% of sales/revenues. Separately, foodstuffs sold at the restaurants account for 3% of revenues and royalties for 2%, suggesting that franchising is practised on a limited scale. A residual 1% covers other items. Out of those 222 restaurants, just 177 were directly run, the rest being franchises.

Rivals/Competitors: The restaurant business, considering chains alone, is a wide-open free-for-all in the big cities and environs thereof. Competitors are numerous and include prospering ventures such as Denny's Japan, MOS Food Services, Kentucky Fried Chicken, Skylark, Jonathan's and, of course, McDonald's. Mr. Yanagi, who is Korean by ancestry, is the businessman in Japan who took up the challenge of creating a barbecue chain, offering spicy food and flames to the masses.

History/Strategy: The company's plan, as explained by the ebullient Mr. Yanagi, is to go for "500 restaurants and annual sales of ¥50 billion by the 21st century". The goals appear ambitious, but he is opening 35 new restaurants yearly. Anrakutei management considers diversifying. The company already sells books and magazines (at a loss). It is looking at options in Japanese and Italian cuisine, no holds barred.

Management: Anrakutei's payroll amounted to 589 staff employees at September '98 plus many part-timers. The company has invested in land to build its restaurants on, and carries a considerable burden of debt, including short-term liabilities on its balance sheet. Overall management is by CEO Yanagi and his younger brother Tokitaka, who serves as Executive Vice-President. Finance is in the hands of the CEO who, with members of his family, accounts for 35.7% of the stock. A major shareholder besides is Itochu; the trading company furnishes Mr. Yanagi with an indispensable item, the meat.

Outlook/Hot News: This is for continued expansion as Anrakutei consolidates its so far unmatched entry into the mass barbecue trade. However, Yanagi-san has to consider how much to go on borrowing as he expands and takes on new commitments. Anrakutei is one of the most highly geared of all the "100 Samurai Companies". The ultimate backer, common sense says, is Itochu Corporation (Japan's and the world's largest trading firm); Itochu is itself in poor financial shape, however. Yanagi-san, watch out!

Tokiki Yanagi / President

Stocks (¥50 par value, 1,000 shares min. trade)

Shares Issued (Nov. 1, '98)	9,517,000 shares
No. of Shareholders (Sep. 30, '98)	617

Major Holders	(%)
Itochu Corp.	10.2
Tokiki Yanagi	9.9
Houzan Kaihatsu	9.3
Tokitada Yanagi	8.1
Tokimoto Yanagi	8.1
Sen Yanagi	3.2
In Yanagi	3.2
Foreign Owners	0.0

Earnings

Period	Sales	Operating Profit	Current Profit	Net Profit	Earnings Per Share	Dividend Per Share
Mar 96	13,257	1,120	744	451	705.3	50.00
Mar 97	15,137	1,332	826	409	63.9	5.00
Mar 98	19,585	1,684	1,063	476	70.8	10.00
**Mar 99	24,000	2,190	1,500	780	82.0	10.00
*Mar 00	30,200	2,750	2,000	1,000	105.1	10.00
Mid-Term						
Sep 98	11,766	1,097	755	400	45.2	5.00
*Sep 99	13,500	1,250	880	440	46.2	5.00

*Estimates; **Company estimates. Per share values in ¥, all other amounts in millions of ¥.*

Balance sheet summary	1995	1996	1997	1998
Current assets	5,487	5,502	6,661	6,740
Fixed assets	8,817	10,672	15,265	19,656
Total assets	14,305	16,175	21,927	26,396
Current liabilities	3,498	5,146	7,291	8,093
Fixed liabilities	10,359	10,161	13,401	15,915
Total liabilities	13,857	15,307	20,692	24,008
Capital Stock	320	320	320	680
Shareholders' equity	448	867	1,235	2,387
Total liabilities and equity	14,305	16,175	21,927	26,396

Note: All amounts in millions of ¥. Balance shet, end March.

Argo Graphics

(Estd. 1985, regd. 1998, stock code no. 7595)
Company address: 5-14 Hakozaki-cho Nihonbashi, Chuo-Ku, Tokyo 103-0015
Tel: 81-3-5641-2020 Fax: 81-3-5641-2012

A powerfully connected company selling CAD/CAM/CAE systems to industrial companies, and furnishing maintenance. Stockholders include Sony and Seiko Instruments. CEO Katsumasa Hotta is 60. He has 130 employees.

Product/Sales breakdown: CAD/CAM (computer-aided design/computer-aided manufacture) systems cover 91% of sales, the rest is in maintenance, as against forecast sales of approx. ¥20 billion in the year ending March '99.

Rivals/Competitors: Argo Graphics claims to be a leader in its field in Japan "as competition among manufacturers in new product development and compressed development cycle becomes even more intense," according to Mr. Hotta. The Argo Graphics chief is an ex-Nihon Unisys sales executive who worked for two decades with that sales subsidiary of the US Unisys.

History/Strategy: Argo Graphics was established in 1985 as a sales vehicle for Argotechnos 21, its main shareholder, employing some 700 people with a plant at Iwaki in Fukushima prefecture. Argo Graphics is a specialist in computer graphics, a particular interest of such key shareholders as Seiko Instruments, once headed by the late Ichiro Hattori. "The company does not sell individual pieces of computer hardware and software, but computer systems," explains Mr. Hotta, "that feature CAD, CAM and CAE (computer-aided engineering)". He adds: "we build applications and systems that cover entire networks . . . and position ourselves as a Technical Solution Provider." The company centres its operation around IBM Japan and held "the top spot among IBM Japan Business Partners for six years through 1997". "Manufacturers' use of CAD is becoming more comprehensive . . ." explains Hotta-san, "we have been successful in securing large-scale orders from traditional customers such as Honda Motor and Sony."

Management: "In the near future . . . the market scope for CAD/CAM/CAE will expand as the move to 3-D CAD gathers pace and CAD technology penetrates the small and medium-sized firm market," continues Mr. Hotta.

Outlook/Hot News: The Argo Graphics' executive concludes: "In the medium to longer term, we look forward to strong growth in business . . . arising from . . . the widespread adoption of PDM (Product Data Management) in order to further shorten lead times." Sales and earnings forecasts, however, foreshadow a slowing down in Argo Graphics' advance (see opposite page) due, no doubt, to the recession. Even the most excellent companies cannot easily surmount what promises to be a collapse in investment in some parts of industry, such as already seen in the semiconductor industry. Maintenance, by the way, is said to be highly profitable. It will be instructive to see how far the maintenance proportion in Argo Graphics' revenues (thus far recorded at under 9%) rises in future.

Katsumasa Hotta / President

Stocks (¥50 par value, 1,000 shares min. trade)

Shares Issued (Nov. 31, '98)	4,940,000 shares
No. of Shareholders (Sep. 30, '98)	23

Major Holders	(%)
Argotechnos 21	23.2
Sony	7.2
Seiko Instruments	7.2
Katsumasa Hotta	6.1
Yoshimaro Fujisawa	4.9
Employees' Stockholding	3.8
JAFCO	3.3
Foreign Owners	0.0

Earnings

Period	Sales	Operating Profit	Current Profit	Net Profit	Earnings Per Share	Dividend Per Share
Mar 96	10,042	826	800	286	139,658.5	10,000.00
Mar 97	13,476	1,281	1,258	644	214,807.1	12,500.00
Mar 98	18,486	1,823	1,828	1,079	3,222.8	125.00
**Mar 99	21,000	4,200	2,020	1,109	224.5	44.90
Mid-Term						
Sep 98	9,677	1,478	1,460	860	193.7	0

**Company estimates. Per share values in ¥, all other amounts in millions of ¥.

Balance sheet summary	1995	1996	1997	1998
Current assets	5,628	6,318	7,193	10,071
Fixed assets	1,232	1,174	1,306	1,063
Total assets	6,860	7,492	8,500	11,135
Current liabilities	4,306	3,657	4,325	5,710
Fixed liabilities	1,197	1,635	1,406	1,151
Total liabilities	5,504	5,293	5,731	6,861
Capital Stock	100	391	391	601
Shareholders' equity	1,355	2,199	2,769	4,273
Total liabilities and equity	6,860	7,492	8,500	11,135

Note: All amounts in millions of ¥. Balance sheet, end March.

ARRK

(Estd. 1968, listed 1996, stock code no. 7873)
Company address: 2-4-3, Kawazura-cho, Tondabayashi City, Osaka Pref. 584-0014
Tel: 81-721-24-0430 Fax: 81-721-20-2051

An Osaka-based industrial design company, strong on consumer items like laptop computers and cellular phones (helps its clients by creating moulds for them). Emphasizes helping manufacturers in the entire design process, from initial idea through to creation of the moulds. Employs 202 staff. President is Tadayoshi Igumi, 51.

Product/Sales breakdown: The company does not divulge much about its own production and current projects, much being confidential, apart from financial statistics. Sales and net profits in the year to March '99 were respectively down at ¥5.87 billion and zero, marking the impact of the recession. The emphasis at ARRK is on consumer-product-related work (52% of revenues), auto-industry stuff (29%, including all types of transport-industry-related products), and other items (19%).

Rivals/Competitors: ARRK operates in an exceedingly competitive area. That its relatively high returns were eroded in this year – with a fall in investment outlays in many industries – is no surprise. The company has performed admirably during most of the long-lived 8-year recession.

History/Strategy: ARRK is well served by its connections with major institutions – its shareholders, Fuji Bank and Sanwa Bank, are sources of long-term finance, secured to the company's property and buildings (long-term loans amounted to ¥3.2 billion,

with due dates in late 1999 for Sanwa and 2004 for Fuji, according to Bloomberg). ARRK has good standing among foreign investors, who held 15.9% of its stock. Chairman Toshihiro Araki, 55, the largest individual stockholder, has played a leading role in the company's history.

Management: An ARRK publicity video shows NC (numerical control) machines churning away making those moulds; emphasizes the importance that executives attach to ARRK's "full-line and global network system"; and states that the company is ready to handle challenging one-off jobs.

Outlook/Hot News: Created 31 years ago, ARRK has made a name for itself in product design. It has watching posts overseas in such places as the West Coast, Toronto, Bangkok and western Europe. Industrial design has long been a Japanese forte – look at those cameras etc., at one time always exhibited in the Museum of Modern Art in New York. Meanwhile, ARRK has a reputation for keeping its customers' secrets. If it can get through the next year . . . When Chairman Araki founded the firm in 1968 there were high hopes for the future. That unusual company name, officials say, was derived from "ark" – as in Noah's Ark or the Ark of the Covenant – to which an extra "r" for "romance" was added in the middle. Is life so romantic now? Perhaps not as long as the recession goes on.

Tadayoshi Igumi / President

Stocks (¥50 par value, 1,000 shares min. trade)

Shares Issued (Nov. 1, '98)	7,123,950 shares
No. of Shareholders (Mar. 31, '98)	517

Major Holders	(%)
Water Systems Co.	33.1
Toshihiro Araki	8.4
Toyo Trust	5.8
State Street Bank & Trust	2.9
Jewel	2.6
Yasuda Trust	2.4
Sanwa Bank	2.1
Foreign Owners	15.9

Earnings

Period	Sales	Operating Profit	Current Profit	Net Profit	Earnings Per Share	Dividend Per Share
Mar 96	5,821	758	637	281	445.8	50.00
Mar 97	6,280	948	756	384	57.0	7.50
Mar 98	6,595	1,106	1,016	498	70.0	10.00
**Mar 99	5,870	N/A	695	0	0.0	7.50
Mid-Term						
Sep 98	2,988	279	200	104	14.7	0

**Company estimates. Per share values in ¥, all other amounts in millions of ¥.

Balance sheet summary	1994	1995	1996	1997	1998
Current assets	3,375	3,327	3,431	5,009	5,206
Fixed assets	5,417	5,038	4,920	4,987	4,715
Total assets	8,793	8,365	8,352	9,996	9,921
Current liabilities	1,099	1,219	1,332	1,442	1,424
Fixed liabilities	4,210	3,643	3,268	2,646	2,169
Total liabilities	5,309	4,863	4,600	4,089	3,594
Capital Stock	813	813	813	1,265	1,265
Shareholders' equity	3,483	3,502	3,752	5,907	6,327
Total liabilities and equity	8,793	8,365	8,352	9,996	9,921

Note: All amounts in millions of ¥. Balance sheet, end March.

Aruze

(Estd. 1973, listed 1998, stock code no. 6425)
Company address: 3-1-25, Ariake, Koto-ku, Tokyo 135-0063
Tel: 81-3-5530-3055 Fax: 81-3-5530-3077

A wall of money hit this slot-machine and pachinko machine maker. Aides to President Kazuo Okada, 56, appear at a loss to account for this phenomenal outcome beyond acknowledging that their machines are popular. Aruze, an established firm in its field, recorded 40–50% margins all of a sudden.

Product/Sales breakdown: Aruze machines sell for ¥350,000 – those of the competition for only ¥250,000. With sales of a given new model capable of running up to 100,000 units, the prospective gross revenues from a smash hit like Aruze's "Thunder V" run up to ¥35 billion. Not every machine is going to do that . . . still Aruze is banking on its slot machines, accounting for 80% of sales, rather than on pachinko machines (10% of sales). The vogue for pachinko is no more. Parts, real estate transactions and royalties account for the residual 10% of revenues.

Rivals/Competitors: Call in on a pachinko/slot-machine parlour. The crash of metal balls is huge, the hubbub enhanced by hard acoustics. Anything may happen in such an atmosphere, a visitor reasons. A couple of years ago a rival machine maker, Yamasa, was on top in the market, Mr. Okada's people tell one. Now, the boot is on the other foot. Aruze has a 40% market share, and no other firm – not even Yamasa

– has more than 10%. Hence those huge profits (see facing page).

History/Strategy: Perhaps the most striking discovery, on a visit to Aruze's top security head office in Ariake, a Tokyo waterfront section, is that Japanese taste in slot machines has veered in a different direction from that in the US. In America customers want to have a big handle and haul down on it; in Japan, the latest slot machines have three buttons (no handle). Gentle manipulation of these buttons is the preferred mode, a touching and a stroking . . . not the ram-bang-crash of the US-style slot machine.

Outlook/Hot News: No one knows, or no one is saying at Aruze's head office, whether reports that Mr. Okada is planning to use some part of his booty to go into computer graphics and/or video games are true. That could be only a rumour. . . . For the time being the one sure thing is that the Aruze boss (that odd company name can be read in Japanese as "it's there", a colloquialism for "grab it") wants to increase his revenues by persuading the police – who regulate slot machines and pachinko – to relax their rules on how much money a player can put into at a machine a time. Young Japanese men – and not a few women – want to blow their cash on the slots!

Kazuo Okada / President

Stocks (No-par value, 1,000 shares min. trade)

Shares Issued (Nov. 1, '98)   84,875,000 shares
No. of Shareholders (Mar. 31, '98)   24

Major Holders	(%)
Kazuo Okada	49.5
Tomohiro Okada	29.5
Hiromi Okada	6.5
Mizuho Seisakusyo	5.6
Hiroko Yokotsuka	3.2
Employees' Stockholding	2.1
Sumitomo Bank	0.7
Foreign Owners	0.0

Earnings

Period	Sales	Operating Profit	Current Profit	Net Profit	Earnings Per Share	Dividend Per Share
Mar 96	25,401	5,644	4,000	607	4,107.3	500.00
Mar 97	52,414	21,972	20,555	5,684	34,506.0	1,000.00
Mar 98	73,371	36,224	35,969	6,159	37,384.8	3,000.00
**Mar 99	110,455	46,047	46,209	23,380	275.5	20.00
Mid-Term						
Sep 97	30,116	13,282	13,071	6,454	39,174.7	0
*Sep 98	46,661	21,106	21,194	9,443	204.5	0

*Estimates; **Company estimates. Per share values in ¥, all other amounts in millions of ¥.*

Balance sheet summary	1994	1995	1996	1997	1998
Current assets	25,300	19,641	21,684	25,863	34,486
Fixed assets	66,651	59,540	59,562	50,961	6,651
Total assets	91,952	79,181	81,247	76,825	41,138
Current liabilities	36,642	26,786	31,639	34,086	13,734
Fixed liabilities	39,447	36,582	33,346	20,966	446
Total liabilities	76,089	63,368	64,985	55,052	14,180
Capital Stock	448	448	460	460	460
Shareholders' equity	15,863	15,812	16,261	21,772	26,957
Total liabilities and equity	91,952	79,181	81,247	76,825	41,138

Note: All amounts in millions of ¥. Balance sheet, end March.

Asahi Intelligence Service

(Estd. 1962, listed 1995, stock code no. 9799)
Company address: 4-2-4, Minami-Senba, Chuo-ku, Osaka 542-0081
Tel: 81-6-6245-7201 Fax: 81-6-6245-7717

A well-respected Osaka company offering advice on management, e.g. systems operations. Founded 37 years ago as a printing machinery maker, it converted itself into a service outfit, helping other companies to analyse their data, for instance. Counts 1,445 employees. The President is Atsuhisa Nishikawa, 63 – Chairman Takashi Ohtsuki, 69, is the top individual shareholder.

Product/Sales breakdown: Sales in the year to March '98 were ¥7.15 billion. The company divides its operations between "systems operations and management", 44%; and "data entries", 27%. Desk-top related services added 6% to revenues. Asahi Intelligence is expanding into software, presently 23% of sales.

Rivals/Competitors: As a company in management consultancy of a sort, with a high-tech bent, it has many rivals in the Kansai. It seeks to distinguish itself from others by its corporate style, an austere culture.

History/Strategy: The company's main strategy has been to ally itself with major institutions – Sumitomo Trust & Banking, Mitsui Trust & Banking, Daiwa Bank, Mitsubishi Trust & Banking and Nippon Life. It encourages long working hours, dedication and earnestness, as do many old-style firms. Its sales and earnings record – with steady but not spectacular increases each year – is just what traditional Japanese businessmen like. Key staff are encouraged to work late (11 pm).

Management: The corporate style is articulated by the dignified Mr. Ohtsuki, a bankerly figure.

Outlook/Hot News: Asahi Intelligence makes a thing of "sincerity" (makoto). Recruiting films for the company display the Chinese character calligraphy and feature company gatherings held around the calligraphy. The emphasis on personal reliability and keeping faith is a good idea for a company whose staff visit other firms to gather data and are trusted with corporate secrets. The company is working hard on new challenges, notably the year 2000 issue in computers. Some hints may be gleaned from trade sources about future activities:

(i) Asahi Intelligence's "data entry business" – helping other old-fashioned companies to keep their data straight – appears to belong in the 19th century; computers today do the job that key-pushers did yesterday;

(ii) the company is suddenly feeling a wind of change – it is hiring a lot of new staff, mainly graduates, and moving its head office to Tokyo. What the strategic shift to Tokyo is about, the company will not say, apart from stating the obvious: "that is where the market is."

Atsuhisa Nishikawa / President

Stocks (¥50 par value, 1,000 shares min. trade)

Shares Issued (Nov. 1, '98)	7,538,000 shares
No. of Shareholders (May. 20, '98)	738

Major Holders	(%)
Kyokusen	16.8
Employees' Stockholding	9.0
Mitsui Trust	5.6
Sumitomo Trust	5.5
Daiwa Bank	4.4
Takashi Ohtsuki	3.5
Mitsubishi Trust	2.6
Foreign Owners	3.6

Earnings

Period	Sales	Operating Profit	Current Profit	Net Profit	Earnings Per Share	Dividend Per Share
Mar 96	4,720	312	322	151	24.4	7.50
Mar 97	5,522	456	322	156	23.1	9.50
Mar 98	7,151	887	818	407	59.5	17.00
**Mar 99	8,530	870	870	390	51.7	17.00
*Mar 00	9,500	980	980	490	65.0	17.00
Mid-Term						
Sep 98	4,136	392	355	128	17.0	0
*Sep 99	4,800	420	380	140	18.6	0

*Estimates; **Company estimates. Per share values in ¥, all other amounts in millions of ¥.*

Balance sheet summary	1994	1995	1996	1997	1998
Current assets	1,653	1,793	2,309	2,569	3,545
Fixed assets	1,277	1,290	1,476	1,440	1,482
Total assets	2,931	3,083	3,786	4,009	5,027
Current liabilities	907	899	993	1,145	1,820
Fixed liabilities		20	100	80	100
Total liabilities	907	919	1,093	1,225	1,920
Capital Stock	543	543	734	734	734
Shareholders' equity	2,023	2,163	2,692	2,784	3,106
Total liabilities and equity	2,931	3,083	3,786	4,009	5,027

Note: All amounts in millions of ¥. Balance sheet, end March.

Aucnet

(Estd. 1984, listed 1991, stock code no. 9669)
Company address: 2-7-26, Kita-Aoyama, Minato-ku, Tokyo 107-8631
Tel: 81-3-3423-6111 Fax: 81-3-3423-2916

A used-car dealer. Employs 172 staff. President is Kiyotaka Fujisaki, 46.

Product/Sales breakdown: A good 54% of its sales comes from auctions. Aucnet uses auctions on satellite TV to sell its cars (President Fujisaki claims that his firm was the first to do this in the world). Another 31% of revenue comes from putting car-owner info about used cars on TV and charging the owner. The remaining 15% comes from "purchased equipment" (parts and the like). Sales will amount to ¥10.5 billion in the current year to Dec. '99 setting net profits at ¥1.5 billion, according to estimates.

Rivals/Competitors: The new owners of rival AM Japan, JAC, announced a sales target of ¥1 trillion. The company already reports sales close to Aucnet's annual estimated revenues of just over ¥10 billion. Competition is hotting up, assuming that JAC delivers. At the same time Aucnet looks well set.

History/Strategy: Aucnet began 15 years ago selling used cars through newspaper ads. It started that way but quickly decided to try selling on TV. "People told us that would be impossible, to sell a car you didn't see," recalls Mr. Fujisaki, "but they were wrong and we were right, because it worked." Aucnet sold 280,000 used cars last year. Out of the nation's 22,800 used-car dealers, 5,400 are registered with Aucnet, the company says. Aucnet is financed to the extent of ¥1 billion in unsecured, long-term loans by a bevy of leading banks (Dai-Ichi Kangyo, Fuji, Sakura, Sanwa, Tokai). They came in because Aucnet's top shareholder is Orient Corp., an auto finance company (the largest in Japan), that spread into consumer finance. Aucnet recorded a large operating profit but a net loss in its year to Dec. '97, due to exceptional expenses incurred by a US branch of Aucnet.

Management: Aucnet is pleased with its success in auctioning cars by satellite TV, and is diversifying into sales of flowers by the same method.

Outlook/Hot News: The company is hugely profitable and looks like staying that way. The challenge from AM Japan is going to stir things up. Both companies are Tokyo-based. Aucnet, for its part, is pressing on:

(i) Fujisaki-san is persisting with tried methods – he set a goal for used-car sales of 350,000 units in 1999;

(ii) at the same time, Aucnet aims to register an additional 50 used-car dealers as members of its national network;

(iii) the company has completed writing off a one-time extraordinary loss of ¥2.5 billion on its US subsidiary;

(iv) Aucnet, with current earnings, can swiftly repay borrowings of ¥2.59 billion on its end-December 1997 consolidated accounts, if it chooses to do so and they are still there. It is in great shape.

Kiyotaka Fujisaki / President

Stocks (¥50 par value, 100 shares min. trade)

Shares Issued (Nov. 1, '98) 10,423,000 shares
No. of Shareholders (Dec. 31, '97) 403

Major Holders	(%)
Orient Corp.	22.5
Flex Co.	13.3
Toyo Trust	8.4
Kiyoko Fujisaki	5.1
Sumitomo Trust	4.4
JBT Inc.	2.5
Mitsui Trust	2.1
Foreign Owners	13.7

Earnings

Period	Sales	Operating Profit	Current Profit	Net Profit	Earnings Per Share	Dividend Per Share
Dec 95	6,069	1,777	1,844	922	107.1	14.50
Dec 96	7,486	2,090	2,118	1,056	112.3	14.50
Dec 97	8,860	2,479	2,507	−443	−42.9	15.50
**Dec 98	9,750	2,720	2,700	200	19.2	15.50
*Dec 99	10.500	3,000	3,000	1,500	143.9	15.50
Mid-Term						
Jun 98	5,009	1,439	1,475	−805	−77.3	0
*Jun 99	5,200	1,480	1,480	750	72.0	0

*Estimates; **Company estimates. Per share values in ¥, all other amounts in millions of ¥.

Balance sheet summary	1993	1994	1995	1996	1997
Current assets	2,908	5,691	6,401	7,236	6,212
Fixed assets	1,986	2,741	2,904	4,320	5,258
Total assets	4,905	8,441	9,312	11,559	11,471
Current liabilities	1,082	2,135	2,313	2,825	3,166
Fixed liabilities	403	211	95	899	1,060
Total liabilities	1,486	2,346	2,408	3,724	4,226
Capital Stock	786	1,866	1,866	1,866	1,866
Shareholders' equity	3,419	6,094	6,903	7,834	7,244
Total liabilities and equity	4,905	8,441	9,312	11,559	11,471

Note: All amounts in millions of ¥. Balance sheet, end December.

Bamiyan

(Estd. 1987, listed 1997, stock code no. 7546)
Company address: 2-10-21, Kyonan-Cho, Musashino City, Tokyo 180-8620
Tel: 81-422-33-1789 Fax: 81-422-33-1567

A Chinese fast-food chain, created by the Skylark group of Musashino City outside Tokyo under the slogan "Affordable, Tasty and Fast". 732 full-time employees. Yasutaka Ito, 49, is President.

Product/Sales breakdown: Almost all the revenues – doubling between 1995 and 1998 – come from the restaurants, some 221 at the end of 1998, mostly in the Tokyo area. Small quantities of food items and cigarettes are sold at Bamiyan outlets, amounting altogether to no more than 2% of income.

Rivals/Competitors: The Skylark group got its major shot in the arm when McDonald's (1971), then Royal Host (1976) and others were allowed to land in Japan (see also below).

History/Strategy: The chain's pleasant-sounding name, Bamiyan, derives from a city of that name, located in Afghanistan on the old Silk Road route; where a celebrated giant Buddha has given a historic flavour to the name Bamiyan . . . The company plan – returning to this day and age – is "to achieve 300 locations by the year 2000 and become a national chain with 1,000 or more locations by 2010". Currently, it has 200 restaurants, served by two giant kitchens, one in Gumma, the other in Saitama. Food is trucked from these centres to the shops and re-heated on the spot.

Management: The policy is to respect Japanese culinary taste: none of Bamiyan's approximately 300 chefs is Chinese, the company notes.

Outlook/Hot News: The success of Bamiyan – swift, widespread – suggests that (i) the Skylark group's decision to decentralize itself, spinning off affiliates – all run out of the same Musashino location, but separated out for management – has paid off in this instance, as in the case of the coffee shop affiliate, Jonathan's; (ii) Japanese consumer taste has diversified to a degree unimaginable a couple of decades ago, when all restaurants were tiny and offered Japanese cuisine; (iii) the fast-food revolution in Japan was kicked off by the arrival in Japan of McDonald's from the United States in 1971, and has taken hold since the end of the Bubble period in 1990/1. Bamiyan's methods are far removed from the old ways; with centralized mass kitchens, each one supposed to serve 100 retail outlets. Yet could they be exported to China – or, more immediately, to America – given their efficiency? One day? "We dream of one day creating a world chain, as a pioneer in the Chinese restaurant trade," says Yasutaka Ito. Something to match McDonald's on its own soil. Meanwhile, as we went to press, there were reports that oh-so-successful Bamiyan will be swallowed back into the Skylark group in mid-1999. Don't ask us what that's all about, we don't know. But it looks as if the important afiliate was so successful that someone got jealous? The owners asserted their right to re-incorporate.

Yasutaka Ito / President

Stocks (¥50 par value, 1,000 shares min. trade)

Shares Issued (Nov. 30, '98)   14,300,000 shares
No. of Shareholders (Jun. 30, '98)   561

Major Holders	(%)
Skylark Co.	50.0
Food Service System R Inst.	32.7
Employees' Stockholding	3.1
Dai-ichi Life Ins.	1.5
Daiwa Bank	1.3
Fiji	0.8
Foreign Owners	2.0

Earnings

Period	Sales	Operating Profit	Current Profit	Net Profit	Earnings Per Share	Dividend Per Share
Dec 95	15,770	1,496	1,399	1,194	170,690.7	0
Dec 96	21,429	1,875	1,806	895	127.9	10.00
Dec 97	26,804	2,214	2,057	1,100	102.6	10.00
**Dec 98	34,000	2,800	2,720	1,360	95.1	16.00
*Dec 99	40,000	3,300	3,200	1,600	101.7	16.00
Mid-Term						
Jun 98	15,658	994	953	481	36.05	8.00
Jun 99	18,000	1,200	1,150	500	31.8	8.00

*Estimates; **Company estimates. Per share values in ¥, all other amounts in millions of ¥.*

Balance sheet summary	1993	1994	1995	1996	1997
Current assets	721	686	898	1,437	1,742
Fixed assets	2,566	3,701	5,694	8,653	12,163
Total assets	3,287	4,387	6,592	10,090	13,905
Current liabilities	3,607	5,063	6,178	8,541	9,621
Fixed liabilities	1,248	194	89	129	368
Total liabilities	4,856	5,258	6,268	8,671	9,989
Capital Stock	300	350	350	350	832
Shareholders' equity	−1,568	−870	324	1,419	3,916
Total liabilities and equity	3,287	4,387	6,592	10,090	13,905

Note: All amounts in millions of ¥. Balance sheet, end December.

C Two-Network

(Estd. 1947, listed 1998, stock code no. 7588)
Company address: 2-2-5, Kanda-Sudacho, Chiyoda-ku, Tokyo 101-0041
Tel: 81-3-5298-6366 Fax: 81-3-5298-5985

A newcomer to the OTC in July 1998, this food wholesaler/retailer was created half a century earlier. As a non-brand operator, low cost and low margin, it fits the times in Tokyo, its base. Payment is in cash. Cash-and-carry keeps the wolf from the door under sprightly President Yasushi Inaida, 45, the chief stockholder, and his team. 112 staff.

Product/Sales breakdown: Processed foods, beverages, frozen items, instant noodles, canned foods – these are the items sold in today's combini ("convenience stores"). C Two-Network is there to supply those stores and/or compete with them. The company attributes 70% of sales (¥22 billion in the year to March '98) to processed food, 9% to sweets and confectionery, 2% to sake and 1% to sundries. Some 19% of revenues come in rents from people who operate stores the company finds.

Rivals/Competitors: As a rapidly expanding outfit in a time of recession (see opposite page for sales and earnings forecasts) this relative newcomer to the OTC stage is setting off waves. But there's little a larger, less speedy competitor such as Seven-Eleven, set in its ways, can do to stop the upstart, so it seems. This small firm is too small to stop. Compare its prospective revenues in the year 2000 (at ¥31 billion) to those of Seven-Eleven – the order of magnitude is different, ditto the motivations.

History/Strategy: That's the strategy, dart in and displace the rivals. The other team goes home at 6? It's possible. It's also possible that key managers at the C Two-Network lot are still in their offices at 10 pm, having spent the day outside running around.

Management: Looking at the stock prices of firms in the wholesale food trade in Japan . . . this company's share price stood head and shoulders above others at the time of writing (December 1998). That's despite its low cost, low margin strategy. They are managing! Others in the food industry with high share prices were Rock Field, a delicatessen-type operation out of Kobe; and Hurxley, an Osaka obento-making outfit, offering hokka-hokka ("hot 'n ready") lunch-boxes. C Two-Network is a lot more basic than these two, and not strictly comparable. It offers strict necessities.

Outlook/Hot News: This very aggressive, cheerful firm is onto something. Moving into the territory long occupied by Seven-Eleven, now being challenged by others, not only by C Two-Network, must be a good strategy. This will not necessarily be an easy act. Lots of work is required to keep C Two-Network's 5 wholesale centres (3 in Tokyo, 1 in Kanagawa, 1 in Saitama) going forward in sync with some 21 retail outlets (also mostly in the Tokyo area – but not all).

Stocks (No-par value, 1,000 shares min. trade)

Shares Issued (Nov. 31, '98)	4,090,000 shares
No. of Shareholders (Mar. 31, '98)	39

Major Holders	(%)
Yasushi Inaida	48.9
Profect Deux Co.	12.0
Yoshihiro Nakatani	5.0
Kunio Kaneda	4.7
Hatsuyoshi Inaida	4.1
Tomoyo Inaida	3.7
Yuji Inaida	2.6
Foreign Owners	0.0

Earnings

Period	Sales	Operating Profit	Current Profit	Net Profit	Earnings Per Share	Dividend Per Share
Mar 96	13,362	401	422	121	65.3	2.50
Mar 97	16,666	506	503	291	142.1	10.00
Mar 98	22,343	748	766	381	106.2	10.00
*Mar 99	27,000	970	980	580	141.8	10.00
*Mar 00	31,000	1,100	1,100	660	161.4	10.00
Mid-Term						
Sep 98	13,216	460	464	293	77.6	0
*Sep 99	13,500	500	500	300	73.3	0

*Estimates. Per share values in ¥, all other amounts in millions of ¥.

Balance sheet summary	1994	1995	1996	1997	1998
Current assets	1,776	1,625	2,401	2,560	2,986
Fixed assets	1,813	1,904	2,117	3,028	3,908
Total assets	3,590	3,529	4,518	5,588	6,895
Current liabilities	1,973	2,349	3,078	3,874	4,669
Fixed liabilities	829	403	552	544	714
Total liabilities	2,803	2,753	3,631	4,419	5,384
Capital Stock	95	95	97	97	97
Shareholders' equity	786	776	886	1,169	1,510
Total liabilities and equity	3,590	3,529	4,518	5,588	6,895

Note: All amounts in millions of ¥. Balance sheet, end March.

Citizen Electronics

(Estd. 1970, listed 1996, stock code no. 6892)
Company address: 1-23-1, Kami-Kurechi, Fujiyoshida, Yamanashi Pref. 403-0001
Tel: 81-555-23-4121 Fax: 81-555-22-9964

An affiliate of Citizen Watch, a major player in the watch industry since 1930. Flowered as an independent entity within the Citizen group, making electronic parts and devices, as well as watch parts. Employees, 522. Rokura Nakasugi, 63, is the President.

Product/Sales breakdown: The company's output breaks down between electronic parts and items, e.g. buzzers (70%), watch parts (21%), health-related equipment, meaning digital thermometers and such (7%), and residual items (2%). A high proportion of sales are exported (24%).

Rivals/Competitors: Citizen Electronics has judged its specialities well, sticking to well-established items for which it made a name such as light emitting diodes (LEDs), a field where Mr. Nakasugi says the company is world market leader. "Our core competence in this area stems from our experience in watchmaking," states Nakasugi-san.

History/Strategy: The company was originally, at the time of its creation in 1970, a joint venture with Bulova Watch of the US. JVs on the whole do not succeed in Japan. This one came to grief after seven years. Two decades later Citizen Watch is a healthy, high-volume manufacturer, with a debtless balance sheet; the substantial investments made in plant over the years have been paid for. The company is still based at its original site, high in the mountains going towards Mt. Fuji from Tokyo, close to Fujiyoshida City.

Management: President Nakasugi worked for Citizen Watch originally. Ultimately, policy is always going to be set by the mother firm, which will very probably continue to provide top executives at its 65.5%-owned affiliate.

Outlook/Hot News: The company has established a name as a successful operation under the aegis of Citizen Watch, but creating its own strategy. Being up there in the mountains – with nothing else around for the most part – encourages independence of mind, as in the cases of Citizen Electronics and neighbouring Fanuc, the renowned robot company. Citizen Electronics got their first, almost a decade ahead of Fanuc. The setting, experience says, encourages long-range vision. Citizen Electronics will surely stick to its specialities, and expand overseas, according to Nakasugi-san. What else? The company went public successfully in 1996 – the funds were used to double shareholder equity, among other things. In its last available consolidated balance sheet, for March 1998, the company showed a grand total of ¥8 million in borrowing against assets of ¥28,470 million – a happy state. How will Nakasugi-san and his successors use their booty? One will see. Little has leaked out.

Rokuro Nakasugi / President

Stocks (¥50 par value, 100 shares min. trade)

Shares Issued (Nov. 1, '98)	11,703,692 shares
No. of Shareholders (Sep. 30, '98)	391

Major Holders	(%)
Citizen Watch	65.5
Employees' Stockholding	2.3
Mitsubishi Trust	1.7
C.O. Nominees	1.6
DKB	1.4
Yasuda Trust	1.3
Foreign Owners	10.4

Earnings

Period	Sales	Operating Profit	Current Profit	Net Profit	Earnings Per Share	Dividend Per Share
Mar 96	28,049	2,092	2,056	749	1,065.8	100.00
Mar 97	31,836	3,116	2,913	1,374	180.7	12.00
Mar 98	36,615	3,477	3,611	1,763	165.7	16.00
**Mar 99	37,700	3,200	3,300	1,800	153.8	16.00
*Mar 00	38,700	3,400	3,400	1,850	158.1	16.00
Mid-Term						
Sep 98	18,375	1,580	1,701	912	78.0	8.00
*Sep 99	19,000	1,700	1,800	950	81.2	8.00

*Estimates; **Company estimates. Per share values in ¥, all other amounts in millions of ¥.

Balance sheet summary	1994	1995	1996	1997	1998
Current assets	11,061	12,628	12,093	17,872	20,296
Fixed assets	2,141	3,990	3,609	3,782	6,009
Total assets	13,203	16,618	15,703	21,654	26,306
Current liabilities	8,874	11,141	9,420	9,620	12,718
Fixed liabilities	1,001	1,197	1,332	1,502	1,457
Total liabilities	9,875	12,338	10,752	11,123	14,176
Capital Stock	496	643	643	1,988	1,988
Shareholders' equity	3,327	4,279	4,950	10,531	12,130
Total liabilities and equity	13,203	16,618	15,703	21,654	26,306

Note: All amounts in millions of ¥. Balance sheet, end March.

Como

(Estd. 1984, listed 1997, stock code no. 2224)
Company address: 505-1, Aza-Shimonotsubo, Oaza-Muranaka, Komaki City,
Aichi Pref. 485-0082 Tel: 81-568-73-7050 Fax: 81-568-73-7089

A local baking operation located outside Nagoya in Aichi prefecture, half way between Tokyo and Osaka. Makes "long-life" croissants and Danish pastries, lasting a month or more, sold in vending machines etc. Has 129 employees. President is Koji Ueda, 58.

Product/Sales breakdown: "Danishes" account for 61% of sales (¥4.63 billion in the year to March '98). Next, croissants (of an Italian variety) 34%. Then, panettones 3%. Remainder, 2%.

Rivals/Competitors: Locally in Aichi prefecture only Como – named after the Italian lake – is offering long-life baked items in quantity. The healthy 10–15% margins that Como products command is an indication that the company found a niche of its own.

History/Strategy: In a recession baked items that last a long time are especially welcome, it seems. Nobody wants to throw anything away, bread included. Como's croissants and pastries are sold in convenience stores, vending machines and factories or offices – places where items may well have to last a few days or even weeks. Como has developed techniques, using yeast imported from Italy and fermented in Japan, that let its products survive reasonably fresh – ready to warm up – for 30 or 60 days. Founded 15 years ago Como had a difficult time in the mid-1990s, barely breaking in, but its numbers – see opposite page – have been on the up ever since then.

Management: Is in the gritty Nagoya tradition. The consumer comes first. The company makes a sales point of the fact that it uses no artificial ingredients to keep its produce from going mouldy. The key to the company's turnaround since 1994 – when the company had negative shareholder value (!) – would appear to be the arrival of a new manager, subsequently the president of the company. Ueda-san started with the firm in 1991, simply as an advisor. His promotion to president 5 years later suggests that he brought the required touch – as witness the improvement in performance.

Outlook/Hot News: Baking is the domain of Yamazaki Baking, a grandfather of the industry in Japan. Compare Yamazaki's ¥700 billion turnover with Como's estimated ¥5.2 billion in the current year. One is a giant, the other a niche-baker. Will Yamazaki allow this minor local challenge to go unnoticed? Probably they will leave best alone. Croissants sold in vending machines? Leave it to those people in Nagoya what they do. What lies ahead? Como is said to be considering putting its wares into railway station kiosks – the next thing you know their long-life danishes will be all over Japan? Give it a try?

Koji Ueda / President

Stocks (¥50 par value, 1,000 shares min. trade)

Shares Issued (Nov. 1, '98)	3,000,000 shares
No. of Shareholders (Sep. 30, '98)	374

Major Holders	(%)
Fuji Sky Service Co.	8.0
Takeshi Funahashi	5.6
Fuji Country Club	4.4
Nichimen Corp.	4.1
Satomi Funahashi	4.0
Michiho Ebihara	4.0
Motoki Ebihara	4.0
Foreign Owners	0.0

Earnings

Period	Sales	Operating Profit	Current Profit	Net Profit	Earnings Per Share	Dividend Per Share
Mar 96	3,982	471	378	3	2,038.2	N/A
Mar 97	4,247	464	409	122	51.0	5.00
Mar 98	4,629	550	435	211	81.5	6.00
**Mar 99	5,260	758	715	303	101.2	7.00
*Mar 00	5,400	830	800	330	110.0	7.00
Mid-Term						
Sep 98	2,210	425	403	138	46.1	0
*Sep 99	2,704	450	405	140	46.7	0

*Estimates; **Company estimates. Per share values in ¥, all other amounts in millions of ¥.*

Balance sheet summary	1994	1995	1996	1997	1998
Current assets	905	951	1,130	1,467	887
Fixed assets	2,522	2,186	2,091	1,787	2,102
Total assets	3,428	3,138	3,221	3,254	2,990
Current liabilities	3,589	2,477	2,647	2,712	2,167
Fixed liabilities		600	450	300	150
Total liabilities	3,592	3,077	3,097	3,012	2,317
Capital Stock	60	60	120	120	222
Shareholders' equity	−164	60	124	242	673
Total liabilities and equity	3,428	3,138	3,221	3,254	2,990

Note: All amounts in millions of ¥. Balance sheet, end March.

Cosel

(Estd. 1969, listed 1994, stock code no. 6905)
Company address: 1-6-43, Kami-Akaemachi, Toyama City, 930-0816
Tel: 81-764-32-8149 Fax: 81-764-41-5324

Take a plane over the Japan Alps, the backbone of Honshu, to Toyama, ride into town and there is one of Japan's model little engineering firms, Cosel. They make electronic switches for industrial purposes, and they are good at it, as witness their 20% profit margins. Cosel has 357 staff. President Hisaharu Ame, 57, founded the company 30 years ago, and is the top shareholder.

Product/Sales breakdown: Mr. Ame has devoted his life to this firm. It's very much a local operation, barely known in the rest of Japan, except to specialists. Ame-san relies on agents to do the selling, both at home and abroad (exports account for 16% of production). The company's forte is what it calls a "standard switch", as opposed to a custom-made one. These account for 78% of revenues (sales were ¥13.5 billion in the year to May '98). Having established his main product as acceptable, Mr. Ame has concentrated on it. The rest of his production – 22% of revenues – comes from "onboard switches".

Rivals/Competitors: Cosel bills itself as the number 2 producer of electronic switches in Japan. The front-runner is Nemic-Lambda, a much bigger company. Mr. Ame believes in playing "Avis" to his rival's "Hertz" (not an image he uses, but that's what it amounts to – Cosel must "try harder"). By running harder Cosel stays up there with the leader, competing on price and service. No other companies are in the same league in Japan.

History/Strategy: If the worst came to the worst – thinking the unthinkable – only one of the two top companies (Cosel or Nemic-Lambda) will survive in electronic switches. However, the betting is that overall the Japanese economy will rebound in 1, 2 or 3 years. Mr. Ame is relaxed. "What vision of the future do we hold?" asks a company brochure, no doubt echoing the boss. "Cosel, a leading developer of innovative technology for over a quarter of a century, envisions a very bright future."

Management: The biggest task – for a strongman founder such as Ame-san – is to provide for the succession (not to assume personal indispensability). Many bosses fall down on this duty. Mr. Ame, however, has designated a successor, a company spokesman confides. Only, the name cannot be announced.

Outlook/Hot News: To be proof against the recession a company like this must have (i) exceptional technology, (ii) sound management and (iii) a decent balance sheet. Cosel fits the profile. The company is all but debtless and performed well over 4–5 years despite the recession. However, the recession threatens to verge into depression in certain industries – e.g. chips – thus Cosel's performance is likely to deteriorate a bit. See opposite page. Yet still with 20% margins, it can hardly complain. The test would come in maintaining those great margins!

Hisaharu Ame / President

Stocks (¥50 par value, 100 shares min. trade)

Shares Issued (Nov. 1, '98)   20,592,000 shares
No. of Shareholders (May. 20, '98)   1,402

Major Holders	(%)
Hisaharu Ame	19.4
Kiyoshi Kaiba	13.8
Yukio Wakatsuchi	8.2
Employees' Stockholding	8.0
Hokuriku Bank	2.7
Michio Meshi	2.3
Akio Moriyama	2.2
Foreign Owners	3.4

Earnings

Period	Sales	Operating Profit	Current Profit	Net Profit	Earnings Per Share	Dividend Per Share
Mar 96	11,609	1,941	2,212	1,107	71.0	12.00
Mar 97	12,296	2,182	2,400	1,217	65.1	13.50
Mar 98	13,543	2,825	3,024	1,509	73.3	14.50
**Mar 99	12,400	N/A	2,590	1,500	72.8	15.50
*Mar 00	13,500	2,900	3,000	1,600	77.7	15.50
Mid-Term						
Nov 97	7,152	1,619	1,757	840	40.8	6.75
Nov 98	6,100	1,200	1,300	700	34.0	7.25

*Estimates; **Company estimates. Per share values in ¥, all other amounts in millions of ¥.

Balance sheet summary	1994	1995	1996	1997	1998
Current assets	6,196	9,337	9,946	10,623	11,006
Fixed assets	2,450	3,421	4,501	4,656	5,873
Total assets	8,646	12,758	14,447	15,280	16,880
Current liabilities	2,392	2,855	3,642	3,428	3,900
Fixed liabilities	248	265	230	260	283
Total liabilities	2,640	3,121	3,873	3,688	4,184
Capital Stock	780	2,055	2,055	2,055	2,055
Shareholders' equity	6,005	9,637	10,574	11,591	12,696
Total liabilities and equity	8,646	12,758	14,447	15,280	16,880

Note: All amounts in millions of ¥. Balance sheet, end May.

Create Medic

(Estd. 1974, listed 1990, stock code no. 5187)

Company address: 2-5-25, Chigasaki-Minami, Tsuzuki-ku, Yokohama 224-0037

Tel: 81-45-943-2611 Fax: 81-45-941-1577

A manufacturer of disposable catheters for hospitals, located in Yokohama. Enjoys a close relationship with the health authorities (the Ministry of Health and Welfare). Managed by owner and founder President Tadao Nishimura 59. 415 employees.

Product/Sales breakdown: A growing business with good margins. Sales (¥6.9 billion in the last full year available, to Dec. '97) break down between various types of catheters, according to Bloomberg. These silicone catheters were 31% for nursing and tests; 29% for urinary organ use; 29% for digestive system usage; and 11% for surgery utilization.

Rivals/Competitors: Catheters of the types made by Create Medic constitute a profitable business, as noted. Rivals exist. They include one or two much larger, aggressive companies (for whom catheters are only one line of business). Terumo Corp. stands out as one such. That company spends as much on R & D alone as Create Medic grosses in revenues – such is the difference in size and scope. Getz Bros., a foreign-owned firm with offices in Aoyama, is prominent as an importer of catheters. This is serious competition, given that Nishimura-san manufactures and bears high Japanese labour costs. Depending on the exchange rates, imported stuff can be a lot cheaper, and still of sound quality.

History/Strategy: The key to Create Medic's profitability since it was established 25 years ago has been its relationship with the hospital authorities, some of them under the aegis of national health authorities. With competition increasing from overseas – and the rise, for example, of a company like Japan Lifeline, yet another importer of catheters – other strategies have become needed (see below).

Management: Create Medic's results have got better each year. Meanwhile, its stock price has not progressed, but rather gone downwards in recent years, taking an opposite direction. Judging by the company's homepage, which includes several charts of the stock price, the owner is unhappy with this development. This seems natural. But what can be the cause?

Outlook/Hot News: The most obvious concern would be that producing catheters in Japan is too expensive a proposition to be valid for very much longer. Nishimura-san, to give him his due, has acted to address this concern by moving production overseas, to China. Trade sources say that Create Medic teamed up with businesses in Beijing to make six different lines of products there. Such a strategy – depending on the products – need not exclude exports, which still accounted for 12% of sales in early 1998, but the tendency would be for these to decrease while imports rise.

Tadao Nishimura / President

Stocks (¥50 par value, 1,000 shares min. trade)

Shares Issued (Nov. 1, '98)	9,664,000 shares
No. of Shareholders (Jun. 30, '98)	943

Major Holders	(%)
Tadao Nishimura	18.0
Hiromasa Nakao	17.4
Fumio Aikawa	4.5
Bank of Yokohama	4.3
Masataka Kasahara	2.9
Masashi Nakao	2.5
Chuo Trust	2.3
Foreign Owners	3.3

Earnings

Period	Sales	Operating Profit	Current Profit	Net Profit	Earnings Per Share	Dividend Per Share
Dec 95	5,716	827	844	388	44.4	10.50
Dec 96	6,241	1,060	1,055	532	60.7	11.50
Dec 97	6,879	1,171	1,144	407	42.6	11.50
**Dec 98	6,900	1,140	1,180	590	61.1	11.50
*Dec 99	7,100	1,200	1,200	630	65.2	11.50
Mid-Term						
Jun 98	3,074	369	423	237	24.6	N/A
*Jun 99	3,100	380	380	200	20.7	N/A

*Estimates; **Company estimates. Per share values in ¥, all other amounts in millions of ¥.

Balance sheet summary	1993	1994	1995	1996	1997
Current assets	4,288	5,813	5,122	5,331	5,833
Fixed assets	1,889	2,778	2,992	3,334	3,569
Total assets	6,177	8,592	8,115	8,665	9,403
Current liabilities	1,203	1,564	1,332	1,623	3,554
Fixed liabilities	1,335	2,962	2,380	2,175	688
Total liabilities	2,538	4,527	3,712	3,798	4,243
Capital Stock	1,303	1,425	1,443	1,461	1,461
Shareholders' equity	3,639	4,064	4,402	4,866	5,159
Total liabilities and equity	6,177	8,592	8,115	8,665	9,403

Note: All amounts in millions of ¥. Balance sheet, end December.

Creo

(Estd. 1974, listed 1990, stock code no. 9698)
Company address: 3-5-1, Shiba, Minato-ku, Tokyo 108-0014
Tel: 81-3-3456-4611 Fax: 81-3-3456-4733

A medium-size, Tokyo-based software development company. Claims independence of big companies. President Takehiko Ohtani, 57, operates under the eye of the founder, now Chairman, Taneyasu Kawabata, 58, the leading shareholder in the firm. They have built up the company together, employing 381 staff.

Product/Sales breakdown: The company divides its activities into software development, often on consignment, 59%; software packages, 31%; and hardware products 10%.

Rivals/Competitors: Software companies are too numerous to mention. Creo's strategy appears to be to seek out special situations where it can develop appropriate software on consignment, offered at a competitive price.

History/Strategy: The company was launched by Kawabata-san in 1974 in anticipation of a national drive to step up software development to the levels of the US. Those were days when America had yet to establish today's dominance in the field. Creo made contacts of its own in the early years in the US, seeking to establish sources of information. It built up a respectful following, both among software managers overseas and eventually in the foreign investment community in Tokyo after the company went public in 1990. Not one to make rash commitments Mr. Kawabata and his successor as President, Ohtani-san, refrained from splashing funds. Today's healthy balance sheet is the result. A consolidated balance sheet for March 1998 recorded borrowing of ¥1 billion against total assets of ¥8.3 billion.

Management: *Creo* (Latin: "I create") is the motto by which this company stands. Trade sources credit the company with an unusual software package for Japanese calligraphy. Just the job for someone who needs a mass of greetings cards done at the New Year with artful brushstrokes?

Outlook/Hot News: For every 100 or perhaps 1,000 software startups in Japan only a handful go on to become public companies. Some remain private by preference, the majority can't hack it and fade away. What made Creo into a survivor? Partly, there was the backing of Fujitsu – and Fuji Bank together. A key factor – long before the appearance of Fujitsu – was the ability of the company to attract good software engineers. The credit goes to Kawabata-san. He created the company 25 years ago. There's nothing mysterious about Creo's success. It survived because its founder was effective. Now a new wave is needed?

Takehiko Otani / President

Stocks (¥50 par value, 1,000 shares min. trade)

Shares Issued (Nov. 1, '98)   5,179,000 shares
No. of Shareholders (Sep. 30, '98)   1,102

Major Holders	(%)
Taneyasu Kawabata	8.7
Fuji Bank	4.9
Fujitsu Ltd.	3.3
Hideo Yamauchi	2.3
Yaeko Inomata	2.1
Northern Trust (AVFC) Authority	1.9
Foreign Owners	8.6

Earnings

Period	Sales	Operating Profit	Current Profit	Net Profit	Earnings Per Share	Dividend Per Share
Mar 96	5,609	190	170	81	15.7	0
Mar 97	6,659	422	353	196	37.9	5.00
Mar 98	7,770	624	554	221	42.9	7.50
**Mar 99	8,000	640	560	100	19.3	7.50
*Mar 00	9,100	850	800	400	77.2	7.50
Mid-Term						
Sep 98	3,973	451	460	54	10.6	0
*Sep 99	4,200	360	360	50	9.7	0

*Estimates; **Company estimates. Per share values in ¥, all other amounts in millions of ¥.*

Balance sheet summary	1994	1995	1996	1997	1998
Current assets	4,973	4,590	5,202	5,199	5,554
Fixed assets	2,298	2,065	2,132	2,437	2,356
Total assets	7,271	6,656	7,334	7,636	7,911
Current liabilities	1,990	1,490	2,096	2,204	2,280
Fixed liabilities	165	41	32	30	32
Total liabilities	2,156	1,531	2,129	2,234	2,313
Capital Stock	2,263	2,263	2,263	2,263	2,263
Shareholders' equity	5,115	5,124	5,205	5,401	5,598
Total liabilities and equity	7,271	6,656	7,334	7,636	7,911

Note: All amounts in millions of ¥. Balance sheet, end March.

Cresco

(Estd. 1988, listed 1997, stock code no. 4674)
Company address: 3-1-12, Mita, Minato-Ku, Tokyo 108-0073
Tel: 81-3-5445-5011 Fax: 81-3-5445-5038

A developer of software and operating systems. Big ambitions in the banking sector. Tokyo-based, in the Mita section near Keio University. 343 employees. President Masahiro Urasaki, 51, runs the show in tandem with Chairman Toshio Iwasaki 58, the co-founder.

Product/Sales breakdown: The company is big on its own products. First and foremost, it boasts of its Usoft Developer ("The Tokyo Financial Big Bang, Deregulation, Market Globalization etc., all of these aggressive changes will make today's system obsolete tomorrow . . . The Usoft Developer with its Business Rule Automation capability offers a highly productive environment etc.") and other "network management solutions". The key to Cresco lies in its clients. President Urasaki shows visitors to his office a pie-chart with the clients' names: IBM Japan (46.39%), Matsushita Communications (19.34%), NTT (7.1%), Hitachi (4.4%) and so forth. The company's ¥6.12 billion sales in 1997/8 were split between "software development" (72%) and "PC systems development" (26%), with a residual 2% in "pre-packaged software".

Rivals/Competitors: These abound in today's Tokyo. Most are medium-small companies. A score or more were registered on the OTC, constituting probably the largest industrial group.

History/Strategy: Cresco's history is so short, it hardly bears repetition from the viewpoint of busy Urasaki-san. He concentrates on the future, in particular he mentions Cresco's interest in supplying new systems to the big banks that will enable the latter to streamline their banking halls, by dispensing with the functions of the older men who sit in the back, quietly affixing their hanko ("seals") to documents already completed by the young girl clerks seated in front of them. "That's got to change, if the banks are to be efficient," says the Cresco chief, "those men in the back have got to go, if the banks are to compete internationally."

Management: Cresco executives are open, frank and direct.

Outlook/Hot News: There are two types of software development companies. Those which aim at the public sector, and those which target the private sector. They inhabit totally different worlds. The first group are circumspect in public, dependent as they are on publicity-shy bureaucrats; the second group – to which Cresco belongs – is open, they have confidence in their technology and their staff. Cresco is still small, very small. But its name, taken from the Latin (*cresco*: "I grow"), is indicative. No one who meets President Masahiro Urasaki, an Okinawan Japanese by birth, can doubt that the company sincerely intends to grow. He is an ebullient person, who talks non-stop. Major decisions within the firm depend on Chairman Toshio Iwasaki, an ex-IBM Japan man, as much as on Urasaki-san, the co-founder. They have a good show going, and their balance sheet is all but debt-free. They are doing something right.

Masahiro Urasaki / President

Stocks (¥50 par value, 1,000 shares min. trade)

Shares Issued (Nov. 1, '98)	4,253,697 shares
No. of Shareholders (Sep. 30, '98)	454

Major Holders	(%)
Toshio Iwasaki	20.9
Masahiro Urasaki	14.2
Employees' Stockholding	8.0
Syun Corp.	7.2
Kenji Tajima	5.9

Foreign Owners	7.5

Earnings

Period	Sales	Operating Profit	Current Profit	Net Profit	Earnings Per Share	Dividend Per Share
Mar 96	4,214	287	277	79	25.8	10.00
Mar 97	4,970	388	383	178	54.3	10.00
Mar 98	6,157	552	587	259	69.2	17.00
**Mar 99	7,400	703	706	305	71.7	15.00
*Mar 00	8,500	800	850	400	94.1	15.00
Mid-Term						
Sep 98	3,437	299	306	111	26.2	7.50
*Sep 99	3,600	310	320	120	28.2	7.50

*Estimates; **Company estimates. Per share values in ¥, all other amounts in millions of ¥.*

Balance sheet summary	1994	1995	1996	1997	1998
Current assets	1,481	1,718	1,650	1,981	3,482
Fixed assets	680	858	705	875	1,025
Total assets	2,161	2,576	2,355	2,857	4,507
Current liabilities	1,252	1,464	1,363	1,395	1,583
Fixed liabilities	183	340	180	88	108
Total liabilities	1,435	1,804	1,544	1,483	1,692
Capital Stock	248	248	248	461	768
Shareholders' equity	725	771	811	1,373	2,815
Total liabilities and equity	2,161	2,576	2,355	2,857	4,507

Note: All amounts in millions of ¥. Balance sheet, end March.

Daika

(Estd. 1936, listed 1992, stock code no. 9926)
Company address: 3-1, Higashi, Kitarokujo Higashi-ku, Sapporo 060-0906
Tel: 81-11-742-4111 Fax: 81-11-721-2985

A Hokkaido wholesale operation specializing in cosmetics and toiletries. Lo and behold, Daika improved its results in 6 out of the last 7 years, an achievement indeed in the recession. Excellent management by President Koichiro Dai, 60, who kept the business growing by mergers, an unusual strategy in Japan.

Product/Sales breakdown: The company divided its 1997/8 annual turnover of ¥91.9 billion between personal care products (including cosmetics) at 31% of sales; paper and sanitary goods, 37%; household items, 15%; and the remainder, including detergents, at 17%.

Rivals/Competitors: Just abound. The rugged Mr. Dai's counter-strategy is to take 'em over. Daika actually began to expand, in 1969, with an act of getting together – seven companies united. Joining up with others became a habit . . . thus in April 1998 Daika gained control of Fuji Shokei and K. K. Tanaka, greatly expanding its operations at a stroke. The move increased annual sales to approx. ¥130 billion in the year to July '99 and prospectively lifted profits by over 50%.

History/Strategy: Daika supplies 6,000 shops, supermarkets and others with items from 400 sources. It has taken over 60 years for Mr. Dai and his predecessors to build up what is now the strongest network of its kind in northern Japan, employing 1,153 people full-time.

Management: For years Daika has dragged along a burden of bank debt (¥8.6 billion, as reported in 1997). Bigger profits would enable Mr. Dai to pay off the loans, if he chose to do so . . . Wholesale has turned profitable, to judge by the emphasis placed on their wholesale departments of late by two Hokkaido supermarket chains, Ralse (foodstuffs) and Tsuruya (drugs).

Outlook/Hot News: Mr. Dai has led Daika through a grisly period when two of its shareholders – Takugin, the main bank in Hokkaido, and the Long-Term Credit Bank – got into trouble. This was bad for confidence in Hokkaido. With this experience behind him, Dai-san is eager to expand the firm's operations outside Hokkaido. But which will come first: growing the firm; or paying off debt? It looks as if the more aggressive strategy suits the boss best. Trade sources reported that Daika aims to open a "distribution centre" in Tsukuba City, north of Toyko, in a move to launch into business in the Tokyo area. Some reports said that Daika intended to create 15 "sales centres" in the Kanto area. All of this is pretty bold, but the way Dai-san sees it the company is already the second largest of its type in Japan, and he believes that now is the time to make it the leader. No fears of a recession here!

Koichiro Dai / President

Stocks (¥50 par value, 1,000 shares min. trade)

Shares Issued (Nov. 1, '98)   23,332,000 shares
No. of Shareholders (Jul. 31, '98)   1,314

Major Holders	(%)
Sakuji Tanaka	9.1
Employees' Stockholding	9.0
Aibisu Co.	6.0
Setsuo Suzuki	3.3
Kyoko Tanaka	2.6
Sumitomo Trust	2.2
Daio Paper	2.1
Foreign Owners	0.4

Earnings

Period	Sales	Operating Profit	Current Profit	Net Profit	Earnings Per Share	Dividend Per Share
Jul 96	67,818	448	1,022	481	47.6	13.50
Jul 97	73,974	509	1,127	491	42.4	13.50
Jul 98	91,938	360	1,136	487	31.4	13.50
*Jul 99	132,000	550	1,780	740	31.7	13.50
*Jul 00	140,400	780	2,000	860	36.9	13.50
Mid-Term						
Jan 98	37,823	217	588	221	19.1	0
*Jan 99	66,400	250	890	360	15.4	0

Estimates. Per share values in ¥, all other amounts in millions of ¥.

Balance sheet summary	1994	1995	1996	1997	1998
Current assets	12,731	13,211	13,954	15,105	26,408
Fixed assets	6,904	8,705	9,098	9,287	14,026
Total assets	19,635	21,917	23,052	24,392	40,434
Current liabilities	10,175	11,174	12,557	14,202	22,119
Fixed liabilities	3,301	4,094	3,496	1,461	3,053
Total liabilities	13,477	15,268	16,053	15,664	25,172
Capital Stock	1,236	1,329	1,329	2,022	3,606
Shareholders' equity	6,158	6,649	6,999	8,728	15,262
Total liabilities and equity	19,635	21,917	23,052	24,392	40,434

Note: All amounts in millions of ¥. Balance sheet, end July.

Daiohs

(Estd. 1969, listed 1996, stock code no. 4653)
Company address: 2-4-1, Hamamatsu-cho, Minato-Ku, Tokyo 105-6123
Tel: 81-3-3438-5511 Fax: 81-3-3438-5515

An office service company, based in Tokyo (Hamamatsu-cho). 536 employees. A strict owner shacho (president), but a very successful one. Shinichi Ohkubo, 57 years old, is a pioneer in his trade. The first person in Japan to offer the service of bringing coffee to people's offices instead of letting the perennial "office ladies" do the job.

Product/Sales breakdown: Coffee furnished directly to offices, 59% of revenues; rental of items for the office, such as air-cleaners and doormats, 41%. Some 31% of Daioh's 1997/8 revenues of ¥10.3 billion was recorded overseas (the company bought a Californian firm, to operate in the same way as in Japan, serving offices).

Rivals/Competitors: Ohkubo-san had no rivals when he began the business of serving coffee and/or furnishing coffee machines in the mid-1970s. These days coffee-drinking has assumed epidemic proportions in Tokyo, and many new firms have leaped into the field. The outstanding competitor would be Unimat Offisco Corp., also an OTC company and a much more recent creation than Daiohs, set up only in 1991. Unimat, which concentrates exclusively or almost exclusively on serving coffee, claims to have nearly half of the national market. Sales are twice those of Daiohs.

History/Strategy: As regards offering coffee in offices, Ohkubo saw his opportunity and never looked back . . . but his start

in business goes back to 1969–70. Ohkubo was one of those, back in that era, who early on applied for a franchise from Duskin, an office service agency that is famous in Japan (as elsewhere) for furnishing companies with doormats, and keeping them clean. Ohkubo-san displayed his energy, and was recognized as the number one salesman in all Japan for Duskin. It was an indication of the energy he possesses, and willingness to pitch in and do a job himself.

Management: The man is something else. In an interview at his office Ohkubo-san polished off all the questions we could throw at him in a brisk 20 minutes.

Outlook: Daiohs was created by the efforts of one man. Can Shinichi Ohkubo keep it up? Margins have come down a bit in recent years, in the recession, but the company expects better results in the year to March '99 (see opposite page). Few firms in Japan have a shacho as hard-working – he is a martinet – as Ohkubo-san. What lies ahead? For one, Ohkubo-san would like in time to see his company quoted on the Nasdaq in New York. But for now he's preoccupied with more immediate concerns. "Respect for the environment" is a great theme for him; what this boils down to is teaching people with offices to let him collect empty carbon cartridges from their fax machines and process them rather than throwing them out on municipal rubbish tips.

Shinichi Ohkubo / President

Stocks (¥50 par value, 1,000 shares min. trade)

Shares Issued (Sep. 1, '98)	5,565,000 shares
No. of Shareholders (Mar. 31, '98)	504

Major Holders	(%)
Daioh Enterprise	43.3
Shinichi Ohkubo	20.4
Yoko Ohkubo	5.6
Hiroshi Ohkubo	4.4
Employees' Stockholding	2.4
Makoto Ohkubo	2.1
Jun Ohkubo	2.1
Foreign Owners	0.7

Earnings

Period	Sales	Operating Profit	Current Profit	Net Profit	Earnings Per Share	Dividend Per Share
Mar 96	8,468	562	572	386	76.1	10.00
Mar 97	9,285	612	615	392	74.0	15.00
Mar 98	10,281	652	695	349	62.8	15.00
**Mar 99	11,359	832	810	404	72.6	15.00
Mid-Term						
Sep 98	5,514	434	446	253	45.5	0

**Company estimates. Per share values in ¥, all other amounts in millions of ¥.

Balance sheet summary	1994	1995	1996	1997	1998
Current assets	2,165	2,322	2,026	3,125	3,262
Fixed assets	2,409	1,775	1,679	1,788	1,819
Total assets	4,575	4,097	3,705	4,914	5,081
Current liabilities	1,955	1,758	1,130	1,130	1,062
Fixed liabilities	1,043	471	319	114	88
Total liabilities	2,999	2,229	1,449	1,245	1,151
Capital Stock	337	337	363	743	743
Shareholders' equity	1,575	1,868	2,255	3,668	3,929
Total liabilities and equity	4,575	4,097	3,705	4,914	5,081

Note: All amounts in millions of ¥. Balance sheet, end March.

Digital Electronics

(Estd. 1972, listed 1997, stock code no. 6884)
Company address: 8-2-52, Nanko-Higashi, Suminoe-ku, Osaka 559-0031
Tel: 81-6-6613-1101 Fax: 81-6-6613-5888

Something there is in the light . . . Brightly lit panels have proliferated in the cities, in ATMs and in ticket machines in train stations, to guide the eye and the brain. The nation's factories these days feature machine tools and other production equipment with glowing computer panels . . . Who makes these? Little Digital Electronics of Osaka, with 455 employees, is a leader in this field.

Product/Sales breakdown: "Operational display equipment" ("graphic panels" is an expression also used) accounts for the lion's share of Digital Electronics' production (sales of ¥14.6 billion in the 1997/8 year), some 69%. The rest is in "control equipment", 12%, "specialty equipment", 11%, and others, 8%. The company, led by President Keizo Wada, 55, one of 4 founders, has pitched into a very rapidly growing industry, sometimes called "control equipment", in which sales have jumped, and are now heading for ¥1 trillion by about 2006, according to industry forecasts that predict yearly increases in demand.

Rivals/Competitors: Figures for 1997 show Digital Electronics as well ahead of rivals. One set of numbers – for so-called "mechatronic parts" used in the panels – shows Digital Electronics as the leader in Japan, with 44% of the market, Mitsubishi Electric running far behind with 15.7% and thereafter Omron with 11.6%. Digital Electronics has published English-language material also, giving itself a handsome lead over other players in 1997 – the company had more than half the market in large panels, and one-third in medium-size ones.

History/Strategy: Unless the eyes (and the numbers) deceive, which few believe, Digital Electronics has hit on a technology that is set to take the company a long way. That technology appears to have been developed in-house, but must be considered non-proprietary? So far royalties do not show up as a source of revenues.

Management: A unique feature of this company is that the largest stockholder is the employees' fund. To be sure, senior directors have large personal holdings, but the employees are ahead of them. "The company has no labour union and enjoys amicable labour relations", says Digital Electronics' report for the year ending March '98. It *is* a freer form corporation. There is one non-Japanese main board director, an unusual feature for a wholly Japanese company.

Outlook/Hot News: Yep, there is something about those luminous panels. Somehow, they dominate and control the spaces where they appear. As a leading maker in the field, Digital Electronics has nothing to lose except that lead . . . One of the companies great strengths would appear to be, as a spokesman mentioned, that the original founders – Wada-san as president, Tadashi Shimizu, Sumio Miyazaki and Masahiro Donoue – have remained together as an executive team with personal shareholdings in the firm, 27 years after its creation.

Keizo Wada / President

Stocks (¥50 par value, 1,000 shares min. trade)

Shares Issued (Nov. 1, '98)	6,613,200 shares
No. of Shareholders (Mar. 31, '98)	823

Major Holders	(%)
Employees' Stockholding	11.0
Keizo Wada	8.0
Tadashi Shimizu	7.2
Sumio Miyazaki	6.9
Masahiro Donoue	6.9
Shuji Fujii	5.3
Yoshiyasu Fujiwara	3.0
Foreign Owners	0.7

Earnings

Period	Sales	Operating Profit	Current Profit	Net Profit	Earnings Per Share	Dividend Per Share
Mar 96	11,641	1,188	1,091	556	1054.0	50.00
Mar 97	12,724	1,198	1,150	604	114.0	5.00
Mar 98	14,659	1,469	1,279	674	119.2	10.00
*Mar 99	14,500	1,200	1,100	600	90.7	10.00
*Mar 00	15,000	1,500	1,400	750	113.4	10.00
Mid-Term						
Sep 98	6,932	666	630	321	53.7	0
*Sep 99	7,000	700	650	350	52.9	0

*Estimates. Per share values in ¥, all other amounts in millions of ¥.

Balance sheet summary	1994	1995	1996	1997	1998
Current assets	4,955	5,557	5,689	6,362	10,138
Fixed assets	2,654	2,599	2,759	4,200	5,892
Total assets	7,610	8,157	8,448	10,563	16,030
Current liabilities	4,598	4,975	5,122	6,270	9,169
Fixed liabilities	1,467	1,509	1,122	1,460	972
Total liabilities	6,065	6,484	6,245	7,731	10,142
Capital Stock	441	441	441	481	1,271
Shareholders' equity	1,544	1,672	2,203	2,831	5,888
Total liabilities and equity	7,610	8,157	8,448	10,563	16,030

Note: All amounts in millions of ¥. Balance sheet, end March.

Fancl

(Estd. 1981, listed 1998, stock code no. 4921)
Company address: 109-1, Iijima-cho, Sakae-ku, Yokohama 247-8577
Tel: 81-45-890-1502 Fax: 81-45-890-1601

Manufacturer of "non-additive" (meaning no artificial preservatives) cosmetics, also "food supplements" (health foods). Based in Yokohama since 1980. 558 employees for Fancl group. Founded by current President Kenji Ikemori, 61.

Product/Sales breakdown: The company divides its revenues between cosmetics (62%), food products (35%), overseas business ventures and other items (3%).

Rivals/Competitors: In the field of non-additive cosmetics Fancl is market leader in Japan with a 37.8% share in the year to March '98, as compared with 12.9% for Shiseido and 6.2% for Kanebo. The long-established companies are having difficulty in competing with Fancl in non-additive cosmetics; to do so would undermine their existing cosmetics, which contain additives.

History/Strategy: The company is the creation of Mr. Ikemori, a former gas company executive. A low-key, highly original person, Ikemori-san did not fit into a corporate mould. Putting it differently, he needed to create a company of his own, Fancl. In the early days, he says, he was treated as a crank. However, he has won through. "Going on the Jasdaq," he remarks, "meant that all of a sudden big companies in distribution – such as Seven-Eleven – took us seriously." His success speaks for itself.

Management: Ikemori-san shows visitors to his office a copy of *The Beauty Bible* by Paula Begoun, an American authority on women's skincare. A note states: "Women with incredibly sensitive skin will no doubt be interested to learn that . . . in Japan the Fancl cosmetics company offers a line of preservative-free skin-care products . . . after being opened their products last about two to four weeks (probably more like two) . . . The Fancl corporation is very straightforward and honest about the limited shelf-life of their products."

Outlook/Hot News: The "hot news" – at the end of 1998 – was that Fancl stock all but doubled in price after it was registered as a newcomer to Jasdaq in July . . . Ikemori-san is meanwhile contemplating future projects. "No one knows what the Japanese economy is going to do, or when it will revive," he told visitors to his Yokohama headquarters in December. "But there are sure-fire situations, where you know pretty exactly what is going to come about – take demographics. We know that the over-65 population is going to soar in Japan through the year 2020; we also know that the ratio of those in their twenties to the population at large will plummet." Ikemori-san shows his visitors tables of statistics to support his remarks, also a copy of a magazine he founded recently, aimed at older people. "This is where the market of the future lies," he concludes. How he will develop that conclusion remains to be seen. He is sure to be original in whatever he does.

Kenji Ikemori / President

Stocks (¥50 par value, 1,000 shares min. trade)

Shares Issued (Nov. 1, '98)	9,900,000 shares
No. of Shareholders (Sep. 30, '98)	66

Major Holders	(%)
Kenji Ikemori	37.5
Hiromitsu Miyajima	13.3
Akiko Miyajima	9.3
Employees' Stockholding	7.6
Masaharu Ikemori	5.7
Taeko Fujiwara	4.3
Reiko Nakajima	3.6
Foreign Owners	0.0

Earnings

Period	Sales	Operating Profit	Current Profit	Net Profit	Earnings Per Share	Dividend Per Share
Mar 96	26,565	2,717	2,964	2,599	618.1	20.00
Mar 97	32,170	4,863	5,134	1,865	443.6	20.00
Mar 98	38,558	6,130	6,260	2,960	323.3	20.00
*Mar 99	45,800	6,800	6,900	3,600	330.3	20.00
*Mar 00	50,000	7,200	7,400	3,900	357.8	20.00
Mid-Term						
Sep 98	22,082	3,663	3,743	2,104	212.6	0
*Sep 99	23,000	3,800	3,900	2,200	201.8	0

*Estimates. Per share values in ¥, all other amounts in millions of ¥.

Balance sheet summary	1994	1995	1996	1997	1998
Current assets	6,055	5,152	6,251	12,923	14,250
Fixed assets	7,658	8,569	8,761	10,912	16,356
Total assets	13,713	13,721	15,013	23,836	30,606
Current liabilities	5,706	4,716	3,560	7,396	8,433
Fixed liabilities	1,065	1,008	911	2,321	4,143
Total liabilities	6,771	5,725	4,471	9,718	12,576
Capital Stock	496	496	496	496	1,017
Shareholders' equity	6,941	7,995	10,541	14,118	18,030
Total liabilities and equity	13,713	13,721	15,013	23,836	30,606

Note: All amounts in millions of ¥. Balance sheet, end March.

Ferrotec

(Estd. 1980, listed 1996, stock code no. 6890)
Company address: 5-24-8, Higashi-Ueno, Taito-Ku, Tokyo 110-0015
Tel: 81-3-3845-1032 Fax: 81-3-3845-1091

A small engineering firm with a specialty in magnetic fluid parts for computer hard disk drives. A leader in its field, with a 40% world market share in "seals" for those disk drives, to keep the dust out. Has 210 employees, of whom 100 work in a factory in Chibba, making the seals. The company is run by founder Akira Yamamura, 54, a distinguished research scientist in his field.

Product/Sales breakdown: Ferrotec analyses its sales – ¥5.3 billion in the year to March 1999 – as 47% in computer seals, 24% in "vacuum seals", a different variety, 2% in magnetic fluids and the remaining 27% in other items. Ferrotec's exports, 43% of revenues, are exceptionally high for a small firm in Japan.

Rivals/Competitors: Its specialities bring Ferrotec within competitive range of rich companies 100 times its size. Thus far Ferrotec has stayed too far ahead in price/performance to be challenged in its main specialty – the seals keep a computer's "brains" free of dust, shutting out the outside atmosphere, dust particles, tobacco smoke etc.

History/Strategy: Ferrotec is run independently by Yamamura-san. Kubota Corporation is Ferrotec's largest shareholder by far.

However, Yamamura-san, a brisk, equable character, is very much the man in charge, as becomes apparent on a visit to his Tokyo office.

Management: Ferrotec's distinction has been its success in developing its seals. Yamamura-san sums up: "Approximately 40% of disk drives produced today incorporate Ferrotec computer seals, as represented by approximately 4 million seals produced each month and over 40 million for calendar year 1997. With the development of MR head technology, disk drives will become more sensitive to electrostatic discharges (ESD), and will require an effective grounding mechanism to protect the head disk assembly. The computer seal with conductive ferrofluid (Ferrotec's product) serves to protect the head disk assembly from the ESD problem."

Outlook/Hot News: Yamamura-san is a rare Japanese shacho (president) who has spent a great part of his career overseas – 15 years in America. With his belief in taking the initiative, the Ferrotec executive should continue to be hugely successful. It's his technology – expertise in ferro-fluids that he developed himself – that puts Yamamura-san in the catbird seat.

Akira Yamamura / President

Stocks (¥50 par value, 1,000 shares min. trade)

Shares Issued (Nov. 1, '98)	9,095,000 shares
No. of Shareholders (Sep. 30, '98)	1,106

Major Holders	(%)
Kubota Corp.	19.7
Akira Yamamura	8.3
Sumitomo Trust	6.3
Bank of Tokyo-Mitsubishi	4.6
JAFCO	4.3
JAFCO Properties	4.1
Kita-Nippon Bank	2.0
Foreign Owners	4.6

Earnings

Period	Sales	Operating Profit	Current Profit	Net Profit	Earnings Per Share	Dividend Per Share
Mar 96	3,640	359	474	255	303.8	50.00
Mar 97	3,878	367	459	239	27.5	7.00
Mar 98	4,659	409	511	310	34.3	7.00
**Mar 99	5,300	500	600	330	36.3	7.00
*Mar 00	5,700	600	750	400	44.0	7.00
Mid-Term						
Sep 97	2,350	188	176	142	15.8	0
*Sep 98	2,400	200	230	130	14.3	0

*Estimates; **Company estimates. Per share values in ¥, all other amounts in millions of ¥.

Balance sheet summary	1994	1995	1996	1997	1998
Current assets	2,012	2,348	2,881	3,165	3,617
Fixed assets	2,112	2,144	2,146	2,673	3,136
Total assets	4,124	4,493	5,028	5,838	6,754
Current liabilities	1,416	1,350	1,704	1,245	1,611
Fixed liabilities	601	710	675	472	771
Total liabilities	2,017	2,061	2,380	1,717	2,382
Capital Stock	1,065	1,109	1,109	1,304	1,310
Shareholders' equity	2,106	2,432	2,647	4,121	4,371
Total liabilities and equity	4,124	4,493	5,028	5,838	6,754

Note: All amounts in millions of ¥. Balance sheet, end March.

Focus Systems

(Estd. 1977, listed 1996, stock code no. 4662)
Company address: 2-7-8, Higashi-Gotanda, Shinagawa-ku, Tokyo 141-0022
Tel: 81-3-5421-7777 Fax: 81-3-5421-3201

A small-medium software company, with ties to the public sector – NTT Data, the ministries. 513 employees, located at Shinagawa, in central Tokyo. President is Masatoshi Ishibashi, 49.

Product/Sales breakdown: The 1997/8 accounts show that this company leans towards a few heavyweight, state-oriented clients. Out of sales of ¥8.37 billion some ¥2.92 billion was related to "communications networks", meaning probably NTT Data (34.9% of sales). The company's largest clients (details are withheld) are perhaps the big ministries in Tokyo, amounting to ¥3.76 billion (44.9%) in the period. Focus Systems says that it is entering the CD-ROM field but so far the result is nil in terms of reported revenues. Ditto for the Internet.

Rivals/Competitors: Rivals abound. Focus Systems' ability to expand would seem to have depended on close, if not cosy, relations with officials in government departments.

History/Strategy: The company made a gentle start after its creation in 1977, taking 9 years to raise its paid-in capital to ¥100 million. The official history, as published on the Net, mentions NTT Data as a client from 1990, but not before. Sales and revenue rose steadily in recent years. Focus Systems is positioned to receive some part of the Ministry of Posts and Telecommunications huge new development budget of ¥7 trillion, intended to boost the economy.

Management: Has seemed a shade timorous in its approach to such new fields for the company as CD-ROM and the Internet.

Outlook/Hot News: Focus Systems is a small-medium size player in an industry that is increasingly dominated by middle-weights – say Fuji ABC Soft, Konami and Nippon System Development. The company is carrying long-term debt on its books equivalent to 15 years of net profits. It needs to grow out of its mindset: that everything takes time. It needs to speed up. There are now indications that this is happening. One sign is that it is recruiting. It will take on an undisclosed number of new graduates in April 1999. Demand for communications software has been going up. NTT and NTT Data have stepped up their demand for applications software, according to trade sources. At the same time there is work from IBM. Maintenance fees are coming in. That is not all: details are lacking, but an increased demand from IBM Japan promises to raise overall revenues to ¥15 billion by the year 2000, as compared with forecasts of under ¥10 billion for the year to March 1999 (see opposite). All this looks like a change of gear, going up!

Masatoshi Ishibashi / President

Stocks (¥50 par value, 1,000 shares min. trade)

Shares Issued (Nov. 1, '98)   6,617,000 shares

No. of Shareholders (Mar. 31, '98)   1,254

Major Holders	(%)
Mitsuhiro Higashi	14.9
Tatsuhiko Kakigi	4.5
Chase Manhattan Bank (London)	3.3
Yoshifumi Hatayama	2.8
Yujiro Tsutsumi	2.8
Masatoshi Ishibashi	2.7
Yasuo Shimizu	2.7
Foreign Owners	8.2

Earnings

Period	Sales	Operating Profit	Current Profit	Net Profit	Earnings Per Share	Dividend Per Share
Mar 96	6,507	453	329	117	31.7	8.00
Mar 97	7,378	599	408	161	40.2	10.00
Mar 98	8,376	664	496	203	34.5	12.00
**Mar 99	9,550	720	600	270	39.3	12.00
**Mar 00	11,100	800	660	314	45.3	12.00
Mid-Term						
Sep 97	3,416	91	21	9	1.8	0
*Sep 98	3,550	100	30	10	1.5	0

*Estimates; **Company estimates. Per share values in ¥, all other amounts in millions of ¥.

Balance sheet summary	1996	1997	1998
Current assets	4,493	4,639	7,122
Fixed assets	4,372	4,448	4,379
Total assets	8,883	9,101	11,610
Current liabilities	4,740	4,933	3,630
Fixed liabilities	2,774	2,032	3,581
Total liabilities	7,514	6,965	7,212
Capital Stock	599	873	1,935
Shareholders' equity	1,369	2,135	4,398
Total liabilities and equity	8,883	9,101	11,610

Note: All amounts in millions of ¥. Balance sheet, end March.

Fuji

(Estd. 1965, listed 1995, stock code no. 7471)
Company address: 1-31-1, Ryutsudanchi-Ichijo, Asahikawa City, Hokkaido 079-8585
Tel: 81-166-47-2818 Fax: 81-166-46-2882

A retail operation based at Asahikawa, the number 2 city in Hokkaido after Sapporo. Family-run firm creating supermarkets and expanding steadily. Low margins in the stores. Run by father (Chairman Hiroshi Muguruma, 71), and son (President Akira Muguruma, 45). 188 employees.

Product/Sales breakdown: Fuji, founded in the mid-1960s and therefore early into the supermarket field, specializes in foodstuffs, mainly processed stuff that stays on the shelves (43% of revenue; sales were ¥17 billion in the year to April 1998), but also perishable foods (29%). The rest is a mixture of daily necessities like toothpaste; liquor; items for the home; and sports goods. In other words these are general stores – the Mugurumas operate them under the chain-names of "Fuji Family Foods" and "Western Power".

Rivals/Competitors: There's plenty of rivalry from other supermarket and chain-store operations in Hokkaido, one reason perhaps why gross margins are low at 3% approx. If anything competition will increase.

History/Strategy: Hokkaido is Big Sky country, the only part of Japan that is. Fuji's general-purpose stores function like such stores anywhere in the world (though the American West springs to mind, with those big open landscapes, largely bereft of people). The stores serve as the closest thing to community centres, churches and recreation spots all wrapped into one, with space available alongside the supermarkets for others to come in, including wholesalers, and sell stuff or offer DIY items. Instead of temples and shrines . . . The Japanese call these "power centres"; well social centres they are.

Management: With his son established in office, founder Hiroshi-san can sit back and relax. The succession is assured. It's important for people to know that in a community where there are no secrets. It helps business. Fuji has borrowed a good deal, half its balance sheet actually – to judge by a credit report that goes back aways – including long-term finance from Hokkaido Bank that goes all the way to 2010, secured on property. That bank, be it noted, is a shareholder in Fuji, as is Asahikawa Shinkin Bank, a local institution.

Outlook/Hot News: A firm like Fuji, with its roots deep in the local community, has nowhere to go but up. The photos of the Mugurumas, father and son, found on their website, are a bit solemn and heavy-featured, but make one feel secure. Hokkaido has emerged as a great place for supermarket chains in recent years . . . much like the Fukuoka area in Kyushu. These are the two parts of Japan that are most hospitable to the new types of retailing, so the word goes.

Akira Muguruma / President

Stocks (¥50 par value, 1,000 shares min. trade)

Shares Issued (Nov. 1, '98)	4,973,000 shares
No. of Shareholders (Apr. 20, '98)	591

Major Holders	(%)
Hiroshi Muguruma	20.7
Maruroku Co.	10.1
Hokkaido Bank	4.2
Asahikawa Shinkin Bank	3.6
Employees' Stockholding	3.5
Dai-ichi Life Ins.	2.8
JAFCO	2.5
Foreign Owners	0.0

Earnings

Period	Sales	Operating Profit	Current Profit	Net Profit	Earnings Per Share	Dividend Per Share
Apr 96	15,014	590	443	273	58.9	12.00
Apr 97	16,000	527	413	223	45.1	12.00
Apr 98	17,578	615	544	276	55.7	15.00
**Apr 99	19,522	N/A	630	338	68.0	15.00
*Apr 00	22,000	840	760	440	88.5	15.00
Mid-Term						
Oct 97	8,723	368	323	163	32.9	0
**Oct 98	9,895	N/A	339	173	N/A	0

*Estimates; **Company estimates. Per share values in ¥, all other amounts in millions of ¥.

Balance sheet summary	1994	1995	1996	1997	1998
Current assets	1,578	1,434	1,593	1,816	1,823
Fixed assets	5,834	6,008	6,440	6,831	7,068
Total assets	7,413	7,442	8,033	8,697	8,917
Current liabilities	2,331	2,393	2,742	2,385	2,550
Fixed liabilities	3,814	3,598	2,934	3,788	3,634
Total liabilities	6,145	5,992	5,676	6,147	6,185
Capital Stock	329	329	605	611	611
Shareholders' equity	1,267	1,450	2,356	2,523	2,731
Total liabilities and equity	7,413	7,442	8,033	8,697	8,917

Note: All amounts in millions of ¥. Balance sheet, end April.

Fujimi

(Estd. 1953, listed 1995, stock code no. 5384)
Company address: 2-1-1, Jiryo, Nishi-Biwajimacho, Nishi-Kasugaigun,
Aichi Pref. 452-8502
Tel: 81-52-503-8181 Fax: 81-52-504-8085

An extremely strong manufacturing company, a maker of silicon wafer polishing materials. Akira Koshiyama, 48, is President and his elder brother Isamu is Chairman of what is still a family business. Employs 355.

Product/Sales breakdown: The company divides its activities between "mirror surface finishing materials" (38%), polishing materials (35%) and other products (9%) and purchased products, mainly polishing machines (18%). It has a wholly-owned manufacturing subsidiary in America, an important market for Fujimi. Silicon wafers are materials used in the manufacture of semiconductors – extremely fine materials required for intricate end results.

Rivals/Competitors: Given the high profits in the specialty, and the difficulty of protecting knowhow in an industry with many players, competition is bound to increase. Fujimi's margins are high, enough to attract jealous eyes.

History/Strategy: The company was created by the father of the Koshiyama brothers, still the owners 46 years after Fujimi's start-up. Its strategy has been bold for a small firm. Impressed by the potential of the market Fujimi set up a US manufacturing subsidiary and a sales JV. It is rare for such a small company to make the leap into production in America, but Fujimi probably did the right thing – there being scope for information gathering over there; to have had some of its best people becoming deeply involved in the US has been a plus for company morale.

Management: Fujimi will remain in the hands of the owning family for the time being.

Outlook/Hot News: The mirror is one of Japan's three imperial regalia. Such a mirror is made of burnished metal ... It seems appropriate that a company that specializes in polishing wafers – the essence of creating a mirror being to polish away – should be prominent in Japan. Fujimi's margins, its export performance (34% of sales, despite the climb in the yen) and its technology combine to make it one of the outstanding small firms in the Nagoya region, long known for producing some of Japan's best engineers. The virtual collapse of capital investment in semiconductors has hurt confidence throughout Japanese industry in latter 1998. Fujimi's earnings prospects are fair, bearing in mind the widening recession ... few mainstream manufacturing companies can boast near 20% margins on sales. The company's balance sheet is all but free of borrowing despite its heavy investment over the years in Japan and in America. Latest prospects – for 1999/2000 – were for sales and earnings to hold level at best, but still those formidable margins stand not to be cut into (see opposite).

Akira Koshiyama / President

Stocks (¥50 par value, 100 shares min. trade)

Shares Issued (Nov. 1, '98)	15,602,470 shares
No. of Shareholders (Sep. 30, '98)	3,031

Major Holders	(%)
Isamu Koshiyama	12.4
Sumitaka Noda	10.8
Asahi Bank	4.6
Koma	3.6
Akira Koshiyama	3.4
Employees' Stockholding	3.1
Tokai Bank	2.3
Foreign Owners	13.7

Earnings

Period	Sales	Operating Profit	Current Profit	Net Profit	Earnings Per Share	Dividend Per Share
Mar 96	18,630	3,649	3,614	1,856	169.5	16.00
Mar 97	21,672	4,268	4,320	2,098	168.0	19.00
Mar 98	26,645	4,876	5,061	2,679	188.9	23.00
**Mar 99	23,700	3,900	4,000	2,300	147.4	11.50
*Mar 00	26,500	4,650	4,900	2,650	169.9	23.00
Mid-Term						
Sep 98	12,882	2,031	1,994	1,173	75.2	11.50
*Sep 99	13,650	2,360	2,200	1,190	76.3	11.50

*Estimates; **Company estimates. Per share values in ¥, all other amounts in millions of ¥.

Balance sheet summary	1994	1995	1996	1997	1998
Current assets	14,204	15,311	19,557	22,076	25,872
Fixed assets	5,893	7,275	9,250	12,326	13,797
Total assets	20,098	22,586	28,808	34,402	39,670
Current liabilities	4,253	6,015	7,609	6,803	9,548
Fixed liabilities	2,021	1,425	1,230	1,418	1,613
Total liabilities	6,274	7,441	8,839	8,221	11,161
Capital Stock	1,117	1,117	2,557	4,753	4,753
Shareholders' equity	13,823	15,145	19,968	26,181	28,508
Total liabilities and equity	20,098	22,586	28,808	34,402	39,670

Note: All amounts in millions of ¥. Balance sheet, end March.

53

Fuji Seal

(Estd. 1958, listed 1997, stock code no. 7864)
Company address: 3-5-26, Kyutaro-machi, Chuo-ku, Osaka 541-0056
Tel: 81-6-6252-6814 Fax: 81-6-6244-4968

"Packaging Tomorrow" is the slogan of this unusual Osaka-based company, a specialist in wrapping, packing, sealing etc. President Tadashi Nakano, 64, runs the show under the eagle eye of Chairman Masaaki Fujio, 68. There are 855 employees.

Product/Sales breakdown: Fuji Seal divides its product between "shrinkage" seals/labels (47%), adhesive seals/labels (16%), machinery (11%), processed products (8%), others (18%). "Shrink-wrap seals and labels" of the first category were developed in the 1970s in what amounted to a packaging revolution. The lightweight material that closes the mouth of a bottle or labels a vessel is "shrunk" into place.

Rivals/Competitors: The company's market share in its specialty packing (50%) makes it dominant. At the same time it has kept prices and margins down, to maintain its market position.

History/Strategy: Fuji Seal was formally established in 1958. However, the company's history goes back to 1897, when the first Fujio commenced business in the Osaka region. The family constitutes a proud dynasty in Osaka business terms worthy of a novel. The ramifying development of Fuji Seal's knowhow – see the company's catalogues for a proud array of different types of seals, "shrink-wrap seals" and the like, as applied to bottles and containers of all shapes and sizes, often small – has given the firm its dominant market share in Japan. Extending its territory, Fuji Seal has built production companies abroad.

Management: The Chairman is actually the one with power in this company. He reigns, President Nakano rules.

Outlook/Hot News: Sooner or later the Fujio family will surrender control of the business. Such is the nature of family businesses . . . However, for now the established line is very much in place in the person of Chairman Fujio, a patriarchal figure. Besides him there are several other Fujio descendants on the main board, three of them figuring as prominent stockholders in the company. Meanwhile, Fuji Seal is working well. The company shows no sign of losing its grip on a business that has attracted the Japanese from time immemorial – packaging is a minor art form in Japan, always has been. Its sealing technology, including its "shrink seal" knowhow, has been patented; this is the company's zaisan, or treasure. Foreign investors like this firm, so do the Japanese themselves. The real strength of Fuji Seal, meanwhile, shows in its activities overseas. The company has gone into production in the US, UK and Thailand. A joint venture in Thailand is operating in the black, having a claimed market share in its specialties of over 50%. Fuji Seal has a 100%-owned subsidiary in the UK, and a 51% joint venture in the US with Nichimen, a trading company.

Tadashi Nakano / President

Stocks (¥50 par value, 100 shares min. trade)

Shares Issued (Nov. 1, '98)	7,609,000 shares
No. of Shareholders (May. 31, '98)	162

Major Holders	(%)
Toumei Ltd.	28.5
Employees' Stockholding	8.3
Masaaki Fujio	6.7
Takashi Fujio	5.7
Yasuhiro Fujio	3.2
Hiroko Fujio	1.8
Hiroo Okazaki	1.8
Foreign Owners	10.8

Earnings

Period	Sales	Operating Profit	Current Profit	Net Profit	Earnings Per Share	Dividend Per Share
Mar 96	34,013	1,762	1,864	674	1,755.8	75.00
Mar 97	37,608	1,987	2,248	763	1,763.5	100.00
Mar 98	40,050	2,309	2,615	1,371	200.8	15.00
**Mar 99	42,500	2,590	2,860	1,495	196.5	12.50
Mid-Term						
Sep 98	22,311	1,747	1,969	1,025	138.5	0

**Company estimates. Per share values in ¥, all other amounts in millions of ¥.

Balance sheet summary	1995	1996	1997	1998
Current assets	12,634	13,879	16,648	17,208
Fixed assets	10,565	11,740	11,456	13,143
Total assets	23,199	25,619	28,105	30,351
Current liabilities	11,431	12,324	14,645	15,634
Fixed liabilities	4,859	5,313	4,763	3,000
Total liabilities	16,290	17,638	19,409	18,635
Capital Stock	514	724	724	1,499
Shareholders' equity	6,908	7,981	8,696	11,716
Total liabilities and equity	23,199	25,619	28,105	30,351

Note: All amounts in millions of ¥. Balance sheet, end March.

Goldcrest

(Estd. 1992, listed 1998, stock code no. 8871)
Company address: 1-18-16, Shimbashi, Minato-ku, Tokyo 105-0004
Tel: 81-3-3504-2111 Fax: 81-3-3504-2110

A Tokyo-based condominium developer, a rare and hardy species in a real estate slump. Founder/President is Hidetoshi Yasukawa, 37. He has 35 employees.

Product/Sales breakdown: Goldcrest's activities break down as between real estate (condo) sales at 79% of turnover, and commissions (on real estate deals) at 21%. No other revenue sources.

Rivals/Competitors: There are half a dozen obvious ones in central Tokyo. In the Shimbashi section, where Yasukawa-san has chosen to be, the rival which comes to mind is Japan's biggest condo developer, Recruit Cosmos, with annual revenues of ¥202 billion (consolidated) in the year to March '98.

History/Strategy: Mr. Yasukawa comes from Recruit Cosmos. He left the firm to create his own company in 1992, shortly after the collapse of Japan's asset bubble. Recruit Cosmos is stuck with the aftermath of the bubble in the shape of loans that it can only just service. Yasukawa-san timed his departure from the company well, setting up a new firm with a clean balance sheet. His strategy – to deal in top-quality condos in first class locations – is one he learned with his former company.

Management: To motivate his employees Mr. Yasukawa has encouraged them to buy stock in the firm. He kept the whip hand with a dominant personal holding (see opposite page).

Outlook/Hot News: Goldcrest's rapid advance into the real estate field – one day Mr. Yasukawa wants to overtake his former employer, Recruit Cosmos – suggests either very great self-confidence or folly. True, real estate values were still on the way down in late 1998. However, the evidence is in favour of the first, happier interpretation: sales of Goldcrest condos are expected to expand at a rapid rate in 1999–2000, see forecasts on opposite page; there are still plenty of people in Tokyo with large amounts of money – in cash – despite the recession; for such private investors a new apartment is the ideal long-term investment. Yasukawa-san has borrowed to get his company moving. The willingness of banks to back him – in the middle of a credit squeeze – suggests that those best informed about the details of Goldcrest's projects (location, price, margin) are impressed. Speculation in real estate, this is not. Banzai!

To be sure, Yasukawa-san's company is still very small. Much depends on the example the boss sets. He qualified as an ikkyu kenchikushi, a quantity surveyor. Prestige is important in this industry – to be perceived to be above average and honest.

Hidetoshi Yasukawa / President

Stocks (¥50 par value, 1,000 shares min. trade)

Shares Issued (Nov. 1, '98)   4,420,000 shares
No. of Shareholders (Sep. 30, '98)   239

Major Holders	(%)
Hidetoshi Yasukawa	60.2
Employees' Stockholding	4.4
Hiroyuki Shimazaki	3.4
Success Factory	3.3
Sakura Bank	2.3
Masao Tai	2.3
Sumitomo Trust	1.8
Foreign Owners	1.2

Earnings

Period	Sales	Operating Profit	Current Profit	Net Profit	Earnings Per Share	Dividend Per Share
May 96	1,954	444	448	231	209,948.2	7,500.00
May 97	1,665	289	320	194	73,572.8	6,250.00
May 98	4,027	642	640	296	74,159.2	7,500.00
*May 99	8,900	1,400	1,250	600	135.7	15.00
*May 00	15,000	2,000	2,000	950	214.9	10.00
Mid-Term						
Sep 98	6,343	1,284	1,247	603	144.6	5.00
*Sep 99	9,300	1,600	1,580	720	162.9	5.00

*Estimates. Per share values in ¥, all other amounts in millions of ¥.

Balance sheet summary	1994	1995	1996	1997	1998
Current assets	1,463	2,065	2,599	6,264	7,360
Fixed assets	49	55	244	528	547
Total assets	1,512	2,120	2,844	6,793	7,907
Current liabilities	1,415	1,846	2,090	4,456	5,467
Fixed liabilities		2	52	1,448	1,247
Total liabilities	1,415	1,849	2,142	5,904	6,714
Capital Stock	30	30	182	182	201
Shareholders' equity	97	271	702	888	1,193
Total liabilities and equity	1,512	2,120	2,844	6,793	7,907

Note: All amounts in millions of ¥. Balance sheet, end May.

57

Graphic Products

(Estd. 1981, listed 1997, stock code no. 6886)
Company address: 2-17-22, Takada, Toshima-ku, Tokyo 171-0033
Tel: 81-3-5656-7302 Fax: 81-3-5956-7303

A specialist in computer-aided design (CAD) and computer-aided manufacturing (CAM) systems. CEO is Masakazu Tabata 47. 163 employees.

Product/Sales breakdown: Output is mainly in CAD/CAM systems (88% of revenues). Maintenance contracts are worth 10% of sales, and DNC (direct numerical control) systems just 2%. Revenues took a dive in 1998, falling by 20% according to estimates at the time of writing. The company is dependent on new orders, these being related to capital investment; at a time when such investment is slowing down or halted, Graphic Products has to pause.

Rivals/Competitors: The company has rivals – Andor, a newcomer to Jasdaq in autumn 1996, also specializes in CAD/CAM for industry, and provides maintenance; the model is the same.

History/Strategy: Tabata-san, who has been with the company since 1985, explains Graphic Products' history in these terms. "Ever since our establishment we have devoted ourselves . . . to the application of computer technology in the production of dies (moulds which are made of metal and used for mass-producing merchandise with identical shapes . . . a critical mainstay of manufacturing industry)." He continues: "It is the dies made in Japan, which have supported the manufacturing industries not only in Japan but throughout the world . . . (Now) leading manufacturers in Japan have been obliged to shift their manufacturing bases offshore. (We) ask ourselves whether it is enough to approach die-making . . . as we have done in the past. We believe that Japan's die manufacturers should now be seriously concerned."

Management: There appears to be no easy answer for management in the CAD/CAM field in the current slowdown (see earnings forecasts opposite).

Outlook/Hot News: Graphic Products has had a terrific start since its creation in the early 1980s, accumulating shareholder value, running ahead without incurring debt over an 18-year period. It is now experiencing a slowdown, as the recession bites into capital equipment spending and demand for its services – for its dies – eases off. Japan has indulged in the biggest splurge in capital investment in industry in history during the 1990s despite the fact that the economy was in a slowdown and, finally, a recession. A company such as Graphic Products is exposed to a slowdown in demand due to a surfeit of investment. How long will the slowdown last? No one knows. For the first time in its short history this company is going to be severely tested by negative macrotrends. The collapse of capital investment in such industries as semiconductor manufacture is real.

Masakazu Tabata / President

Stocks (¥50 par value, 1,000 shares min. trade)

Shares Issued (Nov. 1, '98)   4,508,000 shares
No. of Shareholders (Dec. 31, '97)   593

Major Holders	(%)
Tool Co.	28.6
Kazuo Nishida	8.1
Nippon Life Ins.	6.9
Tooru Takizawa	4.6
Norio Yasue	3.3
Deutscher Auslands-Kassenverei	3.1
Employees' Stockholding	2.3
Foreign Owners	7.8

Earnings

Period	Sales	Operating Profit	Current Profit	Net Profit	Earnings Per Share	Dividend Per Share
Dec 95	3,180	295	321	210	69.9	20.00
Dec 96	4,413	759	771	453	107.8	15.00
Dec 97	4,924	965	907	571	130.7	20.00
*Dec 98	4,000	320	400	200	44.4	20.00
*Dec 99	3,800	200	200	150	33.3	20.00
Mid-Term						
Jun 98	2,284	356	364	217	48.2	N/A
*Jun 99	1,900	100	100	70	15.5	N/A

*Estimates. Per share values in ¥, all other amounts in millions of ¥.

Balance sheet summary	1994	1995	1996	1997
Current assets	2,367	2,928	3,585	5,498
Fixed assets	878	723	823	813
Total assets	3,245	3,651	4,408	6,311
Current liabilities	363	594	936	946
Fixed liabilities	129	124	167	157
Total liabilities	493	719	1,103	1,103
Capital Stock	475	475	475	884
Shareholders' equity	2,752	2,932	3,305	5,208
Total liabilities and equity	3,245	3,651	4,408	6,311

Note: All amounts in millions of ¥. Balance sheet, end December.

Green House

(Estd. 1959, listed 1990, stock code no. 9689)
Company address: 3-20-2, Nishi-Shinjuku, Shinjuku-ku, Tokyo 163-1477
Tel: 81-3-3379-1211 Fax: 81-3-3370-9280

A top-ranking caterer for corporations and government offices, especially in central Tokyo. A family-owned business run by a second generation son, Chiaki Tanuma, 47. His father, the founder Bunzo Tanuma, is non-executive Chairman.

Product/Sales breakdown: The company lists "food catering to offices" as its main line (32%), followed by "catering to factories" (17%). "Other food services" account for 28% of the revenues, "food materials" for 16% and "restaurants" for 7%.

Rivals/Competitors: Catering is a profitable, expanding trade – worldwide – offering steady if not spectacular margins. In Japan the players include: Shidax Food Service, based at Chofu City, outside Tokyo, specializing in meal services for institutional clients; and AIM Services, a joint venture of Mitsui & Co., the trading house, and Aramark of the US. Green House is slightly the smaller of the three in terms of revenues. As the trio expand and others join in, competition will increase.

History/Strategy: Mr. Tanuma said in an interview that he is in what he calls "the 'opium' business", an acronymic pun on the expression "other people's money" that is all but untranslatable (from Japanese English to English). He meant that other companies provide the capital and the buildings (offices, hospitals); his company – here comes the cash flow – furnishes services under con-

tract, for example in the central Tokyo building (Opera City Tower, Shinjuku) where Green House has its head office. Some 8,000 work in the building in question. Many of them take their midday meals upstairs at a communal restaurant. That restaurant, which is open to the general public, is served by Green House. A range of different cuisines (try the 4-dish Chinese lunch at ¥780) is on offer, all furnished under contract by Mr. Tanuma and some of his 1,187 employees.

Management: The CEO is a graduate of the Cornell University catering and hotel management school. He speaks English and knows the great success that catering companies have had in the US, thereby he foresees very considerable growth for the industry in Japan, which lagged behind the US in this field. Mr. Tanuma's style is a blend of American openness and Japanese gentlemanliness. "We care for people, we wish to be loved by people," says the boss, adding that this is the company slogan – thereon permitting himself a slight smile.

Outlook/Hot News: Tanuma-san's thinking does not stop short in Japan. He has subsidiaries, albeit small, in both Canada and the US, the latter specializing in meals for hospitals. Green House aims to be seen as a "food consultant" on an international scale and to inculcate everywhere the principles it follows in Japan: no additives in food, no artificial flavouring!

Chiaki Tanuma / President

Stocks (¥50 par value, 1,000 shares min. trade)

Shares Issued (Nov. 1, '98)	6,757,000 shares
No. of Shareholders (Sep. 30, '98)	483

Major Holders	(%)
Green Kaihatsu	18.5
Chiaki Tanuma	17.3
Yuho Co.	9.9
Green House Foods	9.3
DKB	4.1
Sumitomo Trust	3.0
Bunzo Tanuma	2.5
Foreign Owners	0.9

Earnings

Period	Sales	Operating Profit	Current Profit	Net Profit	Earnings Per Share	Dividend Per Share
Mar 96	30,205	1,035	1,126	513	75.9	20.00
Mar 97	34,448	911	1,032	542	80.3	20.00
Mar 98	37,045	1,225	1,452	544	80.6	20.00
**Mar 99	40,100	1,530	1,600	690	102.1	20.00
*Mar 00	44,000	1,700	1,800	800	118.4	20.00
Mid-Term						
Sep 97	18,198	594	722	286	42.3	0
Sep 98	19,182	625	727	306	45.3	0

*Estimates; **Company estimates. Per share values in ¥, all other amounts in millions of ¥.

Balance sheet summary	1994	1995	1996	1997	1998
Current assets	6,212	6,770	7,056	6,900	6,777
Fixed assets	4,883	6,580	6,718	7,706	7,507
Total assets	11,096	13,350	13,774	14,606	14,284
Current liabilities	3,223	4,394	4,753	5,355	4,929
Fixed liabilities	290	1,000	709	580	320
Total liabilities	3,514	5,395	5,463	5,936	5,250
Capital Stock	2,083	2,083	2,083	2,083	2,083
Shareholders' equity	7,581	7,955	8,311	8,669	9,034
Total liabilities and equity	11,096	13,350	13,774	14,606	14,284

Note: All amounts in millions of ¥. Balance sheet, end March.

Hikari Tsushin

(Estd. 1988, listed 1996, stock code no. 9435)
Company address: 2-1-1, Ohtemachi, Chiyoda-ku, Tokyo 100-0004
Tel: 81-3-3510-2300 Fax: 81-3-3510-2322

A telecom subscription agency. Founded by Yasumitsu Shigeta, 33. Has 911 employees.

Product/Sales breakdown: Sales exploded in the 1995/7 period, as use of cellular phones spread like wildfire all over Japan. Shigeta-san, very much the boss, and still only at the start of his career, has created a network of 500 shops, all franchise operations, throughout Japan, to sell phones and telecom services. Sales break down to 67% in commissions (received from NTT and others), and 32% in "equipment sales", i.e. cellular phones. The remaining 1% of income comes from charges on installations.

Rivals/Competitors: Mr. Shigeta – short, sharp and concise in speech – says that he has 50% approximately of the market he serves, secured through that nationwide network of shops. He aims to have 1,000 such shops by the end of 1999. No rival firm has more than 50 outlets, he said in an interview.

History/Strategy: Shigeta-san dropped out of college – Nihon University in Tokyo – at the age of 22, to set himself up in business with ¥1 million of his own money. A born salesman, he plunged into a rapidly deregulating telecom world that, he says, is in fact "very difficult to understand from outside". Seizing on his opportunity, and deciding on a franchising strategy, implemented with what some saw as ruthlessness – only 5% of his franchisees survived, according to one story

– he built up a business that is still growing. "Those 500 shops we have now sell cellular phones," he says, "in future they will be multi-media shops." He has borrowed to create his business. Loans accounted for nearly one quarter of his balance sheet in early 1998.

Management: Self-confidence is the hallmark of the organization Shigeta-san has created, with its headquarters in the Otemachi financial section of Tokyo in a building nicknamed "the Nomura Bubble building", which is owned by the securities company and noted for its spectacular architecture. A financial PR aide to Shigeta furnished a visitor there with a copy of a company report detailing, among other things, how some disgruntled former sub-agents of Hikari Tsushin are suing the firm for allegedly unpaid commissions. Most of the report details, in glowing terms, the company's recent performance (see opposite page).

Outlook/Hot News: The one play Shigeta-san feels he has missed to date, he asserts unprompted, has been to let foreigners take more of a stake in his company. Expect an aggressive financial PR campaign to raise that stake from 3.1% at end 1998. Shigeta-san, by the way, as one would expect of a salesman, is well able to explain the "secrets" of his success in business. "Low risk, high return," is his motto, he says.

Yasumitsu Shigeta / President

Stocks (¥50 par value, 100 shares min. trade)

Shares Issued (Nov. 1, '98)   29,507,400 shares
No. of Shareholders (Aug. 31, '98)   4,998

Major Holders	(%)
Hikari Power	48.1
Yasumitsu Shigeta	21.3
Kansai Mac	2.6
Tokyo Setsubi	1.3
Toyo Trust	0.8
Sumitomo Trust	0.8
Mitsui Trust	0.5
Foreign Owners	3.1

Earnings

Period	Sales	Operating Profit	Current Profit	Net Profit	Earnings Per Share	Dividend Per Share
Aug 96	56,247	3,540	3,295	1485	176.6	15.00
Aug 97	122,058	6,053	6,351	3198	184.4	50.00
Aug 98	159,619	6,970	10,162	5048	171.1	60.00
**Aug 99	200,000	9,500	12,600	6600	223.7	40.00
*Aug 00	220,000	11,500	14,000	7000	237.2	60.00
Mid-Term						
Feb 98	74,544	3,451	4,151	2051	69.5	10.00
**Feb 99	87,000	3,500	4,200	2200	74.6	10.00

*Estimates; **Company estimates. Per share values in ¥, all other amounts in millions of ¥.

Balance sheet summary	1994	1995	1996	1997	1998
Current assets	5,291	7,047	19,473	27,281	39,150
Fixed assets	3,792	4,210	6,179	15,518	21,697
Total assets	9,083	11,257	25,652	42,799	60,847
Current liabilities	5,121	6,537	8,875	13,333	17,369
Fixed liabilities	2,514	2,415	877	653	11,106
Total liabilities	7,635	8,953	9,752	13,987	28,475
Capital Stock	511	607	2,351	7,325	7,325
Shareholders' equity	1,448	2,304	15,899	28,812	32,372
Total liabilities and equity	9,083	11,257	25,652	42,799	60,847

Note: All amounts in millions of ¥. Balance sheet, end August.

Himiko

(Estd. 1976, listed 1990, stock code no. 9892)
Company address: 6-17-10, Jingumae, Shibuya-ku, Tokyo 150-0001
Tel: 81-3-5485-3711 Fax: 81-3-3486-7660

A shoe designer/developer, wholesaler and retailer, based in Tokyo's fashionable Jingumae section. Owner-President Osamu Shibata, aged 56, is the boss. Employees total only 160. Revenues and profits point upwards, despite the recession.

Product/Sales breakdown: Shibata-san is a lifetime shoe-industry person, he owns the company, with his relatives. Sales of ¥6.9 billion in the last full year to March '98 were set to rise in the succeeding two years. Mr. Shibata is on a bit of a wave? Mostly, he offers women's fashion shoes, but he mixes an occasional "wild card" into his collection. A so-called "water massage shoe" features on Himiko's website. It contains no water, inspection of the website confirms . . . but what the hell, it's amusing to think anyone should offer such a shoe. For men and women. Outrageous.

Rivals/Competitors: Shibata-san ranks his firm number 3 in the shoe wholesale/retail trade. He has carved his way to prominence, he asserts, by offering some very low price numbers in his time, e.g. a so-called "juto" shoe at ¥1,500 the pair got him started in the early days. Himiko does no promotion, takes no spots on TV . . . it simply competes on product. The owner thinks that what has carried the firm upwards has been its management system (see below).

History/Strategy: There is something in Japan called a noren-wake system. Franchis-ing, by another name. You let your "noren" be used by others, the noren being a cotton hanging that tradesmen traditionally put over their entrance door, carrying their sign or name. Shibata-san has let out use of his noren to others: some despatched from his firm to run shops; some going it on their own, renting a place, and buying the shoes, and securing a larger commission. Himiko has played the changes on these two formats, to its advantage. This company is about design *and* marketing.

Management: The success of the firm is surely related to its complex distribution system – in essence, 106 directly run outlets and 60 franchise ones – using 4 brand names.

Outlook/Hot News: Himiko is headed by a pithily original personality, Shibata-san. His home page conveys his life story: how he was fired four times by companies in the shoe trade; travelled to Europe with ¥500,000 of his wife's money; and went on to found Himiko – he took the name from Japanese mythology, Himiko being the name of Japan's first legendary ruler, and only queen – and made a success of it. Will he attain his ultimate ambition and get the company listed on the Tokyo Stock Exchange? Hard to say, but the numbers point upwards (see opposite page for earnings and sales forecasts). His company is all but debtless. People still need shoes in a recession; even if they can do without a new wardrobe, they *need* shoes.

Osamu Shibata / President

Stocks (¥50 par value, 1,000 shares min. trade)

Shares Issued (Nov. 1, '98)	10,387,000 shares
No. of Shareholders (May. 31, '98)	766

Major Holders	(%)
Osamu Shibata	17.4
Osamu Ltd.	12.6
Masao Shibata	7.3
Eri Shibata	7.3
Motoko Shibata	5.7
Daiwa Bank, Tokyo	3.9
Yasuda Trust	2.6
Foreign Owners	9.3

Earnings

Period	Sales	Operating Profit	Current Profit	Net Profit	Earnings Per Share	Dividend Per Share
Mar 96	5,130	787	865	414	64.0	10.50
Mar 97	6,313	1,226	1,208	686	85.0	9.50
Mar 98	6,904	1,221	1,292	743	71.7	10.00
*Mar 99	7,600	N/A	1,460	770	74.1	10.00
Mid-Term						
Sep 98	4,117	836	818	422	40.6	N/A

*Estimates. Per share values in ¥, all other amounts in millions of ¥.

Balance sheet summary	1994	1995	1996	1997	1998
Current assets	2,682	3,506	3,904	6,391	6,410
Fixed assets	2,681	3,572	3,520	3,739	4,758
Total assets	5,363	7,078	7,425	10,130	11,169
Current liabilities	955	783	1,197	1,159	1,395
Fixed liabilities	58	1,744	1,300	352	410
Total liabilities	1,013	2,527	2,498	1,512	1,806
Capital Stock	1,007	1,007	1,007	2,547	2,589
Shareholders' equity	4,350	4,550	4,926	8,618	9,362
Total liabilities and equity	5,363	7,078	7,425	10,130	11,169

Note: All amounts in millions of ¥. Balance sheet, end March.

H.I.S.

(Estd. 1980, listed 1995, stock code no. 9603)
Company address: 5-27-7, Sendagaya, Shibuya-ku, Tokyo 151-0051
Tel: 81-3-5360-4793 Fax: 81-3-5360-4797

Sells airline tickets at discounts. Nation's largest specialist in cheap international travel. Employees, 2,014. President Hideo Sawada, 47, well-known as an aggressive leader, eager to diversify.

Product/Sales breakdown: Some 97% of the company's business is in discount tickets for international flights. Huge volume – with annual revenues up to ¥153 billion in the year to Oct. '98. Low margins. H.I.S. – a shorthand for "Hideo-san's International Service" – is widely believed to offer the cheapest tickets in a hotly contended trade.

Rivals/Competitors: The travel trade is a hive of tiny agents. Sawada-san is credited by his rivals with having knocked out at least one major competitor (Jet Tour) by tactics.

History/Strategy: Airline tickets were over-priced for so long, someone had to take note of the reality. Credit goes to Sawada-san as the one who saw the business opportunity, and realized it much to the advantage of millions of Japanese travellers. Thereby, he established a reputation for offering the best deals (rivals claim, of course, that their tickets are usually cheaper). Bluster, bravado and balls have built up Sawada's empire. His efforts to diversify into other fields – in the mid-1990s he planned to build up an international hotel chain; in 1996 he founded a domestic airline to compete with long-established competition – now stand to be tested.

Management: The hallmarks of Sawada-san's management are that (i) he makes himself a master of detail; (ii) he personally is always in control; and (iii) he is constantly on the look-out for new opportunities.

Outlook/Hot News: In a country that has so far produced no Richard Branson, Mr. Sawada is doing his best to emerge. For the first time in 35 years Japan has a new player in the domestic airline market . . . long live deregulation. As of autumn 1998, Sawada-san was operating on only one domestic route (Tokyo–Fukuoka) and boasted ownership of only two aircraft, Boeing 767's. Yet he was quickly joined by other start-up independents, also flying only a route apiece (Tokyo–Sapporo and Fukuoka–Okinawa) but preparing to pool facilities to share overhead costs. Tickets were priced well below levels set by Japan Air Lines and All Nippon Airways to date. Nor was that all . . . Sawada-san separately announced his purchase of a securities company, readying himself to branch out into brokerage. Here is a man who sees himself creating an American Express or Thomas Cook of Japan.

Hideo Sawada / President

Stocks (¥50 par value, 1,000 shares min. trade)

Shares Issued (Nov. 1, '98)	17,033,000 shares
No. of Shareholders (Apr. 30, '98)	592

Major Holders	(%)
Hideo Sawada	33.1
Hide Inter	5.6
Takeo Ryu	4.1
Sumitomo Trust	3.3
Toyo Trust	3.2
Yasuda Trust	2.9
Daiwa Bank	1.8
Foreign Owners	17.9

Earnings

Period	Sales	Operating Profit	Current Profit	Net Profit	Earnings Per Share	Dividend Per Share
Oct 95	87,346	2,865	2,939	1,436	122.5	11.00
Oct 96	112,522	3,761	4,068	1,855	136.5	12.00
Oct 97	141,182	4,471	4,915	2,599	167.7	15.30
Oct 98	153,898	4,612	5,092	2,614	153.4	15.40
**Oct 99	177,000	5,180	5,610	3,000	176.12	15.00
Mid-Term						
Apr 98	64,771	1,232	1,527	824	48.4	0
**Apr 99	74,500	1,410	1,540	830	N/A	N/A

**Company estimates. Per share values in ¥, all other amounts in millions of ¥.

Balance sheet summary	1994	1995	1996	1997	1998
Current assets	8,300	14,974	20,606	28,190	31,186
Fixed assets	2,373	3,949	8,716	10,309	12,437
Total assets	10,673	18,924	29,322	38,500	43,624
Current liabilities	6,363	9,553	12,876	14,615	17,376
Fixed liabilities	176	210	243	5,274	5,319
Total liabilities	6,540	9,764	13,119	19,889	22,696
Capital Stock	541	1,715	4,384	4,384	4,384
Shareholders' equity	4,133	9,159	16,202	18,610	20,927
Total liabilities and equity	10,673	18,924	29,322	38,500	43,624

Note: All amounts in millions of ¥. Balance sheet, end October.

Hokuto

(Estd. 1964, listed 1994, stock code no. 1379)
Company address: 138-1, Aza-Murahigashi, Oaza-Minamihori, Nagano City, 381-8533
Tel: 81-26-243-3111 Fax: 81-26-243-1680

A Nagano-based mushroom grower, located in a mountainous prefecture with a cool, humid climate suited to the specialty. Emphasizes R & D. Came out a few years ago with a *pink* mushroom. An effective and profitable small firm run by Masayuki Mizuno, 58, the feisty soul who founded the firm.

Product/Sales breakdown: Mushrooms of many different varieties make up the bulk of Mr. Mizuno's revenues (67%). He has a line in packaging materials (accounting for 22% of sales). Agricultural and other materials, not defined, account for 10% of revenues; and there's a miscellaneous 1% ... The variety of Hokuto's mushrooms impresses. Company brochures abound with colour photos of mushroom clusters, like bursts of fireworks in the sky.

Rivals/Competitors: Mizuno, an energetic, direct man, says that he controls about 30% of the Japanese mushroom market. He doesn't want more than that. So he keeps his prices where they are, not reducing them to increase volume. Many of his competitors are small, ageing farmers, close to retirement. Mizuno chooses not to put pressure on them. "If I get up to a 50% market share," he says, "it will be much harder to go higher." He has one competitor of roughly his size – a firm called Yukiguni Maitake, based in Niigata, a neighbouring prefecture. "Yukiguni" means "snow country", and is the title of a novel by Yasunari Kawabata, Japan's first winner of a Nobel Prize for literature. That gives the rival firm a little cachet in some eyes, perhaps. But Hokuto is more profitable.

History/Strategy: The company had an unusual start. In the summer of 1964 an earthquake struck the region – "the Niigata earthquake". It caused tremendous damage to the mushroom farmers, mostly small people, by cracking the glass jars they used to grow their produce. In desperation, some of the farmers turned to Mr. Mizuno, the owner of a firm making packing materials, to ask him to furnish them with some of the synthetic material sheets he traded in at the time, to save their mushrooms. He obliged, and in doing so became drawn into the trade, changing his specialty to mushrooms.

Management: Hokuto's hallmark is R & D. Mizuno employs 32 researchers – out of a total payroll of 429 – who work on new species of mushroom, experimenting with bacteria. The firm's famous pink mushroom was developed in-house – "it tastes like chicken", Mr. Mizuno says – but was not pushed as a sales item because it deteriorates "after 12 hours".

Outlook/Hot News: The outlook for Hokuto is fair, despite the recession, because the Japanese believe that mushrooms are good for their health, and the population is ageing. Simple.

Masayuki Mizuno / President

Stocks (¥50 par value, 100 shares min. trade)

Shares Issued (Nov. 30, '98) 13,500,000 shares
No. of Shareholders (Sep. 30, '98) 4,125

Major Holders	(%)
Hokuto Co.	16.4
Masayuki Mizuno	14.6
Hachijuni Bank	4.7
State Street Bank & Trust	4.0
Mitsubishi Trust	3.8
Sakura Bank	3.0
Mitsui Chemicals	2.9
Foreign Owners	10.0

Earnings

Period	Sales	Operating Profit	Current Profit	Net Profit	Earnings Per Share	Dividend Per Share
Mar 96	14,067	1,442	1,267	632	95.3	12.00
Mar 97	18,223	2,718	2,615	1,266	134.2	12.00
Mar 98	20,775	3,191	3,208	1,597	122.9	21.00
**Mar 99	22,700	3,900	3,800	2,050	116.8	20.00
**Mar 00	25,000	4,700	4,600	2,400	136.7	20.00
Mid-Term						
Sep 98	10,225	902	839	526	40.1	10.00
**Sep 99	11,000	1,000	950	550	31.3	10.00

**Company estimates. Per share values in ¥, all other amounts in millions of ¥.

Balance sheet summary	1994	1995	1996	1997	1998
Current assets	3,653	4,837	4,697	9,875	9,393
Fixed assets	7,403	8,652	9,892	12,624	14,713
Total assets	11,056	13,490	14,590	22,499	24,107
Current liabilities	3,329	3,603	4,833	5,600	6,361
Fixed liabilities	5,442	5,880	5,169	4,709	4,182
Total liabilities	8,772	9,484	10,002	10,309	10,543
Capital Stock	827	1,300	1,300	4,600	4,600
Shareholders' equity	2,283	4,006	4,587	12,190	13,563
Total liabilities and equity	11,056	13,490	14,590	22,499	24,107

Note: All amounts in millions of ¥. Balance sheet, end March.

ISB

(Estd. 1970, listed 1990, stock code no. 9702)
Company address: 5-1-11, Ohsaki, Shinagawa-ku, Tokyo 141-0032
Tel: 81-3-3490-1761 Fax: 81-3-3490-7718

A software development company deeply marked by the personality of its strong-minded founder, Moriyasu Wakao – a Hitachi engineer who left his company 29 years ago to found ISB.

Product/Sales breakdown: 82% of the company's business in its last full year was in software development, most of the balance was in "facility management" service.

Rivals/Competitors: Mr. Wakao, a bearded, sharp-eyed man of 62, makes no bones about it. ISB hit a bad patch in the early 1990s, losing money for four years in a row. The company accumulated losses of ¥1.15 billion – they are still on the books – during that period. It also, says Mr. Wakao, used up the money it gained from sale of its shares at its IPO in 1990. "Management delayed taking action to restructure," says the ISB founder, taking responsibility.

History/Strategy: The company's situation today is hard to grasp, say Japanese in the know, without an awareness of its history. Mr. Wakao comes from Yamanashi prefecture (though he now lives overseas). One of his strengths as a company boss was his network of friends from his native prefecture. They included the late Shin Kanemaru, a conservative politician who was considered the most powerful person in Japan in his heyday (the late '80s and early '90s, up until his fall from grace on corruption charges). ISB had its best year in business in 1989, a time when its public-sector business peaked, perhaps with the help of introductions, over the years, from Mr. Kanemaru on Mr. Wakao's behalf, as other Japanese believe.

Management: Those years are now a decade away, and ISB faces the future under different leadership. Although Mr. Wakao is still there as Chairman (and chief shareholder), responsibility for running the company rests on Masaaki Komatsu, 54, the president of ISB since 1995. The latter tells visitors to ISB's office in Tokyo – a photo of Mr. Kanemaru still hangs on the wall – that he pins his hopes on the company securing new business from the government. Mr. Komatsu gives no specifics, but he mentions a massive ¥7 trillion telecoms promotion budget that the Obuchi Cabinet has approved, as one of the government's chief measures to get the Japanese economy going again, to end the recession.

Outlook/Hot News: As was the case a decade ago much will depend on what connections ISB management has established at the MPT (the powerful Ministry of Posts and Telecommunications), which is responsible for the ¥7 trillion budget. All that is certain is that Mr. Wakao, living now in Canada, will not play a major part in the outcome. It's up to Mr. Komatsu and other key executives among his staff of 605. The outlook, says Wakao-san, is good.

Masaaki Komatsu / President

Stocks (¥50 par value, 1,000 shares min. trade)

Shares Issued (Nov. 1, '98)	4,470,000 shares
No. of Shareholders (Jun. 30, '98)	761

Major Holders	(%)
Moriyasu Wakao	34.3
Wakao Shoji	7.3
Asahi Bank	3.2
Employees' Stockholding	2.6
Mitsui Trust	2.5
Chiyoda Life Ins.	2.4
Toyo Trust	1.4
Foreign Owners	2.4

Earnings

Period	Sales	Operating Profit	Current Profit	Net Profit	Earnings Per Share	Dividend Per Share
Dec 95	4,624	−77	−78	−152	−34.1	0
Dec 96	5,639	159	190	153	34.3	0
Dec 97	7,591	351	370	253	56.7	0
**Dec 98	9,000	500	500	480	107.4	0
**Dec 99	10,000	600	600	400	89.5	0
Mid-Term						
Jun 98	4,113	258	276	256	57.4	0
**Jun 99	4,500	250	250	176	33.6	0

*Company estimates. Per share values in ¥, all other amounts in millions of ¥.

Balance sheet summary	1992	1993	1994	1995	1996
Current assets	2,504	2,242	2,271	2,426	2,496
Fixed assets	1,640	1,656	1,608	1,516	1,489
Total assets	4,145	3,898	3,879	3,942	3,985
Current liabilities	712	912	1,157	1,344	1,282
Fixed liabilities	63	38	105	134	86
Total liabilities	776	951	1,263	1,479	1,368
Capital Stock	1,416	1,416	1,416	1,416	1,416
Shareholders' equity	3,369	2,947	2,616	2,463	2,617
Total liabilities and equity	4,145	3,898	3,879	3,942	3,985

Note: All amounts in millions of ¥. Balance sheet, end December.

Ishii Tool & Engineering

(Estd. 1979, listed 1996, stock code no. 6314)
Company address: 2-1-3, Higashi-Ohmichi, Oita City 870-0823
Tel: 81-97-544-1001 Fax: 81-97-554-5035

A glance at Ishii Tool's earnings (see page opposite) tells you that something is wrong. The widening recession hit the semiconductor manufacturing equipment industry smack on in 1998. Here's a challenge for President Mitoshi Ishii, 63, and the firm's 274 employees.

Product/Sales breakdown: Semiconductor-related manufacturing equipment and moulds account for almost the entire business, some 97% of revenues (¥6.3 billion in the 1997/8 year). This overwhelming concentration on one specialty – the firm is still very young – has exposed Ishii Tool to trouble, namely in this case a sudden decline in orders from Japan's big semiconductor makers. "This year, bang, they stopped ordering," says an aide to Mr. Ishii.

Rivals/Competitors: All the companies in the industry lost orders. Some were hit badly. Tescon – a well-known company in the semiconductor-making equipment industry, based in Kanagawa outside Tokyo – suddenly went belly up, for example. "All the semiconductor makers were in the red in their 1998 midterms," says Ishii Tool's spokesman. "Normally, the orders came in from them during the summer," he added, "not this year."

History/Strategy: The company was set up originally in the 1970s by the Ishii family – the family still own 45% of the stock, one of them is the President and CEO. The Ishii-san in question sums up the firm's history: "It was around 1970 when large electri-cal manufacturing companies built semiconductor factories all over Kyushu (the south-western island where Ishii Tool is located). That was when we decided to (enter) the business of precision dies and equipment dedicated to semiconductor production. (The) semiconductor industry is evolving very quickly – continuously advancing." The words were uttered (and put up on the company's website) a little while ago . . .

Management: A robust, excellent company, no doubt, Ishii Tool has fallen victim to one of the major macro-industrial management failures in Japan in decades. The *Financial Times* commented in an 8 December 1998 annual review of Japanese industry that: "none of the big five integrated electronics conglomerates has pulled out of chip production despite huge losses". The newspaper quoted a Tokyo consultant, Koichi Hori, President of the Boston Consulting Group, as saying: "There has been no real domestic restructuring . . . We have had seven years since the crash in 1991, and we have had seven years of inaction."

Outlook/Hot News: Here's a fine mess, a high-tech industry suddenly caving . . . Contacted on the phone the Ishii Tool people make it clear that trouble came so fast, they hardly knew what had hit them. They have little idea what lies ahead. The good side, commented a company official, is that Ishii Tool is debtless. It has not gone deep into the red to get where it is, unlike Tescon.

Mitoshi Ishii / President

Stocks (¥50 par value, 100 shares min. trade)

Shares Issued (Nov. 1, '98)   7,800,000 shares
No. of Shareholders (Sep. 30, '98)   2,819

Major Holders	(%)
Mitoshi Ishii	33.1
Techtron Co.	8.4
Employees' Stockholding	5.4
Daiwa Bank	2.5
Morgan Nom. Lending	2.2
JAFCO	1.8
Toyo Trust	1.7
Foreign Owners	5.1

Earnings

Period	Sales	Operating Profit	Current Profit	Net Profit	Earnings Per Share	Dividend Per Share
Mar 96	5,016	1,195	1,186	420	95.7	10.00
Mar 97	6,035	1,471	1,317	677	141.9	10.00
Mar 98	6,342	1,513	1,518	769	118.5	10.00
**Mar 99	4,000	N/A	300	150	19.2	10.00
Mid-Term						
Sep 98	1,974	133	127	52	6.8	0

**Company estimates. Per share values in ¥, all other amounts in millions of ¥.*

Balance sheet summary	1994	1995	1996	1997	1998
Current assets	1,843	2,807	3,511	6,274	6,971
Fixed assets	1,306	1,363	1,239	1,433	1,733
Total assets	3,150	4,171	4,750	7,707	8,705
Current liabilities	885	1,425	1,805	1,526	1,783
Fixed liabilities	795	733	555	278	299
Total liabilities	1,681	2,159	2,360	1,804	2,082
Capital Stock	409	607	607	1,186	1,186
Shareholders' equity	1,468	2,011	2,389	5,903	6,623
Total liabilities and equity	3,150	4,171	4,750	7,707	8,705

Note: All amounts in millions of ¥. Balance sheet, end March.

Iuchi Seieido

(Estd. 1962, listed 1995, stock code no. 7476)
Company address: 4-15-5, Tenma, Kita-ku, Osaka 530-8560
Tel: 81-6-6354-1512 Fax: 81-6-6356-3095

A wholesaler of scientific and medical items (incl. lately books) via catalogue and now a website. Osaka-based family business headed by the aggressive Hideo Iuchi, 57, son of the founder. Has 204 employees.

Product/Sales breakdown: This tautly disciplined firm – no fat in terms of extra staff there – divides its attention between 30,000 items listed in its catalogue, inclusive of scientific equipment. A coherent, pithy breakdown is not available, the company says.

Rivals/Competitors: An Iuchi Seieido spokesman, requested to name rival companies, mentioned Misumi Corporation and Trusco Nakayama Corporation, both first-section companies on the Tokyo Stock Exchange.

History/Strategy: The company started up selling plastic items, using a catalogue. That was in 1962, as stated above. Then, gradually, it expanded the range. It tended towards chemistry and experimental research equipment; stationery; items for hospitals and nursing homes (of late, things for old people's homes); items for the semiconductor industry, a wide sweep. The company's "secret", what makes it work, is its distribution. In Japan, you can't sell things cold via a catalogue sent through the mail, so it is said. Iuchi Corp. is in contact with the general public via 5,000 "distributors"

(individuals, some with little shops or businesses). These intermediaries receive commissions, fairly generous ones, perhaps. Iuchi has made an increasingly solid business out of this trade.

Management: The feisty CEO, not content with today's near 10% margins would like to go to 30% ones, he says. For a (mere) distributor that sounds greedy, but that's Osaka business.

Outlook/Hot News: The company's main new thrust, which makes eminent sense as it wants to sell more (often highly specialized scientific and medical) books, in English as well as Japanese, is to set up a virtual store via its website. Iuchi has picked up a hint from amazon.com in America – to sell books you go via the Internet. How the new strategy will fare remains to be seen. Iuchi-san bases his personal confidence, as projected in interviews, on a belief that his operation is recession-proof. He says that the catalogue's contents include many "defensive products" for which there is demand in good times or bad, rain or shine. "Our motto is 'satisfy the customers' ", he says. Very probably, he will. Iuchi's success would appear to be based on (i) the selection of the highly specialized items in the catalogue, (ii) constant updating of the catalogue, (iii) keeping in touch with the scientific/academic community, and (iv) its distribution system, perhaps above all.

Hideo Iuchi / President

Stocks (¥50 par value, 500 shares min. trade)

Shares Issued (Nov. 1, '98)	10,375,000 shares
No. of Shareholders (Sep. 30, '98)	664

Major Holders	(%)
Hideo Iuchi	25.9
Misako Iuchi	11.0
Seiei Co.	5.1
Asahi Bank	4.3
Toyo Trust	3.2
Employees' Stockholding	3.1
Tsutomu Kimura	2.9
Foreign Owners	9.1

Earnings

Period	Sales	Operating Profit	Current Profit	Net Profit	Earnings Per Share	Dividend Per Share
Mar 96	19,006	1,298	1,251	644	129.2	10.00
Mar 97	21,946	2,049	1,721	850	120.1	11.00
Mar 98	24,149	2,277	2,155	1,017	112.8	13.00
*Mar 99	25,190	N/A	2,260	1,230	118.6	12.00
Mid-Term						
Sep 98	11,749	1,066	1,002	568	54.8	6.00

*Estimates. Per share values in ¥, all other amounts in millions of ¥.

Balance sheet summary	1994	1995	1996	1997	1998
Current assets	8,666	9,782	12,194	13,955	15,757
Fixed assets	5,124	5,209	5,519	5,749	5,909
Total assets	13,790	14,991	17,714	19,704	21,666
Current liabilities	6,124	6,896	7,691	7,198	8,308
Fixed liabilities	4,322	3,677	3,646	2,380	2,354
Total liabilities	10,446	10,573	11,337	9,579	10,662
Capital Stock	373	705	1,149	2,661	2,661
Shareholders' equity	3,344	4,418	6,376	10,125	11,004
Total liabilities and equity	13,790	14,991	17,714	19,704	21,666

Note: All amounts in millions of ¥. Balance sheet, end March.

Jamco

(Estd. 1949, listed 1988, stock code no. 7408)
Company address: 6-11-25, Ohsawa, Mitaka City, Tokyo 181-8571
Tel: 81-422-31-9111 Fax: 81-422-31-6998

The "world's largest manufacturer of galleys and lavatories for commercial airplanes" says a rubric in the *Japan Company Handbook*, published by Toyo Keizai. Based outside Tokyo at Mitaka, Jamco has powerful stockholders, including Japan's two main airlines. 1,339 employees. President Takashi Kawashina, 53, is a Japan Air Lines man by background.

Product/Sales breakdown: Jamco, originally an aircraft maintenance division of C.Itoh, the trading company, still does a lot of maintenance – equivalent to 22% of sales worth ¥34.8 billion on consolidated figures in 1997/8. The company also does some equipment supply, chalking up 8% of sales to "machinery and equipment". Its main line is in "interior decorations", a phrase which covers those airline loos and galleys and accounts for 66% of all revenues, with a residual 4% attributed to parts supply. Jamco's clients are commercial airlines. It has one big state client, the Japanese Self-Defense Forces, a steady source of income.

Rivals/Competitors: Jamco is in fact a world leader in aircraft loos, claiming 60% of the world market in that regard – as compared with 30% of the world market in galleys. The company acknowledges only one serious competitor (see below).

History/Strategy: The company, as mentioned, was originally part of C.Itoh, now Itochu Corp., the world's largest trading company and Jamco's largest stockholder to date. Jamco got its breakthrough overseas in 1979, an order from Boeing for B767 lavatory

modules, according to the company's website. But its real start as an "interior decorator" came nine years earlier, when ANA ordered "galleys and insert for eight B727-200s and three B737s". From there on it was up to Itochu salesmen to carry the news to Boeing HQ in America that there was this good company in Japan making the necessaries.

Management: Jamco has a big company ethos. Its managers are corporation men, given its shareholders. Now nearly half a century old, Jamco is sitting pretty in a steadily growing market long-term.

Outlook/Hot News: Jamco gained entry to the Tokyo stock exchange (second section) as this work was going to press, achieving a goal nurtured by management for a decade since the company was registered on the OTC. As to future performance, very much depends on the $/¥ exchange rate, given Jamco's huge dependence on exports in general (56%) and on the US market – where Boeing and McDonnell Douglas, two of the company's major clients, are now one. President Kawashina's team are projecting substantial increases in sales and profits this year (1998/9) and next, a good result when one considers the financial pressures on its big clients – ANA and Japan Air Lines at home; and Boeing overseas. Jamco's strong point is that it has built up a reputation for quality. Sell of Germany comes to mind as a competitor, says a Jamco spokesman, but there are not many really strong companies in the field.

Takashi Kawashima / President

Stocks (¥50 par value, 1,000 shares min. trade)

Shares Issued (Nov. 1, '98)   26,863,974 shares
No. of Shareholders (Mar. 31, '98)   1,503

Major Holders	(%)
Itochu Corp.	23.1
Japan Airlines	22.4
All Nippon Airways	22.4
Employees' Stockholding	2.8
Daiwa Bank, Tokyo	1.3
Nippon Dantai Life Insurance Ltd.	0.9
Sumitomo Trust	0.9
Foreign Owners	3.6

Earnings

Period	Sales	Operating Profit	Current Profit	Net Profit	Earnings Per Share	Dividend Per Share
Mar 96	22,113	656	506	544	21.5	5.00
Mar 97	27,781	995	1,066	915	36.1	6.00
Mar 98	33,486	2,313	2,184	1,036	40.9	6.00
*Mar 99	43,700	N/A	3,800	2,000	74.5	8.00
*Mar 00	43,800	3,900	3,700	1,900	70.7	8.00
Mid-Term						
Sep 98	19,511	1,999	1,777	956	37.7	N/A
*Sep 99	19,000	1,900	1,700	900	33.5	N/A

*Estimates. Per share values in ¥, all other amounts in millions of ¥.

Balance sheet summary	1994	1995	1996	1997	1998
Current assets	23,080	19,671	14,635	18,750	26,157
Fixed assets	8,491	8,023	7,738	7,514	7,838
Total assets	31,572	27,695	22,373	26,264	33,996
Current liabilities	11,448	10,299	5,957	10,555	13,990
Fixed liabilities	8,812	7,839	6,391	4,896	8,348
Total liabilities	20,260	18,139	12,349	15,451	22,338
Capital Stock	4,605	4,605	4,605	4,605	4,605
Shareholders' equity	11,311	9,555	10,024	10,812	11,657
Total liabilities and equity	31,572	27,695	22,373	26,264	33,996

Note: All amounts in millions of ¥. Balance sheet, end March.

Japan Business Computer

(Estd. 1964, listed 1990, stock code no. 9889)
Company address: 1-53, Nisshin-cho, Kawasaki-ku, Kawasaki 210-0024
Tel: 81-44-210-2211 Fax: 81-44-210-2209

An IBM sales affiliate, said to be the largest IBM sales agency in the country. With 1,331 staff this 36% IBM Japan-owned company operates out of a Kawasaki location (between Tokyo and Yokohama) doing a bit of production under its own brand name, "JBCC", in printers, and engaging in software development. Run by Haruo Kuriu, 63.

Product/Sales breakdown: The company analyses its sales as 59% in computers, 10% in software, 15% in maintenance and the balance in computer-related areas. With annual sales of ¥63 billion (consolidated) it is receiving just over 5% on average in gross margins. The parent, IBM Japan, is not being greedy and pressing 'em down.

Rivals/Competitors: Serving IBM Japan's often long-established clients is a snip in competitive terms, now that the entire IBM world is healthier, following a bad patch in the early 1990s. Sales and earnings projections (see opposite page) show that JBC is on a steady upward path, going at a measured pace. Long-established clients such as Bank of Tokyo-Mitsubishi and Fuji Bank – they are shareholders as well, and also serve as ongoing sources of finance – are not going to run away in the night.

History/Strategy: If times were bad . . .

Mr. Kuriu might have a nasty job on his hands to get costs down by the only means, letting staff take early retirement (a strategy adopted by IBM Japan in 1992/5, until things got better). The average age of JBC's staff looks high for a Japanese corporation. It is 39 . . . Incidentally JBC's profits took a dive in the last recorded full year (to March '98) – profits fell due to extraordinary charges. But that performance is not to be repeated, earnings forecasts say (see page opposite).

Management: The monolithic appearance of the world of IBM Japan and its affiliates – the lack of an international atmosphere within the system, as also at JBC, where few Americans or other non-Japanese ever sat on the board, strikes outsiders as odd but, lo and behold, it works!

Outlook/Hot News: The future looks fair for Japan Business Computer as part of the huge, extended family of IBM Japan (a home, still, to over 20,000 staff despite years of cutbacks). The overall performance of the group has come up sharply – for 4 years running – since that trough in the early 1990s. That is thanks to growth in the demand from Japanese corporations, large and small, for computers, software and services. JBC has piggy-backed on the parent, it has a secure place in a secure firmament.

Haruo Kuriu / President

Stocks (¥50 par value, 1,000 shares min. trade)

Shares Issued (Nov. 1, '98)   19,250,000 shares
No. of Shareholders (Sep. 30, '98)   2,102

Major Holders	(%)
IBM Japan	36.0
Kazuo Taniguchi	2.9
Employees' Stockholding	2.2
Kimiyo Taniguchi	1.5
Bank of Tokyo-Mitsubishi	1.4
Fuji Bank	1.4
Saeko Katsuyama	1.3
Foreign Owners	4.7

Earnings

Period	Sales	Operating Profit	Current Profit	Net Profit	Earnings Per Share	Dividend Per Share
Mar 96	45,053	1,753	1,391	2,211	114.9	0
Mar 97	57,378	2,771	2,390	1,209	62.9	0
Mar 98	61,848	3,428	3,238	1,283	66.7	7.50
**Mar 99	63,400	3,400	3,250	1,300	67.5	10.00
*Mar 00	72,000	4,400	4,200	1,800	93.5	10.00
Mid-Term						
Sep 97	30,023	1,436	1,351	571	29.7	0
Sep 98	30,624	1,718	1,675	701	36.4	0

*Estimates; **Company estimates. Per share values in ¥, all other amounts in millions of ¥.*

Balance sheet summary	1994	1995	1996	1997	1998
Current assets	18,688	18,206	18,772	21,867	25,164
Fixed assets	7,239	6,078	5,810	5,445	4,977
Total assets	25,927	24,285	24,582	27,313	30,141
Current liabilities	13,959	12,968	11,747	13,136	17,519
Fixed liabilities	5,458	5,595	4,902	5,034	2,196
Total liabilities	19,418	18,563	16,649	18,170	19,715
Capital Stock	4,562	4,562	4,562	4,562	4,562
Shareholders' equity	6,509	5,721	7,932	9,142	10,425
Total liabilities and equity	25,927	24,285	24,582	27,313	30,141

Note: All amounts in millions of ¥. Balance sheet, end March.

Japan Lifeline

(Estd. 1981, listed 1997, stock code no. 7575)
Company address: 2-38-1, Ikebukuro, Toshima-ku, Tokyo 171-0014
Tel: 81-3-3590-1620 Fax: 81-3-3590-2124

One of Japan's more unusual trading houses; specializes in imported pacemakers, artificial organs. President Takeshi Masumoto, 56, founded the business, importing from the US, 18 years ago. He has built up a substantial firm employing 286, a leader in its field in Japan.

Product/Sales breakdown: The company identifies two main lines of business: artificial internal organs, accounting for 72% of sales; disposable catheters for 26%; with a residual 2% in other items.

Rivals/Competitors: Starting off early in what was then a relatively undeveloped field, Masumoto-san has stayed ahead of the competition, it now seems. All of a sudden Japan Lifeline is a company name that people recognize.

History/Strategy: Japan Lifeline has got ahead thanks (i) to picking a good supplier in the US, namely Sulzer Medica, and (ii) an aggressive policy of rapid expansion, based on financing. By last year dependence on borrowing, relative to the balance sheet, was sharply down, but remained substantial. Japan Lifeline seemed to cross the hazy line that separates risk-taking advance from prudent investment in the future in 1997/8, and is now in the latter territory, to judge by the numbers; borrowing fell in absolute terms, total assets rose substantially as did shareholders' equity.

Management: The credit for this success belongs to Masumoto-san. It has been an 18-year haul from obscurity and insecurity up to a certain eminence.

Outlook/Hot News: Japan has the fastest ageing population in the world. Accordingly, the demand for health services in all forms can be expected to increase mightily – by the year 2020 35% of the population will be over 65. How a society functions under such circumstances has yet to be seen. Companies such as Japan Lifeline – a brilliant choice of name – seem to be onto a sure thing. Demand for its services, notably those pacemakers, can only rocket up. Judging by its 1998 results and the earnings forecasts (see opposite page) Japan Lifeline has nowhere to go but up. The nation *needs* a lifeline, that's for sure. Disposable catheters will remain in heavy demand, for all that competition in that area is tough. To beef up his marketing within Japan, Masumoto-san set up a nationwide network of 8 branches and 23 offices. Meanwhile, as this work went to press, the company was about to announce new long-term plans to do with the sourcing of products in America. Sulzer, it was understood, had been taken over; Masumoto-san had decided to negotiate an end to a long-term contract for supply of products from the US and possible sourcing in future from within Japan.

Takeshi Masumoto / President

Stocks (¥50 par value, 100 shares min. trade)

Shares Issued (Nov. 1, '98)   12,236,000 shares
No. of Shareholders (Sep. 30, '98)   481

Major Holders	(%)
Takeshi Masumoto	27.4
Keisuke Suzuki	10.2
Sulzer Medica USA Holding Co.	9.0
T.K. Agency	6.6
Employees' Stockholding	3.7
Daiwa Bank	2.6
Tokai Bank	1.3
Foreign Owners	14.2

Earnings

Period	Sales	Operating Profit	Current Profit	Net Profit	Earnings Per Share	Dividend Per Share
Mar 96	12,983	1,904	1,916	766	161.2	20.00
Mar 97	14,857	2,107	2,389	1,151	207.6	20.00
Mar 98	18,008	2,362	2,671	1,239	108.3	20.00
*Mar 99	25,407	N/A	4,776	2,446	199.9	20.00
Mid-Term						
Sep 98	13,251	2,631	2,695	1,378	112.7	0

*Estimates. Per share values in ¥, all other amounts in millions of ¥.

Balance sheet summary	1994	1995	1996	1997	1998
Current assets	12,428	10,283	12,423	13,465	17,129
Fixed assets	3,497	3,825	3,640	5,420	5,345
Total assets	15,925	14,109	16,064	18,886	22,475
Current liabilities	6,584	6,788	6,956	7,023	10,124
Fixed liabilities	3,212	998	988	2,786	1,074
Total liabilities	9,796	7,786	7,945	9,810	11,198
Capital Stock	1,009	1,009	1,580	1,580	2,095
Shareholders' equity	6,128	6,322	8,119	9,076	11,276
Total liabilities and equity	15,925	14,109	16,064	18,886	22,475

Note: All amounts in millions of ¥. Balance sheet, end March.

Japan Process Development

(Estd. 1967, listed 1992, stock code no. 9651)
Company address: 1-5-1, Ohmori-Kita, Ohta-ku, Tokyo 143-0016
Tel: 81-3-3768-5601 Fax: 81-3-3768-2209

A Tokyo-based computer software company "heavily dependent upon heavy electric machinery manufacturers, with about 90% of system development bound for them", according to Toyo Keizai's *Japan Company Handbook*. Run by Mikio Kayagawa, 65. Has 231 employees.

Product/Sales breakdown: The company divides its activities between "control systems" (43%), "basic operating systems" (29%) and "application systems" (28%).

Rivals/Competitors: In a highly competitive field, JPD stands to survive thanks to the connections of its senior executives.

History/Strategy: JPD was founded in the late 1960s, a time when the authorities – the push came from MITI and the MPT among the big government departments – strove to launch Japan into new high-tech directions as the drive into heavy industry showed signs of peaking out, as seen by government planners. The funding for JPD came from the private sector; Japan Process Management, the single large shareholder in the company (see opposite page), is owned by the family of the late Toshio Ohbu, who headed the company and was its largest shareholder up to his death in 1998. JPD's main clients appear to have been mainly big electrical machinery makers. Still, the tendency at JPD has been to depend on orders that come, directly or indirectly, through the impulse of the public sector. When the economy as a whole flagged in the early 1990s and fiscal stimulus packages still emphasized the infrastructure – in the old style – companies like JPD temporarily weakened, too.

Management: The incoming chief executive has the task of nurturing a company that was very much the baby of the late Ohbu-san, its founder.

Outlook/Hot news: The company went through a grisly period in the early to mid-1990s. JPD went public on the Jasdaq in 1992, only to have this move coincide with the onset of a bad time. For years the company made no money. The pattern is observable at other computer software companies, for example ISB, another firm that floundered in the early 1990s, took its time over restructuring, used up the funds obtained from the public offering, and then gradually crept back to health, so that today a decent return is forthcoming. JPD came through its lean years without accumulating debt, that is one good thing. Its prestigious shareholders – Dai Ichi Life, Sumitomo Bank – have stuck with it. That's another plus. The foreign investment community is not unimpressed (foreign investors owned 5% of the firm at end 1998). Can JPD justify its hopes and get back to a situation where it boasts margins of close to 20%? See earnings forecasts on opposite page. Much depends on how far the huge investments being shovelled into the economy by the government come to bear on JPD's order book, directly or indirectly. These days such drives go not into infrastructure but telecoms – high-tech investments of various kinds. The whole thrust of Keynesian pump-priming measures has changed in such a way as to help firms like JPD. Good luck!

Mikio Kayagawa / President

Stocks (¥50 par value, 1,000 shares min. trade)

Shares Issued (Nov. 1, '98)	5,984,000 shares
No. of Shareholders (May. 31, '98)	448

Major Holders	(%)
Japan Process Management	43.6
Toshio Ohbu	10.7
Dai-ichi Life Ins.	3.7
Sumitomo Bank	3.3
Employees' Stockholding	3.1
Sakura Bank	2.1
Morgan Stanley Trust	2.0
Foreign Owners	5.3

Earnings

Period	Sales	Operating Profit	Current Profit	Net Profit	Earnings Per Share	Dividend Per Share
May 96	2,197	50	116	57	9.7	7.50
May 97	2,399	243	299	126	21.1	10.00
May 98	2,630	504	504	2	0.4	7.50
**May 99	2,660	320	400	220	36.7	7.50
*May 00	2,800	490	570	310	51.8	7.50
Mid-Term						
Nov 97	1,264	173	99	65	10.9	0
**Nov 98	1,389	179	223	143	23.9	0

*Estimates; **Company estimates. Per share values in ¥, all other amounts in millions of ¥.*

Balance sheet summary	1994	1995	1996	1997	1998
Current assets	5,731	5,532	5,972	6,159	6,297
Fixed assets	1,259	1,238	1,338	1,412	1,185
Total assets	6,991	6,770	7,329	7,584	7,489
Current liabilities	497	275	332	505	468
Fixed liabilities	0	0	490	490	490
Total liabilities	497	275	822	995	958
Capital Stock	1,485	1,485	1,485	1,485	1,485
Shareholders' equity	6,493	6,494	6,507	6,588	6,531
Total liabilities and equity	6,991	6,770	7,329	7,584	7,489

Note: All amounts in millions of ¥. Balance sheet, end May.

Jonathan's

(Estd. 1979, listed 1986, stock code no. 8204)
Company address: 1-6-14, Nishi-Kubo, Musashino City, Tokyo 180-8588
Tel: 81-422-37-6111 Fax: 81-422-37-6127

A coffee and light repast chain set up by the Skylark group in the late 1970s. 935 employees. President Kiwamu Yokokawa, 61, is a member of the family owning Skylark.

Product/Sales breakdown: The whole thing's in the family, bearing in mind that Skylark owns 54.5% of Jonathan's stock, and Mr. Yokokawa is one of four large stockholders in Skylark, each owning 7.9%. Almost all of Jonathan's turnover is in the restaurants (96%), the balance is in items bought in these Western-style eateries.

Rivals/Competitors: The café trade is always competitive, margins are not high outside a few delicatessens. Yet Japanese houses are small and the pattern is to meet people outside the home. Jonathan's, which opened its places in the suburbs mainly, offered a slight touch of gentility that Japanese families appreciated, it seems.

History/Strategy: The strategy pursued by the Yokokawas – to spin off as separately-run chains those specialty restaurants that had character – has prospered, with their Japanese and Chinese chains (the latter is Bamiyan, also a Jasdaq company) flourishing far beyond any reasonable expectations. No other family-owned restaurant business

in Japan has accomplished this feat; the Yokokawas deserve credit for having spotted what this eternally middle-class Japan finds acceptable in food.

Management: Yokokawa-san looks like a stayer – as a permanent feature at Jonathan's – given that he is not only a major stockholder in parent Skylark but also chairman of Skylark. His writ runs large in the group as a whole.

Outlook/Hot News: Jonathan's increased its sales and net profits by roughly 50% in the years 1995/8. Is the momentum still there? The company thinks so. Management believes that Jonathan's has found a niche for itself in the market, somewhere between Denny's and Royal Host on one side and McDonald's on the other. Jonathan's is more dynamic than its Skylark parent – it is already one third the size of the parent company. And the future? Jonathan's is doing a rare thing. Some of its 249 branches – 248 are directly run, only one is franchised – stay open all night, the company says, in keeping with the new downtown lifestyle in Tokyo (the capital has of late become a 24-hours-a-day-awake city). Jonathan's is on a surge of growth. Plans call for the creation of a 500-shop chain by the year 2003.

Kiwamu Yokokawa / President

Shares Issued (Nov. 1, '98)	23,796,000 shares
No. of Shareholders (Jun. 30, '98)	4,038

Major Holders	(%)
Skylark Co.	54.4
Employees' Stockholding	2.7
DKB	1.9
Fuji Bank	1.9
LTCB	1.9
Norinchukin Bank	1.9
Sumitomo Trust	1.6
Foreign Owners	1.4

Earnings

Period	Sales	Operating Profit	Current Profit	Net Profit	Earnings Per Share	Dividend Per Share
Dec 95	34,017	1,700	1,663	702	40.1	13.00
Dec 96	38,928	2,002	2,132	911	44.0	13.00
Dec 97	45,947	2,092	2,245	922	38.9	16.00
Dec 98	50,260	2,052	2,255	980	41.3	18.00
**Dec 99	54,000	N/A	2,650	1,100	46.2	18.00
Mid-Term						
Jun 98	23,779	617	736	331	14.0	9.00
**Jun 99	25,000	N/A	800	250	N/A	9.00

**Company estimates. Per share values in ¥, all other amounts in millions of ¥.

Balance sheet summary	1993	1994	1995	1996	1997
Current assets	4,359	4,098	5,675	5,476	5,865
Fixed assets	8,499	9,863	11,928	14,744	18,809
Total assets	12,859	13,961	17,678	20,258	24,675
Current liabilities	5,508	6,189	4,874	6,819	8,959
Fixed liabilities	143	164	3,058	813	2,310
Total liabilities	5,652	6,353	7,932	7,632	11,270
Capital Stock	2,670	2,670	3,483	4,612	4,724
Shareholders' equity	7,206	7,608	9,745	21,625	13,405
Total liabilities and equity	12,859	13,961	17,678	20,258	24,675

Note: All amounts in millions of ¥. Balance sheet, end December.

K K People

(Estd. 1973, listed 1996, stock code no. 4643)
Company address: 8-5-30, Akasaka, Minato-ku, Tokyo 107-0052
Tel: 81-3-3475-4471 Fax: 81-3-3475-4580

Decades ago there wasn't a single "fitness club" in Tokyo, apart from a place run by Clark Hatch for American businessmen. Sometime in the early 1970s the light dawned that Japanese office workers needed to exercise. Then began a boom in swimming pools, followed by fitness clubs. President Satoru Ishihara of People, 53, is a veteran of this industry. His experience goes back to before 1973, the year in which he joined People Co. The Akasaka, Tokyo-based company has 857 employees at its 124 different pools and clubs.

Product/Sales breakdown: Swimming pools and gymnasia, 28%. Fitness clubs (and also tennis schools) 55%; other activities account for the remaining 17%. Turnover reached ¥39.8 billion in 1997/8 on a non-consolidated basis, compared with ¥42.6 billion on consolidated figures, making this the leading company in its field in Japan. "No one of our centres and clubs is quite like another," says a company spokesman, making the point that People is a company with a diverse culture.

Rivals/Competitors: Ishihara-san says (in an interview on the company's website) that People was a latecomer into the swimming pool trade. By 1982 People was managing 45 pools out of a nationwide total of 1,200 pools in private hands, and wasn't competitive. Therefore the company shifted its strategy to creating fitness clubs, opening a first

one in Aoyama, Tokyo, in 1984. Competition heated up in the industry, many fell by the wayside during the bubble years, the late 1980s, and thereafter. People emerged as number one in the field, but profits were lean, entering the 1990s.

History/Strategy: The CEO traces the success of People today to a reorganization he undertook in 1995. The membership system and pricing was revised; the locations of new clubs were decided on the basis of demographics (a population of 70,000 can support one such club, experience showed). Money was invested in new equipment. Young women emerged as the biggest class of new customers, according to Ishihara-san, who took over as President in 1994.

Management: People is a subsidiary of the Mycal group, an Osaka-based retail chain specializing in clothing – and suffering from slow sales in the recession. Mycal management has let Ishihara-san get on with the job and initiate a strategy that is paying off.

Outlook/Hot News: Those fitness clubs have proved to be more than just a fashion. Young women with ¥20,000 or so in extra spending money a month will come to the clubs, People found, as an alternative to yoga, jazz-dancing etc. Women get married later than before in Japan these days, or they remain single. People has tapped into an opportunity, thanks to its experienced management. Ishihara-san could take this success a step further.

Satoru Ishihara / President

Stocks (¥50 par value, 100 shares min. trade)

Shares Issued (Sep. 1, '98)	14,587,200 shares
No. of Shareholders (Aug. 31, '98)	868

Major Holders	(%)
MYCAL Corp.	51.0
Estate MYCAL Corp.	7.1
K & K	5.3
Employees' Stockholding	3.4
State Street Bank & Trust	2.4
Mitsui Trust	1.7
Foreign Owners	14.5

Earnings

Period	Sales	Operating Profit	Current Profit	Net Profit	Earnings Per Share	Dividend Per Share
Feb 96	29,787	1,843	1,331	636	68.2	10.00
Feb 97	33,484	2,385	1,932	885	90.2	15.00
Feb 98	39,841	2,781	2,548	1,240	114.5	15.00
**Feb 99	44,880	4,093	3,400	1,670	114.5	20.00
*Feb 00	49,000	4,150	3,900	1,950	133.7	15.00
Mid-Term						
Aug 98	22,462	1,792	1,638	814	55.9	10.00
*Aug 99	24,000	2,050	1,900	950	65.1	7.50

*Estimates; **Company estimates: Per share values in ¥, all other amounts in millions of ¥.

Balance sheet summary	1994	1995	1996	1997	1998
Current assets	2,923	3,060	2,639	4,832	2,414
Fixed assets	21,329	20,545	20,673	21,188	23,439
Total assets	24,252	23,605	23,314	26,093	25,894
Current liabilities	12,139	12,713	13,673	14,960	13,368
Fixed liabilities	6,404	5,514	3,155	1,120	1,521
Total liabilities	18,543	18,228	16,829	16,080	14,889
Capital Stock	2,400	2,400	2,635	3,255	3,255
Shareholders' equity	5,709	5,377	6,485	10,013	11,004
Total liabilities and equity	24,252	23,605	23,314	26,093	25,894

Note: All amounts in millions of ¥. Balance sheet, end February.

Kaneko Seeds

(Estd. 1947, listed 1981, stock code no. 1376)
Company address: 1-50-12, Furuichi-machi, Maebashi City, Tokyo 371-8503
Tel: 81-27-251-1617 Fax: 81-27-290-1073

A very large outfit for its field – market gardening, with a hint of biotechnology in the offing. Saijuro Kaneko, 72, is President. He has 481 employees.

Product/Sales breakdown: The company divides up its sales between "agricultural materials" (e.g. fertiliser) at 32%, flowering plants at 33%, flower gardening supplies at 19%, seeds and seedlings at 14% and landscape gardening at 2%. The company is best known for its seeds, hence its name. But its products are multifarious, as befits a firm of this type and size, with regional sales offices all over Japan.

Rivals/Competitors: Competition (from small rivals) is intense – witness the low margins on Kaneko's business. Its turnover (for a market gardener)is huge at ¥38.6 billion in the year to March '98 – it operates on an industrial scale; the gross margin on sales was 2.58% in that year.

History/Strategy: The company is one of the very few in Japan that is still in the hands of the same family after 100 years. The history of Kaneko Seeds goes back to its beginnings in Gumma prefecture late in the 19th century. Yet today there are three Kanekos listed among its largest eight stockholders. One of the company's strengths is its cultivation of ties with long-established customers; it must be one of the very few firms in Japan that encouraged its clients to join in as stockholders – the holding accounts for 3.7% of the issued capital. Another of Kaneko Seeds' fortes is that the company has remained very much a local firm, doing its banking in Gumma.

Management: For the time being Kaneko Seeds will stay in the hands of the founding family. The owner has no plans to retire, a company spokesman avers.

Outlook/Hot News: "With the beginning of the 21st century near at hand, a new kind of agriculture has begun to emerge . . . as a general enterprise trading in agriculture and a total landscape planner," states the company's English-language brochure. Kaneko Seeds sees a great future for itself, with its roots in Gumma prefecture (its actual start there was 100 years ago, though the company dates itself officially to 1947), and its future the world at large. "It won't be long before epoch-making vegetables and flowers produced by the use of biotechnology begin to appear," the company asserts. With a vision of this kind, seeing itself as "a seed-breeding company", what limits are there for Kaneko Seeds in its own eyes? Perhaps financial ones. With borrowing of ¥5 billion, a lot of it short-term, that being the equivalent of many years of net profits at current levels, Mr. Kaneko has to stay on the right side of the Gumma Bank, a large shareholder. Or has he got some "epoch-making" move up his sleeve that will change everything?

Saijuro Kaneko / President

Stocks (¥50 par value, 1,000 shares min. trade)

Shares Issued (Nov. 1, '98)   11,772,000 shares
No. of Shareholders (May. 31, '98) 1,666

Major Holders	(%)
Saijuro Kaneko	5.0
Customers' Stockholding	4.3
Gunma Bank	4.1
Masahiro Kaneko	3.9
Etsuzo Kaneko	2.9
Akagi Kogyo	2.6
Towa Bank	2.6
Foreign Owners	2.7

Earnings

Period	Sales	Operating Profit	Current Profit	Net Profit	Earnings Per Share	Dividend Per Share
May 96	32,900	743	727	276	26.2	10.00
May 97	36,508	873	875	422	40.0	11.00
May 98	38,647	998	1,020	234	20.2	10.00
**May 99	40,500	N/A	800	350	29.7	10.00
*May 00	41,000	850	820	360	30.6	10.00
Mid-Term						
Nov 97	16,044	212	219	−136	−11.6	0
Nov 98	16,745	229	216	139	11.9	0

*Estimates; **Company estimates. Per share values in ¥, all other amounts in millions of ¥.*

Balance sheet summary	1994	1995	1996	1997	1998
Current assets	18,431	18,309	20,489	23,351	24,534
Fixed assets	5,177	6,181	6,577	6,652	7,185
Total assets	23,649	24,511	27,067	30,003	31,720
Current liabilities	16,650	17,187	19,606	23,792	24,040
Fixed liabilities	2,462	2,168	2,124	514	1,754
Total liabilities	19,113	19,355	21,731	24,306	25,794
Capital Stock	1,256	1,467	1,482	1,487	1,491
Shareholders' equity	4,536	5,155	5,336	5,696	5,925
Total liabilities and equity	23,649	24,511	27,067	30,003	31,720

Note: All amounts in millions of ¥. Balance sheet, end May.

KEL

(Estd. 1962, listed 1990, stock code no. 6919)
Company address: 6-17-7, Nagayama, Tama City, Tokyo 206-0025
Tel: 81-42-374-5810 Fax: 81-42-374-5889

A flourishing maker of electrical connecting devices ("connectors" in the trade), based in Tama City on the edge of Tokyo. Kept up a momentum – until this year – despite the recession. Shunzo Watabe, 65, heads the firm. 268 employees.

Product/Sales breakdown: Connectors come in many different shapes and sizes. KEL specializes in connectors for OA (office automation), accounting for 74% of its output. Racks, also miniature devices, account for another 14%; and sockets for 6%, with other items also 6%.

Competitors/Rivals: A main competitor of KEL is Yamaichi Electronics, somewhat larger in sales volume (¥23.4 billion at Yamaichi in contrast with KEL's ¥10.6 billion, in the year to March '98). Yamaichi is dominant in so-called "IC sockets", having a 40% market share; KEL has been unable to expand there. As to connectors: KEL specializes in one type (for OA), Yamaichi in another ("pressure welding connectors"). There is no direct competition in this instance, but the potential thereof. Of the two, Yamaichi expanded more rapidly, borrowing more heavily than conservative KEL

History/Strategy: The market for miniature electrical/electronic devices promises to expand forever. This was a basic perception, long ago, that led to the creation of KEL in the early 1960s, an era when the centre of gravity of Japanese industry shifted from the heavy, traditional end (steel, shipbuilding, textiles) to the high-tech field, notably with the advance of consumer electronics. KEL found its opportunity in a specialized area (OA) that took time to grow. For many years its progress was slow. Now, with the surge in OA demand over the last decade, KEL has come forward, spending money on product development, pushing into further improvements of existing items.

Management: KEL's performance suddenly veered downwards in the current business year ending March '99. Sales are falling by a quarter, margins are sagging from over 10% to under 5%, and net profits are being slashed by 82%, according to forecasts (see opposite page). This represents the greatest challenge faced by KEL management in years.

Outlook/Hot News: Competition has hotted up – hence the lower margins – the recession has cut into demand. The current year, starting in April 1999, looks only a little better. This is a situation reminiscent of the collapse in semiconductor manufacturing equipment demand. Suddenly the skies clouded over. Its shareholders, including Bank of Tokyo-Mitsubishi and other city banks, will see KEL through these difficult times, one may assume. Competitor Yamaichi, it may be noted, has also been hard hit, with its net profits dropping by two thirds.

Shunzo Watabe / President

Stocks (¥50 par value, 1,000 shares min. trade)

Shares Issued (Nov. 1, '98)	8,415,000 shares
No. of Shareholders (Sep. 30, '98)	1,159

Major Holders	(%)
Hiroko Kobayashi	6.0
Bank of Tokyo-Mitsubishi	4.5
Shunzo Watabe	4.0
Tokai Bank	3.7
Eizo Ozaki	3.6
Kozo Takashina	3.3
DKB	3.1
Foreign Owners	3.9

Earnings

Period	Sales	Operating Profit	Current Profit	Net Profit	Earnings Per Share	Dividend Per Share
Mar 96	8,403	820	694	385	45.9	15.00
Mar 97	9,597	1,223	1,080	406	48.3	15.00
Mar 98	10,677	1,253	1,237	593	70.5	22.00
**Mar 99	8,056	N/A	391	110	13.0	15.00
*Mar 00	8,600	500	450	200	23.8	15.00
Mid-Term						
Sep 98	3,743	132	137	33	4.0	0
*Sep 99	4,100	150	150	100	11.9	0

*Estimates; **Company estimates. Per share values in ¥, all other amounts in millions of ¥.*

Balance sheet summary	1994	1995	1996	1997	1998
Current assets	4,803	4,983	7,033	6,047	6,537
Fixed assets	5,270	5,453	5,699	6,321	6,441
Total assets	10,074	10,436	12,960	12,537	13,088
Current liabilities	1,411	2,050	2,255	2,492	2,641
Fixed liabilities	2,052	1,690	3,730	2,812	2,777
Total liabilities	3,464	3,740	5,985	5,305	5,419
Capital Stock	1,617	1,617	1,617	1,617	1,617
Shareholders' equity	6,610	6,695	6,974	7,231	7,669
Total liabilities and equity	10,074	10,436	12,960	12,537	13,088

Note: All amounts in millions of ¥. Balance sheet, end March.

Kourakuen

(Estd. 1970, listed 1997, stock code no. 7554)
Company address: 1-1, Aza-Kawakubo, Kanaya, Tamura-machi, Koriyama City,
Fukushima Pref. 963-0725
Tel: 81-249-43-3351 Fax: 81-249-43-3726

A fast-food chain company operating in Fukushima prefecture, a largely rural area, north of Tokyo. Notable for its high 8% margins, seeing that it is a chain, created more or less in the middle of nowhere, and specializing in humble items – ramen (Chinese-style noodles) and gyoza (dumplings). Tsutae Niida, 54, is the boss. He has 299 employees.

Product/Sales breakdown: The company breaks down its activity between direct-run establishments, accounting for 88% of turnover, and franchise ones for a small amount (sales to franchise stores, and food materials account for 11% of sales. Royalties from those franchisees bring in 1% of revenues).

Rivals/Competitors: Mr. Niida plunged into a most competitive business. He prospered, on his own account, by undercutting others. He was able to do this, and still not borrow much from the banks, by cutting costs; that achievement was made possible by centralizing material preparation and keeping as much of the operation under his personal control as possible. His company brochures convey an impression of modernization and centralization that no old-fashioned little ramen and gyoza place could ever aspire to, on its own. Most such places are small, owner-run shops and restaurants, with the proprietor and his wife doing the cooking. Such operations do not allow economies of scale, however earthily charming they may be; they are vulnerable to a strategy such as Mr Niida's.

History/Strategy: The strategy has been to keep expanding, taking advantage of the economies of scale. Latest numbers available on Mr. Niida's energetically updated website – he takes things personally, showing photos of himself along with texts on the virtues of expansion and the needs of the 21st century (food at reasonable prices) – show the number of shops run by Kourakuen as 83.

Outlook/Hot News: Kourakuen seems destined to keep growing under the feisty Mr. Niida's management. His sales targets are ambitious – 14% in the year to March 1999, 18% in the year following. But how many Fukushima-based companies, starting up from scratch 30 years ago, have made it to a listing on the Jasdaq during that time? Fast food has created an entrée for Mr. Niida and his people into a wider world, and he has seized his opportunity. Judging by the energy with which he has done that – opening new shops every month – his momentum is sufficient to carry on for a very long time.

Tsutae Niida / President

Stocks (¥50 par value, 1,000 shares min. trade)

Shares Issued (Nov. 1, '98)	4,383,768 shares
No. of Shareholders (Mar. 31, '98)	638

Major Holders	(%)
Tsutae Niida	39.2
Enu Tii Syoji Co.	10.9
Daito Bank	4.9
Employees' Stockholding	3.7
Toho Bank	2.2
Takeo Niida	1.7
Kensaku Niida	1.6
Foreign Owners	0.0

Earnings

Period	Sales	Operating Profit	Current Profit	Net Profit	Earnings Per Share	Dividend Per Share
Mar 96	4,135	324	327	66	325.8	100.00
Mar 97	4,957	411	427	201	728.6	100.00
Mar 98	5,962	483	471	216	50.9	15.00
**Mar 99	6,800	540	540	236	53.8	10.00
**Mar 00	8,000	620	620	300	50.7	10.00
Mid-Term						
Sep 98	3,239	216	225	94	21.7	0
*Sep 99	3,800	260	250	120	27.4	0

*Estimates; **Company estimates. Per share values in ¥, all other amounts in millions of ¥.

Balance sheet summary

Balance sheet summary	1994	1995	1996	1997	1998
Current assets	794	926	823	1,174	1,289
Fixed assets	1,451	1,568	1,870	2,210	2,617
Total assets	2,245	2,494	2,694	3,384	3,907
Current liabilities	603	684	769	939	1,180
Fixed liabilities	1,021	917	994	829	694
Total liabilities	1,624	1,601	1,764	1,768	1,874
Capital Stock	140	231	231	491	610
Shareholders' equity	620	892	929	1,616	2,032
Total liabilities and equity	2,245	2,494	2,694	3,384	3,907

Note: All amounts in millions of ¥. Balance sheet, end March.

Kyoden

(Estd. 1983, listed 1997, stock code no. 6881)
Company address: 482-1, Mitsukamachi, Minowa-machi, Kamiina-gun,
Nagano Pref. 399-4603
Tel: 81-265-79-0012 Fax: 81-265-79-8008

It's remarkable how the Japanese create high-tech jobs in the middle of nowhere – imagine an operator such as Kyoden springing up in say N. Devon. What do they do? Printed circuit boards at short notice, if necessary they will run you up a PCB in 24 hours. 491 employees, privately owned and run by Hiroshi Hashimoto, 46, the founder.

Product/Sales breakdown: Some 94% of sales are in PCBs (printed circuit boards) – the balance of 6% is in CAD software for PCBs and other items. The work requires a high degree of automation, and continuous R & D. There's fiddly work too. Short-term contracts. Batch production – meaning one small lot only, the type of work that Kyoden specializes in – requires human hands and eyes. Hence the large payroll.

Rivals/Competitors: Kyoden's advantages up there in Nagano prefecture are: somewhat lower wages, as with anywhere on the Japan Sea side of the Japan Alps; a settled labour environment, which means, when translated, that people have good work habits, turn up when expected etc, and are ready to work long hours at short notice. Job openings are limited in the "snow country"; 3–4 months a year the local economy is snow-bound. Kyoden has plenty of competitors, but how many can match its delivery schedules? Probably few even try?

History/Strategy: The firm is the brainchild of President Hashimoto. He still dominates the place and, also, the shareholders' roster. He seems to have made one strategic error, however. In 1993 he bought into Showa Mining, purchasing 50% of the stock of this company, to get additional PCB-making capacity. Showa is not contributing much to profits, the accounts suggest. On the other hand Kyoden has established a tie-up with PC notebook maker Sotec. This looks like a better move. The agreement dates to July 1998; it calls for Sotec to design the equipment as a whole and for Kyoden to handle the PCB side, designing that.

Management: Given his relative youth, Hashimoto-san is set there for another 10–15 years of management at least, all being well.

Outlook/Hot News: Kyoden has established a reputation in a short time. It has a tie with Sony, and another with Sotec. The company's debt-to-asset ratio is high, which means it has to keep working hard, however. Foreign ownership was 6% of the company when last checked. Not bad for a firm in the back of beyond. Not that the boss is content to rest on his laurels. He wants to quintuple sales on a consolidated basis to exceed ¥100 billion a year by 2002, the year Hashimoto-san reaches 50.

Hiroshi Hashimoto / President

Stocks (¥50 par value, 1,000 shares min. trade)

Shares Issued (Nov. 1, '98)	13,041,000 shares
No. of Shareholders (Mar. 31, '98)	507

Major Holders	(%)
Hiroshi Hashimoto	34.7
Kurafoto Co.	33.5
Nippon Credit Bank	3.2
Shoko Chukin Bank	1.9
Employees' Stockholding	1.4
Toyo Trust	1.4
Yasuda Trust	0.9
Foreign Owners	6.0

Earnings

Period	Sales	Operating Profit	Current Profit	Net Profit	Earnings Per Share	Dividend Per Share
Mar 96	6,016	731	659	178	248.0	75.00
Mar 97	9,021	1,477	1,432	548	762.3	75.00
Mar 98	10,878	2,207	2,061	1,038	115.3	10.00
**Mar 99	12,025	N/A	2,132	1,084	83.0	15.00
*Mar 00	13,500	2,500	2,350	1,220	93.6	15.00
Mid-Term						
Sep 98	5,253	984	950	471	36.2	N/A
*Sep 99	5,800	1,050	1,000	490	37.6	N/A

*Estimates; **Company estimates. Per share values in ¥, all other amounts in millions of ¥.

Balance sheet summary	1995	1996	1997	1998
Current assets	3,628	2,876	3,422	5,385
Fixed assets	6,462	6,745	7,295	8,871
Total assets	10,091	9,621	10,717	14,257
Current liabilities	6,091	5,355	5,785	6,979
Fixed liabilities	1,566	1,689	1,860	1,669
Total liabilities	7,657	7,044	7,645	8,649
Capital Stock	1,120	1,120	1,120	1,855
Shareholders' equity	2,434	2,576	3,071	5,608
Total liabilities and equity	10,091	9,621	10,717	14,257

Note: All amounts in millions of ¥. Balance sheet, end March.

Kyoritsu Electric

(Estd. 1959, listed 1998, stock code no. 6874)
Company address: 6-33, Nakada-Honcho, Shizuoka City, 422-8686
Tel: 81-3-54-288-8899 Fax: 81-54-285-1105

A family business active in FA (factory auto-mation), offering both systems and machin-ery. Run by Masahiro Nishi, 49, a member of the owning family. Has 282 employees.

Product/Sales breakdown: The company breaks down its activities as between "intelli-gent FA systems" (48%), "FA equipment" (24%), "purchased products" (27%), and others (1%).

Rivals/Competitors: Kyoritsu has to look lively to beat off a host of rivals, many of them small size.

History/Strategy: FA was in fashion from the late 1970s onward. Every manufacturer wanted to streamline production and organ-ize workshops more efficiently, to cut costs and thereby keep pace with the steady, some-times vertiginous, climb in the yen; for exporters there was no alternative but mass-ive introduction of FA systems, this com-pany's forte. However, Kyoritsu had to compete not only on price, but with its con-nections. The latter appear to have been excellent, thus enabling Kyoritsu to do satis-factory business, not just to survive. Its margins are not high, but its profit perform-ance, after hitting a bad patch in the early 1990s, has been satisfactory. Thereby, Kyor-itsu, while investing heavily in its own plant – to sell FA systems to others you have to be impeccable yourself – avoided increasing its indebtedness. The company is all but debtless.

Management: For the time being Kyoritsu continues as a family business. President Nishi set the tone of future business as the company prepared to go public in 1998. In an interview in July of the previous year Nishi-san related how proud the manage-ment is that Kyoritsu had been awarded a coveted quality recognition, the ISO 9002, indicating that the firm is up to a global standard. As compared with the early 1980s, he said, the company had grown 10 times in size, supplying mainly the auto and pharma-ceutical industries.

Outlook/Hot News: For a company that has been around for 40 years, Kyoritsu Elec-tric bided its time. It waited for 39 years before deciding to go public, having pro-duced a stream of good results – 7 successive years of increasing profits. The better per-formance gave management confidence to open a sales office in Nagoya, the centre of the machinery industry (rather than Kyor-itsu's location in Shizuoka City, a bit out of the way). This is bold timing – with the economy dipping deeper into recession; with the bad news spreading from the banking and real-estate sectors to industry, specifi-cally the machinery industry which Kyoritsu aspires to help in FA systems and equipment. Japan indulged in an orgy of over-investment in industry in the 1990s, experts say, creating much excess capacity. Kyoritsu no doubt has illustrious clients, but at a time when even Toyota, according to its management, is making no money at home (or practically nothing), who needs to invest in new fac-tories? A company such as Kyoritsu pins its hopes on re-doing existing plants, and on maintenance contracts ... a stream of business that extends into the future.

Masahiro Nishi / President

Stocks (¥50 par value, 100 shares min. trade)

Shares Issued (Nov. 1, '98)	3,341,000 shares
No. of Shareholders (Jun. 30, '98)	1,098

Major Holders	(%)
MNS Co.	29.6
Masahiro Nishi	9.1
Nobuyuki Nishi	8.2
Mitsuyo Nishi	6.1
Yokogawa Electric	2.4
Bank of Tokyo-Mitsubishi	2.0
Employees' Stockholding	1.7
Foreign Owners	0.1

Earnings

Period	Sales	Operating Profit	Current Profit	Net Profit	Earnings Per Share	Dividend Per Share
Jun 96	11,100	291	255	121	851.6	50.00
Jun 97	13,287	455	436	238	1,034.0	50.00
Jun 98	14,217	501	464	272	93.0	10.00
**Jun 99	15,000	500	500	285	85.3	10.00
*Jun 00	16,300	600	600	320	95.8	10.00
Mid-Term						
Dec 97	6,862	256	237	142	49.4	0
**Dec 98	7,100	263	240	145	43.4	0

*Estimates; **Company estimates. Per share values in ¥, all other amounts in millions of ¥.*

Balance sheet summary	1994	1995	1996	1997	1998
Current assets	3,474	4,389	5,032	5,739	6,287
Fixed assets	2,258	2,183	2,241	2,207	2,414
Total assets	5,732	6,576	7,274	7,946	8,701
Current liabilities	4,132	4,277	5,697	5,832	5,425
Fixed liabilities	818	1,396	559	3	203
Total liabilities	4,951	5,674	6,256	5,836	5,629
Capital Stock	85	124	124	553	688
Shareholders' equity	781	902	1,017	2,110	3,071
Total liabilities and equity	5,732	6,576	7,274	7,946	8,701

Note: All amounts in millions of ¥. Balance sheet, end June.

Marche

(Estd. 1972, listed 1996, stock code no. 7524)
Company address: 2-20-14, Hannan-cho, Abeno-ku, Osaka 545-0021
Tel: 81-6-6624-6123 Fax: 81-6-6624-6118

An Osaka-based chain of restaurants for evening entertainment – Izakaya "pubs" and "Hakkenden" barbecue spots. Family-owned. Has 339 employees plus 1,312 employed on contract basis. President Tadaaki Tanigaki, 56, is the chief shareholder.

Product/Sales breakdown: Marche has 575 shops, restaurants and franchised locations – out of this total 84% are franchise basis, 16% under direct management. Revenues at the directly run places are bigger than at the restaurants run on franchises. Overall, 60% of revenues are accounted for by directly run locations, only 7% by royalties. Other sources of earnings are sales of liquor (9%), foodstuffs (18%) and other items (6%).

Rivals/Competitors: The restaurant trade is hotly competed for, nowhere more so than in Osaka, the culinary centre of the nation. Mr. Tanigaki has accomplished an extraordinary job of building up his chain from a standing start 27 years ago.

History/Strategy: The company has slogans, as do many Japanese firms. Tanigaki's credo is: "Challenge, originality, humanity" – the words are in English in the original. In other words: try your hardest. Earnings and revenues have climbed steadily in recent years, despite the recession, to the point where the company must be coming close to listing itself on the Osaka and Tokyo Stock Exchanges. Its performance has impressed the tough banking community in Osaka. Sumitomo Bank has granted Tanigaki-san long-term finance through to 2006. Asahi Breweries has opted for a small shareholding, as has Marubeni Corp., a trading company.

Management: Those with franchises say that Marche's support is impressive. "If you ask them to deliver even just one daikon (giant radish), they will do it," says a franchiser quoted on a company video.

Outlook/Hot News: Marche will go on expanding, to the point where it will have "1,000 outlets by the year 2000", says President Tanigaki. To reach that goal may not be possible as soon as that, but expansion looks like a certainty. Marche's strength is that it offers people what they want, say the Japanese who like its places – namely, "pubs" to go to in early evening, with snacks to eat, on a per-person budget of ¥2,000–3,000 on own account. Expense account entertaining still goes on – the tradition is honoured – but it has tapered off in the recession. One of Marche's lucky breaks in recent years has been that the beer company it is associated with, Asahi Beer, had a giant marketing success, moving up to overtake Kirin as Japan's number one beer.

Tadaaki Tanigaki / President

Stocks (¥50 par value, 1,000 shares min. trade)

Shares Issued (Nov. 1, '98)	5,720,000 shares
No. of Shareholders (Sep. 30, '98)	477

Major Holders	(%)
Tadaaki Tanigaki	24.1
Masahiro Tanigaki	9.8
Asahi Breweries	4.8
Marubeni Corp.	4.4
Employees' Stockholding	2.9
Marubeni Foods Co.	2.9
Yaeko Tanigaki	2.1
Foreign Owners	0.0

Earnings

Period	Sales	Operating Profit	Current Profit	Net Profit	Earnings Per Share	Dividend Per Share
Mar 96	11,195	815	686	291	633.4	50.00
Mar 97	12,074	867	729	360	74.9	12.00
Mar 98	13,212	1,004	932	449	78.6	12.00
**Mar 99	14,400	1,090	1,060	540	94.4	12.00
Mid-Term						
Sep 98	7,033	499	492	252	44.2	6.00

**Company estimates. Per share values in ¥, all other amounts in millions of ¥.

Balance sheet summary	1994	1995	1996	1997	1998
Current assets	1,218	1,679	1,797	2,145	2,491
Fixed assets	5,878	6,099	6,318	6,898	7,118
Total assets	7,097	7,779	8,116	9,043	9,610
Current liabilities	2,236	2,144	2,496	2,207	2,844
Fixed liabilities	3,879	3,922	3,637	3,491	3,068
Total liabilities	6,116	6,067	6,133	5,699	5,913
Capital Stock	373	700	700	1,057	1,057
Shareholders' equity	981	1,711	1,982	3,344	3,697
Total liabilities and equity	7,097	7,779	8,116	9,043	9,610

Note: All amounts in millions of ¥. Balance sheet, end March.

Matsumotokiyoshi

(Estd. 1975, listed 1990, stock code no. 9875)
Company address: 9-1, Shinmatsudo-Higashi, Matsudo City, Chiba 270-8501
Tel: 81-47-344-5111 Fax: 81-47-342-8446

A retail outfit running drugstores, supermarkets and "home centres", i.e. do-it-yourself stores. Famed for its rapid rise. Kazuna Matsumoto, 59, serves as President of this family business. He employs 2,261 staff.

Product/Sales breakdown: The firm breaks down its main sales items as medicine and cosmetics (42%), foodstuffs (25%), sundry goods (25%) and DIY goods (7%), with a residual 1% for franchise chain income and other items. Mainly the company runs its own outlets. It has 351 shops, of which 20 are franchises.

Rivals/Competitors: In the frenziedly competitive atmosphere that used to prevail in Tokyo, Matsumotokiyoshi's advance into retailing would have been bitterly contested by the established firms – anyone who felt threatened. But customers demanded a different type of establishment, emphasizing ease of access, speed at the cashier's desk and a limited range of goods at bargain prices, and Matsumotokiyoshi sensed as early as anyone that there had been a sea change in consumer shopping habits. Others have sought to follow, they were mostly too late to compete until now.

History/Strategy: A retail outfit as hot as Matsumotokiyoshi – named after its late founder – appears once in a generation in Tokyo. Certainly, the name is a mouthful. The person who created the firm was evidently full of himself, yet with reason. The corporate culture that Kiyoshi Matsumoto created in the 1970s was strong enough to outlive the man. For the future, having established itself on sturdy foundations, all that management has to do is to ring the changes between the drugstores, the supermarkets and the DIY home centres, as necessary, responding to fluctuations in demand for individual products. Not complicated in principle, but a lot of work.

Management: Can the company maintain the momentum, as suggested by its earnings forecasts? Perhaps yes. The current Matsumotos have acquired great confidence as a result of seeing themselves rocket past the traditional upmarket outlets, the big department stores. Go into one of the Tokyo department stores these days and you will find everywhere but the food sections – and the toy departments – quite deserted. Habits have changed. Customers want to walk in off the street and shop at that level. They are put off by empty spaces . . .

Outlook/Hot News: The company has borrowed to finance expansion, mainly from a local bank, Chiba Bank. Repaying the ¥10 billion in loans – equivalent to three years of net profits at the level reached in the term ended in March 1998 – is surely going to be no problem. The firm – which is actually run by Kiyoshi Kuniyuki, one of Kazuna Matsumoto's senior executives, while the latter plays local politics rather than business – aims at having 500 shops in the near future. The company wants to boost its sales of medicines and drugs and to that end is adding more pharmacists to its payroll. It already has 450 such professionals.

Kazuna Matsumoto / President

Stocks (¥50 par value, 100 shares min. trade)

Shares Issued (Nov. 1, '98)	23,667,000 shares
No. of Shareholders (Sep. 30, '98)	2,503

Major Holders	(%)
Tetsuo Matsumoto	12.7
Namio Matsumoto	9.0
Kazuna Matsumoto	8.7
Nankai Kosan Co.	3.7
Syowa Kosan Co.	3.6
Chiba Bank	3.5
Sumitomo Trust	2.6
Foreign Owners	26.0

Earnings

Period	Sales	Operating Profit	Current Profit	Net Profit	Earnings Per Share	Dividend Per Share
Mar 96	111,979	4,468	4,385	2,177	118.5	23.00
Mar 97	127,634	6,092	6,683	3,390	163.8	30.00
Mar 98	149,717	6,946	7,507	3,592	156.2	36.00
*Mar 99	173,000	7,200	7,700	3,800	160.6	22.00
*Mar 00	195,000	7,400	7,900	3,900	164.8	22.00
Mid-Term						
Sep 98	84,621	3,316	3,695	1,924	82.4	10.00
*Sep 99	92,000	3,400	3,800	1,900	80.3	10.00

*Estimates. Per share values in ¥, all other amounts in millions of ¥.

Balance sheet summary	1994	1995	1996	1997	1998
Current assets	24,896	25,413	29,421	29,798	28,177
Fixed assets	43,878	45,225	48,411	54,634	60,093
Total assets	68,775	70,638	77,832	84,433	88,271
Current liabilities	28,888	26,507	33,010	33,770	36,947
Fixed liabilities	20,466	22,978	21,559	13,477	9,068
Total liabilities	49,354	49,486	54,569	47,247	46,016
Capital Stock	6,014	6,188	6,334	11,847	12,956
Shareholders' equity	19,420	21,152	23,263	37,185	42,256
Total liabilities and equity	68,775	70,638	77,832	84,433	88,271

Note: All amounts in millions of ¥. Balance sheet, end March.

Matsuya Foods

(Estd. 1980, listed 1990, stock code no. 9887)
Company address: 4-1-7, Shimo-Syakujii, Nerima-ku, Tokyo 177-0042
Tel: 81-3-3904-1121 Fax: 81-3-3904-3876

A fast-food chain, basically offering gyudon (rice topped with beef). Tokyo-based, operating in the capital. Boss is Toshio Kawarabuki, 57. He employs 469 staff.

Product/Sales breakdown: 95% of what they do is gyudon, according to the company. Ramen (Chinese-style noodles) accounts for 1% of revenues, food materials 3%. Finally, royalties bring in 1% of the company's money – Matsuya Foods does only a minimal amount of franchising. Most outlets are directly run.

Rivals/Competitors: Gyudon is a specialty that others offer, an area of ferocious competition. Leading the pack in Tokyo is Yoshinoya D & C, a Saison group company established in 1958 and roughly four times the size of Matsuya in terms of sales. Yoshinoya's net profits were 10 times as large as Matsuya Foods' in some recent years; and it is debtless, while Matsuya owes the banks substantial amounts.

History/Strategy: Matsuya was created by the Kawarabuki family, 3 of whom are listed as stockholders (see opposite page), including the CEO, with a whacking 41.5%. Toshio Kawarabuki is the person who made this company happen . . .

Management: Kawarabuki-san is a brave man to have plunged into the gyudon trade in Tokyo decades after others – notably Yoshinoya – had established their turf. Yet his decision is paying off. The appetite of Tokyoites for gyudon is seemingly all but inexhaustible. His banks have expressed confidence in Matsuya Foods' aggressive strategy and its management by lending the company substantial sums long-term; Bloomberg reports that Matsuya secured loans going up to 2011, offered by major banks. The March 1998 balance sheet records borrowing of ¥7.3 billion, equivalent to many years of net profits at current levels.

Outlook/Hot News: Evidently, Kawarabuki-san is confident that steady expansion will take care of those loan repayments. His company earnings' forecasts call for revenues and earnings to keep rising. The fact is that in hard times people still want a little beef on their rice! Not too much, at not too high a price, but *something*. Kawarabuki-san and staff have found the way to do it, it seems. Yoshinoya, for its part, is putting its energy into going overseas, starting with the US. This takes some of the pressure off other gyudon chains back in Japan. Matsuya has increased its net profit figure in all but one of the last 10 years. That has created the confidence to reach out and expand into the rest of the country. By late 1998 Kawarabuki-san had 190 outlets, including only 11 franchise ones, the rest being directly run. Some 50 additional new outlets are supposed to open in 1999, including some in Osaka. If the CEO has his way he will go much further than this by making Matsuya Foods into a national name with its restaurants everywhere. This is an ambitious man in a hurry: that's the impression!

Toshio Kawarabuchi / President

Stocks (¥50 par value, 1,000 shares min. trade)

Shares Issued (Nov. 1, '98)	7,714,000 shares
No. of Shareholders (Mar. 31, '98)	791

Major Holders	(%)
Toshio Kawarabuki	41.5
TKK Co.	17.5
Kazutoshi Kawarabuki	4.5
Kaoru Kawarabuki	3.8
Shoko Chukin Bank	3.1
Sumitomo Trust	0.9
Sakura Bank	1.8
Foreign Owners	1.9

Earnings

Period	Sales	Operating Profit	Current Profit	Net Profit	Earnings Per Share	Dividend Per Share
Mar 96	13,251	1,339	1,211	596	77.3	15.00
Mar 97	15,044	1,378	1,245	632	82.1	15.00
Mar 98	18,540	1,777	1,586	806	104.6	20.00
**Mar 99	23,200	N/A	1,900	910	118.0	20.00
Mid-Term						
Sep 98	10,754	800	707	312	40.6	0

**Company estimates. Per share values in ¥, all other amounts in millions of ¥.

Balance sheet summary	1994	1995	1996	1997	1998
Current assets	3,132	2,115	2,209	1,063	1,668
Fixed assets	7,927	9,267	10,657	13,165	15,823
Total assets	11,060	11,382	12,867	14,228	17,491
Current liabilities	2,228	2,066	3,126	2,677	4,171
Fixed liabilities	3,557	3,637	3,560	4,871	5,966
Total liabilities	5,786	5,704	6,687	7,548	10,138
Capital Stock	1,277	1,277	1,277	1,277	1,277
Shareholders' equity	5,274	5,678	6,179	6,680	7,353
Total liabilities and equity	11,060	11,382	12,867	14,228	17,491

Note: All amounts in millions of ¥. Balance sheet, end March.

MegaChips

(Estd. 1990, listed 1998, stock code no. 6875)
Company address: 4-5-36, Miyahara, Yodogawa-ku, Osaka 532-0003
Tel: 81-6-6339-2884 Fax: 81-6-6399-2886

Consider the success of Masahiro Shindo, the 58-year-old President, founder and chief shareholder of MegaChips – a tiny Osaka startup with a staff of 89.

Product/Sales breakdown: MegaChips makes LSIs – large-scale integrated devices – of its own design. These customised LSIs account for 83% of its revenues, while "custom systems" represent a further 7% of revenues, "standard LSIs" 8% and other items 2%. As a "fabless" (or factory-less) firm MegaChips designs the chips, and "outsources" the task of manufacture. But who or what is the one big, fat client – a firm that bought an estimated 90% of MegaChips' annual sales of ¥25.7 billion in 1997/8, its last full year?

Rivals/Competitors: The customer is Nintendo, a Kyoto-based maker of "home-use game machines" – such as, in the past, Game Boy, which is so good for small children's eyesight. The boss of Nintendo, Hiroshi Yamauchi, and/or his acolytes, struck a deal with Mr. Shindo under which they, in effect, "bought" the company; it being a rule in business that, if you are a manufacturer and depend largely on one customer, you lose your independence.

History/Strategy: Shindo-san is experienced. He started his career at Mitsubishi Electric, spending 16 years there; his next employer was Ricoh. His eventual decision to set up on his own came in a moment of hopefulness. "Around 1989, I began to realize that times were changing for the Japanese electronics industry," says Mr. Shindo. "In 1990, I consequently established Mega-Chips with seven other persons who shared my vision of building an R&D-oriented, fabless high-tech firm turning out system LSIs born of a fusion of LSI and system knowledge." He is a good chap – with his vision – but how does he bargain with one customer, 40 times his size in terms of revenues, if the going ever gets tough?

Management: For the time being all is sweetness and light. The numbers keep racing up. MegaChips' performance under Shindo-san looks exemplary – 50% annual increases in turnover, net profits doubling every year. *No one* has performance like this in Japan these days – albeit at a cost. MegaChips has built up borrowings on its balance sheet, investing to get started. The company's non-consolidated accounts showed borrowing of ¥7.6 billion in March 1998.

Outlook/Hot News: With Nintendo striding forward, there is no reason for MegaChips, mighty mouse that it is, to put on the brakes. Quite the contrary. Masahiro Shindo is in no mood to look back, having put his shoulder to the wheel 8 years ago and seen it budge. Wisely, Shindo-san seems to be trying to diversify his clientele. Trade sources say that he set up a sales company with help from Mitsui and Co., the giant trading company. Furthermore, he is said to have created a sales company in the US and to have opened a branch office in Taiwan, as well as an R & D centre in Matsuyama, Shikoku. Shindo-san is trying to extricate himself from total dependence on one major client. That's what it looks like, anyway!

Masahiro Shindo / President

Stocks (¥50 par value, 1,000 shares min. trade)

Shares Issued (Nov. 1, '98)	11,589,840 shares
No. of Shareholders (Mar. 31, '98)	47

Major Holders	(%)
Masahiro Shindo	13.1
Shindo Corp.	11.1
Shigeki Matsuoka	10.0
Ritsuko Shindo	7.9
Employees' Stockholding	6.8
Ines Corp.	4.9
JAFCO	4.0
Foreign Owners	0.0

Earnings

Period	Sales	Operating Profit	Current Profit	Net Profit	Earnings Per Share	Dividend Per Share
Mar 96	10,774	242	178	44	44,216.5	7,500.00
Mar 97	16,846	561	464	240	1,640.1	75.00
Mar 98	25,691	1,137	1,043	511	66.5	8.00
**Mar 99	29,439	1,823	1,603	846	76.5	10.00
*Mar 00	32,000	2,100	2,000	1,040	89.7	8.00
Mid-Term						
Sep 98	11,734	614	470	310	29.5	0
*Sep 99	12,500	700	650	340	29.3	0

*Estimates; **Company estimates. Per share values in ¥, all other amounts in millions of ¥.*

Balance sheet summary	1994	1995	1996	1997	1998
Current assets	241	841	6,940	9,786	12,599
Fixed assets	150	122	165	324	571
Total assets	400	967	7,109	10,111	13,170
Current liabilities	213	491	4,569	7,720	10,270
Fixed liabilities	57	276	2,062	1,534	1,059
Total liabilities	270	768	6,631	9,254	11,330
Capital Stock	53	53	179	262	518
Shareholders' equity	130	199	477	857	1,840
Total liabilities and equity	400	967	7,109	10,111	13,170

Note: All amounts in millions of ¥. Balance sheet, end March.

Moritex

(Estd. 1973, listed 1997, stock code no. 7714)
Company address: 3-1-14, Jingumae, Shibuya-ku, Tokyo 150-0001
Tel: 81-3-3401-9711 Fax: 81-3-3401-9776

Yuhko Morito, founder and president of Moritex, is a swarthy engineer of 53, a bit of a performer. Ensconced at a table at his head office – located in a back street in the Jingumae section of Tokyo – he discloses the secret of his success.

Product/Sales breakdown: "Total honesty, directness," he says. "I go naked before my banks." He names the banks as Industrial Bank of Japan and Bank of Tokyo-Mitsubishi. "They trust me because I tell them everything," he adds, listing his lines of business – 33% in optical fibre products, 27% in visual equipment (microscopes etc), 7% in optical communications, 5% in biotech equipment, purchased products 27% and others 1%. Morito-san has diversified because he has learned from experience – he went bust twice – that it is best not to put all your eggs in one basket.

Rivals/Competitors: To survive in a brutal world you have to be ready to do anything. Morito-san tells visitors how he cleaned up sewage for big trading companies (Mitsui, Marubeni) that were too proud to dirty their hands. Another time he turned to hauling plastic junk, selling it off to Chinese dealers, and using the proceeds to bring himself back into the high-tech world that he prefers. "They called me the King of Rubbish Mountain," he recalls.

History/Strategy: But how is Morito-san doing now, in the middle of a prolonged recession? His surprising answer: just fine, he has obtained backing from – who else? – the State. The MPT (Ministry of Posts and Telecommunications) is agreeing to finance four R&D projects of his, he mentions – it's under the ministry's famous ¥7 trillion plan to build a SuperHighway in telecoms. The money is *supposed* to come in; it need not be returned. Meanwhile the authorities in Tochigi prefecture – Morito-san was born at Nikko in the mountains there – have financed him for the construction of a quartz fibre plant he opened there, with much ballyhoo, in August 1998. A white model of the plant sits in front of him on the table. It is a "heads I win, tails you lose" strategy. Morito-san owns the land and the plant, and if he makes a profit the money's his; if the plant fails, the prefecture loses the funding provided.

Management: Morito-san is an engineer, as stated. To keep track of the financing, he has hired Yozo Kotani, a suave banker, who sits next to him at table. Kotani-san took over as finance director in the spring of 1999. So the banks have put in their man. Good for all concerned.

Outlook/Hot News: Kotani confirms that 1998/9 will not be a good year. Profits will fall. On sales of ¥9 billion, net profits are due to fall below the 1997/8 figure of ¥353 million (see opposite page). With 300 on his payroll, plus 50 part-timers, spread between Moritex's various facilities, including a new plant at Yaita, Tochigi, the team in charge have got to look after the interests of the shareholders, notably Ajinomoto Co., Inc.

Yuhko Morito / President

Stocks (¥50 par value, 1,000 shares min. trade)

Shares Issued (Nov. 1, '98)	4,600,000 shares
No. of Shareholders (Sep. 30, '98)	367

Major Holders	(%)
Yuhkoh Morito	21.0
Ajinomoto Co.	20.3
Employees' Stockholding	4.1
Japan Energy	2.5
Dai-ichi Life Ins.	1.9
Sumitomo Trust	1.5
Toyo Trust	1.5
Foreign Owners	4.7

Earnings

Period	Sales	Operating Profit	Current Profit	Net Profit	Earnings Per Share	Dividend Per Share
Mar 96	6,581	352	312	45	113.3	50.00
Mar 97	7,722	587	523	201	503.4	50.00
Mar 98	9,009	817	708	353	83.6	15.00
**Mar 99	8,700	450	400	200	43.5	10.00
**Mar 00	10,000	880	800	400	86.9	10.00
Mid-Term						
Sep 98	3,808	195	151	91	19.9	5.00
**Sep 99	4,500	300	260	130	28.2	5.00

**Company estimates. Per share values in ¥, all other amounts in millions of ¥.

Balance sheet summary	1995	1996	1997	1998
Current assets	3,279	3,656	4,029	4,588
Fixed assets	2,513	2,284	2,409	3,502
Total assets	5,793	5,941	6,438	8,090
Current liabilities	2,667	3,035	3,582	4,153
Fixed liabilities	1,518	1,273	1,041	1,055
Total liabilities	4,185	4,308	4,623	5,208
Capital Stock	635	635	635	935
Shareholders' equity	1,607	1,633	1,814	2,881
Total liabilities and equity	5,793	5,941	6,438	8,090

Note: All amounts in millions of ¥. Balance sheet, end March.

N.I.C.
(Estd. 1968, listed 1992, stock code no. 9652)
Company address: 3-2, Kanda-Sakumacho, Chiyoda-ku, Tokyo 101-8638
Tel: 81-3-3864-3311 Fax: 81-3-3832-0884

The company is the number 2 in Japan in medical clerical services. CEO Niimura-san, 68, is also the owner. Staff employees number 408, plus there are some 3,000 part-timers.

Product/Sales breakdown: The great bulk (71%) of N.I.C.'s revenues comes from doing clerical, including accounting, work, mainly at prefectural, i.e. local authority, hospitals. The doctors and nurses care for the patients. They "out-source" the keeping of records, including crucial billing functions – work for which the hospital staff have little time and less inclination. N.I.C. (the company's name stands for "Nippon Iryo-Jimu Centre", or "Japan Medical Office Centre") despatches its people to the hospitals (a function accounting for an extra 14% of revenues). The firm also does consulting functions and other work, helping hospitals to organize themselves (8% of sales); and finally the firm trains people who want to learn medical clerical work (7%).

Rivals/Competitors: N.I.C. has been overtaken in this small, but strongly growing, industry by Niichi Gakkan, also a Jasdaq firm, but it's none the less a formidable company.

History/Strategy: These two firms do exactly equivalent work and adopt similar strategies. Competition between the two is limited, however, because they have contracts with different institutions. The contracts will come up for renewal but, lacking any contentious issues, they are more or less certain to be renewed, the way things are done in Japan. Once the connection has been made . . .

Management: The Japanese public is ageing, that is certain. As to the economy, no one can be sure what lies ahead; as to demographic trends, no one is in doubt. The proportion of the population over 65 is going to increase sharply in the next couple of decades. A company specializing in medical clerical work stands to be on an upward path, if management is sound, as at N.I.C. and reputation is maintained.

Outlook/Hot News: N.I.C.'s results are continually improving, a credit to President Niimura. As the CEO and chief shareholder he has an exceptional responsibility for ensuring that N.I.C.'s work, particularly the billing, is done scrupulously. Companies such as N.I.C. are there to ensure that there is no cheating, for example on national insurance. The sums of money involved in medical care are huge. Everything must be done impeccably. Such functions as staff training are accordingly important – and profitable to N.I.C. Looking ahead, what portends? Niimura-san is said to be interested in diversifying into prescriptions. He so far has 33 pharmacists on his staff. Plans call for N.I.C. to take on an additional 10 pharmacists a year. Niimura-san is also said to be considering catering – though the competition there from established caterers could be strong, thinking of Shidax and Green House, two Jasdaq companies.

Katsuyoshi Niimura / President

Stocks (¥50 par value, 1,000 shares min. trade)

Shares Issued (Nov. 1, '98)	8,238,000 shares
No. of Shareholders (Mar. 31, '98)	687

Major Holders	(%)
Katusyoshi Niimura	13.6
Kensho Ltd.	10.1
Yasuda Life Ins.	6.0
Employees' Stockholding	4.9
Sakura Bank	3.1
Morgan Stanley Trust	3.0
Yasuda Trust	3.0
Foreign Owners	13.7

Earnings

Period	Sales	Operating Profit	Current Profit	Net Profit	Earnings Per Share	Dividend Per Share
Mar 96	14,440	761	817	287	34.9	11.00
Mar 97	16,466	986	900	353	43.0	11.00
Mar 98	18,725	1,077	1,070	453	55.1	11.00
*Mar 99	21,800	1,450	1,450	650	78.9	11.00
*Mar 00	24,800	1,500	1,500	680	82.5	11.00
Mid-Term						
Sep 98	10,773	820	823	363	44.1	0
*Sep 99	12,200	850	850	380	46.1	0

*Estimates. Per share values in ¥, all other amounts in millions of ¥.

Balance sheet summary	1993	1994	1995	1996	1997
Current assets	2,282	4,070	5,585	6,274	5,620
Fixed assets	1,629	2,300	3,937	4,295	5,437
Total assets	3,912	6,370	9,663	10,640	11,058
Current liabilities	1,539	1,555	1,470	2,276	2,606
Fixed liabilities	329	1,989	801	753	587
Total liabilities	1,868	3,545	2,272	3,029	3,194
Capital Stock	631	915	3,176	3,176	3,176
Shareholders' equity	2,043	2,825	7,391	7,610	7,864
Total liabilities and equity	3,912	6,370	9,663	10,640	11,058

Note: All amounts in millions of ¥. Balance sheet, end March.

Nadex

(Estd. 1950, listed 1995, stock code no. 7435)
Company address: 9-27 Furuwatari-cho, Naka-Ku, Nagoya 460-8338
Tel: 81-52-323-2211 Fax: 81-52-322-3059

Nadex trades in machinery of many types. The company also manufactures – welding control equipment. President is Kenroku Tani, 59. He has 209 employees.

Product/Sales breakdown: The company identifies its interests as: electronic control equipment and parts (41%); industrial machinery (34%); welding control equipment and parts (12%); welding equipment and materials (8%); others (5%). It does a little exporting – 4% of sales.

Rivals/Competitors: As one of many such companies in the Nagoya – and no outstanding specialty – Nadex survives by virtue of its long-standing business relationships, fostered by a powerful owner (see below).

History/Strategy: Nagoya is traditionally the home ground of engineers in Japan, just as Birmingham, Coventry and other Midlands cities are in England. Machinery is to Nagoya what politics is to Tokyo or the textile industry was to Osaka (no longer); it is the centre of life. Few engineers know how to sell. Nadex's role has been to act as an intermediary between inarticulate "makers" and the customers, including Toyota group members. As such, it has charged small margins, and kept its cost down; it has not taken on staff it didn't need. This type of frugal management is the way they do things in Nagoya, a flinty tradition. Nadex has not shone, but it has plugged on steadily upwards, as one of the few independent traders in its field to survive into what promise to be difficult times ahead.

Management: Chairman Masatoshi Furukawa, as a prominent stockholder, is the dominant figure in the company – and one of the few company-owners who insisted on having his photograph printed here.

Outlook/Hot News: These are not easy times. The auto industry, centring on Nagoya, is in trouble. Even Toyota makes basically no money inside Japan. The capital equipment industry is going deeper into the down part of the demand cycle. Nadex, thanks to prudent management, has kept borrowing low. It will survive the hard times ahead, with any luck. Others may not do so. But what will be the keys to the survival of this family business? Several considerations suggest themselves: (i) the company needs, as it plans, to diversify out of machinery into the broader FA systems – to put efficiency first in the workplace; (ii) as a trader Nadex needs to go outside its traditional Nagoya area and the auto industry. The buzzword used in and about Nagoya these days is "total FA systems". As a final matter Nadex needs to strengthen its financial controls even further in the light of the ¥2.6 billion in borrowing in its consolidated accounts for end April 1998. This is no time to be owing money.

Masatoshi Furukawa / Chairman

Stocks (¥50 par value, 1,000 shares min. trade)

Shares Issued (Nov. 1, '98)	10,000,800 shares
No. of Shareholders (Apr. 30, '98)	755

Major Holders	(%)
Art Gallery Fujimi	17.9
Masatoshi Furukawa	4.1
Tokuji Furukawa	2.9
Employees' Stockholding	2.4
Sumitomo Bank	1.9
Toyo Trust	1.7
Koji Wakamiya	1.5
Foreign Owners	0.6

Earnings

Period	Sales	Operating Profit	Current Profit	Net Profit	Earnings Per Share	Dividend Per Share
Apr 96	15,112	481	534	300	28.6	10.00
Apr 97	16,820	701	741	363	34.7	11.00
Apr 98	18,815	847	850	410	39.9	14.00
**Apr 99	19,150	803	794	404	40.4	14.00
**Apr 00	19,600	850	840	410	41.0	14.00
Mid-Term						
Oct 97	8,965	431	421	222	21.2	7.00
Oct 98	9,472	368	346	184	18.4	7.00

**Company estimates. Per share values in ¥, all other amounts in millions of ¥.

Balance sheet summary	*1994*	*1995*	*1996*	*1997*	*1998*
Current assets	5,508	7,583	8,232	9,182	10,655
Fixed assets	2,569	2,442	2,472	2,501	2,311
Total assets	8,107	10,075	10,778	11,751	13,007
Current liabilities	3,333	4,838	5,411	6,118	7,344
Fixed liabilities	433	247	228	260	307
Total liabilities	3,767	5,086	5,640	6,378	7,651
Capital Stock	790	1,028	1,028	1,028	1,028
Shareholders' equity	4,340	4,989	5,138	5,373	5,356
Total liabilities and equity	8,107	10,075	10,778	11,751	13,007

Note: All amounts in millions of ¥. Balance sheet, end April.

Nagano Japan Radio

(Estd. 1949, listed 1997, stock code no. 6878)
Company address: 1163, Shimohigano, Inasato-cho, Nagano City 381-2288
Tel: 81-26-291-1111 Fax: 81-26-291-1013

A diversified electronics firm – making communications equipment, power supply units and parts – established up in rural Nagano during the Second World War, originally by Japan Radio, a classic company linked to the Japanese shipping industry and to the military as a First World War-era supplier. 1,200 employees. President is Yukio Ishikawa, 60, a Japan Radio executive from Tokyo.

Product/Sales breakdown: With year-to-March 1998 sales of ¥51.3 billion, the company grew by a quarter in two years. Net profits quadrupled during 1996/8. The going items were power sources (of various types), accounting for 39% of sales; OA equipment (20% of sales); telecom items (15%); other electronic equipment (12%); and parts (14%). Some 8% of its production is exported. The range of products is wide.

Rivals/Competitors: To the extent that the company supplies its parent Japan Radio – with 18% of sales – it is subject to protection from the mother firm but also to transfer price decisions (within the Japan Radio group) that outsiders cannot know about. However, with 82% of the production going elsewhere the Nagano company has to fight it out in the market. Its advantages? Somewhat lower labour-cost structures, a controlled labour environment, and a climate where there's not much else to do besides work, for much of the year – as at Kyoden, also a Nagano-based company in electronics.

History/Strategy: The reasons for this spin-off into Nagano half a century ago by Japan Radio have to do with history. Nagano was a safe place, spared American bombs during the Pacific War. Nagano Japan Radio was originally set up in 1942, as part of the war effort, making condensers and other items. The company was granted its formal independence and set up in its present form only in 1949. It attracted good-quality engineers from the start. Morale was high. The company's history shows how it continually sought to break into new fields. As early as 1953 it was working on transistors. It got into the facsimile field in 1977. It took up research in sensors in 1986.

Management: Nagano Japan Radio, as an offshoot of the venerable Japan Radio (established 1915), has confirmed its separate identity as of 1996, with its IPO in that year, but it is still much of a Japan Radio affiliate, and must listen to its parent in Tokyo, as such – it is one of many, if one of the biggest, affiliates within the Japan Radio family of companies.

Outlook/Hot News: Nagano Japan Radio has established a sound performance in recent years, with net profits rising to about one quarter of the parent company's profits. Will it continue? The revenues and earnings forecasts (see opposite page) are not especially bright, given the recession, but the firm is hopeful that the volume of orders will not tail off.

Yukio Ishikawa / President

Stocks (¥50 par value, 1,000 shares min. trade)

Shares Issued (Nov. 1, '98)   29,420,000 shares
No. of Shareholders (Sep. 30, '98)   1,406

Major Holders	(%)
Japan Radio	25.9
Nisshinbo Industries	21.9
Mitsubishi Electric	9.9
Employees' Stockholding	9.7
Hokuriku Bank	4.9
Fuji Xerox	3.8
Mitsubishi Trust	3.0
Foreign Owners	0.0

Earnings

Period	Sales	Operating Profit	Current Profit	Net Profit	Earnings Per Share	Dividend Per Share
Mar 96	41,882	883	652	213	82.5	40.00
Mar 97	47,484	1,421	1,237	622	240.0	60.00
Mar 98	51,352	1,769	1,575	835	30.2	7.00
*Mar 99	52,000	1,800	1,650	850	28.9	6.00
*Mar 00	53,000	1,900	1,750	900	30.6	6.00
Mid-Term						
Sep 98	25,861	939	857	452	15.4	3.00
*Sep 99	26,000	950	800	450	15.3	3.00

*Estimates. Per share values in ¥, all other amounts in millions of ¥.

Balance sheet summary	1994	1995	1996	1997	1998
Current assets	27,442	26,810	30,633	31,154	33,502
Fixed assets	8,249	7,810	7,501	7,516	8,104
Total assets	35,692	34,620	38,135	38,670	41,606
Current liabilities	24,983	23,942	29,753	27,826	28,244
Fixed liabilities	4,062	3,949	1,531	3,560	3,481
Total liabilities	29,046	27,891	31,285	31,386	31,726
Capital Stock	1,788	1,788	1,788	1,788	2,768
Shareholders' equity	6,646	6,729	6,849	7,283	9,880
Total liabilities and equity	35,692	34,620	38,135	38,670	41,606

Note: All amounts in millions of ¥. Balance sheet, end March.

Net One Systems

(Estd. 1988, listed 1996, stock code no. 7518)
Company address: 2-2-8, Higashi-Shinagawa, Shinagawa-ku, Tokyo 140-8621
Tel: 81-3-5462-0800 Fax: 81-3-5462-0840

A provider of computer network systems and integrator thereof. Set up by Mitsubishi Corp. and others in the late 1980s. Big company shareholders. The President is Atsuhiko Asada, 57, a former Mitsubishi Corp. man. Has 401 employees.

Product/Sales breakdown: The company identifies its activities in the half year to September 1998 as 71% for "network equipment", 1% for "network computing", 9% for "media products", and 19% for "services" – not a very explicit list.

Rivals/Competitors: Net One Systems, commissioned to do the work in hand by its shareholders, has no rivals. It has to negotiate fees, which it does with its shareholders, insofar as they are clients. To judge by the profit/performance figures (see opposite page) these inside-track negotiations have boosted Net One Systems' standing. Going public in 1996 may be taken as an indication of an intention to actively seek business outside the charmed circle of shareholders, a mark of self-confidence.

History/Strategy: Trading companies are key intermediaries in Japan, a society where "connecting" is the heart of life, and essential in business. People have got to know each other for something to be achieved. No other country depends on trading companies to stitch things together, the way they do in Japan. Net One Systems is a case in point.

It looks like it. Mitsubishi Corp., probably the most important trading house in Japan today, if not quite the largest, brought together its bank, Bank of Tokyo-Mitsubishi (as it is named today), a major industrial client (Kawasaki Steel), and others to create a "provider of network systems" in the jargon, to integrate network systems used by the firms in question. Net One Systems is that company. It was created to improve and seal communications between widely differing companies that yet wish to work together. With the powerful backing it received Net One Systems grew rapidly and successfully during the first decade of its existence.

Management: Net One Systems exists in a controlled management environment, and functions to strengthen it. As such, it was bound to succeed.

Outlook/Hot News: Net One Systems' strategy, according to company sources, has been to offer its services on three fronts: (i) in planning network systems; (ii) in constructing the same; and (iii) in maintenance – the latter being potentially the most lucrative. Not that the business environment is easy at this point. Cost-cutting programmes have impacted the most prestigious and prosperous companies. In its half year to September 1998, sales dropped by about one fifth. What is going on? Possibly this is a short-lived blip. Net One Systems has been on a steadily climbing slope for years.

Atsuhiko Asada / President

Stocks (¥5,000 par value)

Shares Issued (Nov. 1, '98)	78,495 shares
No. of Shareholders (Mar. 31, '98)	2,142

Major Holders	(%)
Mitsubishi Corp.	33.5
Kawasaki Steel	17.2
Bank of Tokyo-Mitsubishi	3.5
Sumitomo Trust	2.6
IBJ	2.2
Yasuda Trust	1.8
Meiji Life Ins.	1.5
Employees' Stockholding	1.2
Foreign Owners	3.9

Earnings

Period	Sales	Operating Profit	Current Profit	Net Profit	Earnings Per Share	Dividend Per Share
Mar 96	16,109	1,256	1,119	439	77,115.6	10,000.00
Mar 97	20,971	1,657	1,273	837	138,546.8	15,000.00
Mar 98	22,751	1,464	1,720	856	15,666.3	1,500.00
*Mar 99	25,000	1,600	1,700	900	11,538.5	1,000.00
*Mar 00	32,000	2,100	2,200	1,000	12,820.5	1,000.00
Mid-Term						
Sep 97	11,001	627	653	355	11,444.7	0
*Sep 98	9,493	119	238	127	1,623.7	0

*Estimates. Per share values in ¥, all other amounts in millions of ¥.

Balance sheet summary	1994	1995	1996	1997	1998
Current assets	7,181	7,155	11,225	17,576	16,661
Fixed assets	2,593	2,747	2,946	2,150	2,759
Total assets	9,774	9,902	14,171	19,727	19,420
Current liabilities	7,488	7,723	11,140	6,444	5,745
Fixed liabilities	623	87	536	455	79
Total liabilities	8,111	7,810	11,677	6,899	5,825
Capital Stock	925	925	925	2,138	2,151
Shareholders' equity	1,662	2,092	2,494	12,828	13,595
Total liabilities and equity	9,774	9,902	14,171	19,727	19,420

Note: All amounts in millions of ¥. Balance sheet, end March.

Nichii Gakkan

(Estd. 1973, listed 1995, stock code no. 9792)
Company address: 2-9, Kanda-Surugadai, Chiyoda-ku, Tokyo 101-8688
Tel: 81-3-3291-2121 Fax: 81-3-3291-6876

Handles documentation and secretarial work for hospitals. Claims 53% market share in the field. Also in pharmaceuticals trade. Has 1,868 employees. President Akihiko Terada, 62, has a winner.

Product/Sales breakdown: 69% of revenues are attributable to work as a "consignee of medical clerical works". Nichii Gakkan staff – usually young women – are potentially found at the reception desks of about 1 hospital in 10; most hospitals do their own clerical work, but not all. Terada-san has leaped into the small opening. Some 22% of revenues are attributed to "clinic and dispensing pharmacy consignment". Terada-san's staff take care of the paperwork, but not the dispensing per se. Education of hospital staff – a rapidly growing activity – accounts for the remaining 9% of revenues.

Rivals/Competitors: Judging by its market share Nichii Gakkan has moved into this great opportunity far ahead of others. The company has judged its point of entry into the hospitals – doing the clerical work, as noted, and helping with cleaning and sterilizing hospital equipment. It also joins in medical testing. Further, it receives fees for training staff to work in hospitals, possibly with Nichii Gakkan itself. The company has had its manual – a textbook on its specialities – approved by the Ministry of Labour.

History/Strategy: The company has been in business for 26 years, long enough to consolidate its position in the hospitals of Japan. It has refrained from going into some

hospital service areas that Terada-san considered unattractive, e.g. serving meals (Nichii Gakkan is not in the catering trade, many others are) or doing the laundry (another specialized, mostly low margin field). All hospital laundry is handled by outside contractors, none by Nichii Gakkan, according to the company.

Management: Terada-san's early inspiration came from his understanding of the phenomenon of Japan's ageing population – the most rapidly ageing population in the world, it is said – and the likelihood, therefore, that hospitals would be inundated with a demand for services. Home nursing care is a field that Nichii Gakkan may expand into.

Outlook/Hot News: As a company entrenched in the health care field Nichii Gakkan is well placed to move forward. Given its experience it should be able to avoid running into conflict with established interests – the doctors, nurses, pharmaceutical companies and health authorities. It has received a welcome from the health community, and should be able to build on this. Forecasts indicate that revenues and earnings will continue to rise. One promising area, as indicated above, lies in training. Enormous numbers of young women feel the call to work in hospitals, if not as nurses then as helpers, who need less training. Nichii Gakkan's training enrolment increased by 40% in 1998, according to the company. With three different courses made available, a total of 30,812 enlisted in 1998, according to a company spokesman.

Akihiko Terada / President

Stocks (¥50 par value, 100 shares min. trade)

Shares Issued (Nov. 1, '98)	15,685,075 shares
No. of Shareholders (Mar. 31, '98)	666

Major Holders	(%)
Akihiko Terada	20.6
Meiwa Co.	19.9
Toyo Trust	3.5
Yasuda Trust	3.3
Sanwa Bank	2.4
Employees' Stockholding	2.3
Chase Manhattan London	2.2
Foreign Owners	16.2

Earnings

Period	Sales	Operating Profit	Current Profit	Net Profit	Earnings Per Share	Dividend Per Share
Mar 96	44,452	3,187	2,998	1,407	109.9	15.00
Mar 97	52,193	3,775	3,833	1,729	112.2	15.00
Mar 98	58,977	4,297	4,522	2,378	151.7	15.00
**Mar 99	68,000	4,500	4,700	2,720	173.4	12.00
*Mar 00	78,000	5,000	5,200	2,950	188.1	15.00
Mid-Term						
Sep 98	33,252	2,222	2,307	1,408	89.8	0
*Sep 99	37,000	2,350	2,400	1,450	92.4	0

*Estimates; **Company estimates. Per share values in ¥, all other amounts in millions of ¥.

Balance sheet summary	1993	1994	1995	1996	1997
Current assets	4,764	7,043	7,907	12,100	18,310
Fixed assets	7,138	7,577	8,818	9,770	10,587
Total assets	11,902	14,621	16,725	21,870	28,897
Current liabilities	4,472	5,610	6,712	9,282	8,572
Fixed liabilities	5,175	3,567	3,502	835	834
Total liabilities	9,647	9,177	10,215	10,117	9,407
Capital Stock	516	1,744	1,744	3,000	6,119
Shareholders' equity	2,254	5,443	6,510	11,753	19,490
Total liabilities and equity	11,902	14,621	16,725	21,870	28,897

Note: All amounts in millions of ¥. Balance sheet, end March.

Nippon Systemware

(Estd. 1966, listed 1996, stock code no. 9739)
Company address: 31-11 Sakuragaoka-cho, Shibuya-ku, Tokyo 150-8577
Tel: 81-3-3770-1111 Fax: 81-3-3770-2362

One of Japan's longest-established software development houses, a firm established by the current, first-generation President in Tokyo over 30 years ago. Nippon Systemware boasts a close relationship with NEC, the communication, computer and consumer electronics giant, fostered over the years by CEO Naoto Tada, 64. He and his family own the firm.

Product/Sales breakdown: The company lists a powerful selection of clients, including the mighty MPT (Ministry of Posts and Telecommunications). It breaks down its items on offer as "software development" (45%), "device development" (26%), "data processing" (17%) and "system equipment" (12%).

Rivals/Competitors: The relationship with NEC, accounting for a reported 50–60% of turnover, serves to protect Nippon Systemware from undue pressure in what has become a crowded industry in Japan, albeit one that struggles in the face of international competition. Tada-san's firm, with sales of ¥23.9 billion in the year to March 1999, is a fraction of the size of NEC, which has turnover of ¥5.2 trillion.

History/Strategy: Its long record of service and its early arrival in a key industry have secured Nippon Systemware a leading role in its field. The early bird . . . The company employs 1,704 people; it has built its own head office on land it owns in central Tokyo. At the same time the accounts show substantial borrowing relative to assets; Nippon Systemware reports long-term loans of ¥2.7 billion, secured against property, plus greater amounts of short-term debt.

Management: The company has been built up by one man, Tada-san. He crowned his years at the helm by listing Nippon Systemware on the Tokyo Stock Exchange (second section) in late 1998, and by opening a research facility in Yamanashi prefecture.

Outlook/Hot News: The CEO is a founding father of software in Japan, most of his contemporaries have retired. The question of the succession arises. Tada-san is optimistic over the future, saying that, while Japanese software companies slipped far behind those in America, they will catch up. A revival of the fortunes of NEC, a laggard in recent years in competition with Sony, is hoped for. Here, the latest news is discouraging. NEC is in its worst shape in years, is reporting heavy losses, and is being criticized for management failures – notably an inability to foresee the plunge in the prices of personal computers in world markets, e.g. the US. All this is harder for Nippon Systemware, in that NEC's ills look like taking years to go away given the company's apparent unwillingness to address its management issues. This means in turn that Nippon Systemware, which is expanding its staff and is generally optimistic, is looking for more business outside NEC.

Naoto Tada / President

Stocks (¥50 par value, 1,000 shares min. trade)

Shares Issued (Nov. 1, '98)	7,150,000 shares
No. of Shareholders (Sep. 30, '98)	406

Major Holders	(%)
Naoto Tada	37.7
Nakaya Ltd	20.9
Naoki Tada	2.7
Shoji Tada	2.7
Employees' Stockholding	2.1
NEC Corp.	2.0
Fiji	1.3
Foreign Owners	6.1

Earnings

Period	Sales	Operating Profit	Current Profit	Net Profit	Earnings Per Share	Dividend Per Share
Mar 96	17,357	977	804	386	59.0	12.00
Mar 97	18,654	1,252	889	341	48.0	12.00
Mar 98	20,389	1,317	1,190	591	82.7	16.00
**Mar 99	23,900	N/A	1,500	750	97.9	20.00
*Mar 00	26,500	2,000	1,700	850	118.9	20.00
Mid-Term						
Sep 98	11,000	678	623	255	35.8	10.00
*Sep 99	12,000	750	700	300	42.0	10.00

*Estimates; **Company estimates. Per share values in ¥, all other amounts in millions of ¥.

Balance sheet summary	1994	1995	1996	1997	1998
Current assets	9,008	7,922	8,900	11,133	10,307
Fixed assets	7,884	7,856	7,709	7,816	8,846
Total assets	16,892	15,779	16,610	18,949	19,154
Current liabilities	8,525	7,275	8,160	7,433	7,259
Fixed liabilities	3,087	3,032	2,667	3,448	3,352
Total liabilities	11,613	10,308	10,828	10,882	10,611
Capital Stock	1,125	1,125	1,125	1,716	1,716
Shareholders' equity	5,278	5,470	5,782	8,067	8,542
Total liabilities and equity	16,892	15,779	16,610	18,949	19,154

Note: All amounts in millions of ¥. Balance sheet, end March.

Nishimatsuya Chain

(Estd. 1956, listed 1997, stock code no. 7545)

Company address: 266-1, Sho, Shikito-cho, Himeji City, Hyogo Pref. 671-0218

Tel: 81-792-52-3300 Fax: 81-792-52-3307

A chain-store operation specializing in clothes for children and babies, based in Western Honshu in a historic city known for its castle. Owned and run by CEO Yoshihiro Mori, aged 67. Has 196 employees. An expanding firm, secure in its specialty, showing spectacular growth in a recession time.

Product/Sales breakdown: The company identifies its main lines of business as "children's clothing", 38%, "infant and accessory goods", 43%, and baby and maternity wear, 19%.

Rivals/Competitors: The big department stores are traditionally where parents go for these items in Japan. A firm that designs and retails children's and infants' clothing exclusively is a rarity, which may be the root of Nishimatsuya's success. The company has 104 stores mainly in the Osaka/Kobe regions: a network that was steadily built up over 40 years. To run these outlets, which are mostly small, Mori-san employs 373 part-timers and 2 contracted employees, the company says.

History/Strategy: After several decades of effort Mr. Mori broke through in business in the late 1990s. Few operations experienced such explosive growth in retail sales outside special cases and apart from, say, the new supermarkets and small "convenience stores". Nishimatsuya's emergence on the national retail scene was crowned by its Jasdaq registration in 1997. As a public com-

pany, it achieved name-recognition from suppliers and rivals, for the first time from the company's own standpoint.

Management: Mori-san has announced no plans for a successor, a company official noted in response to an enquiry.

Outlook/Hot News: The success of Nishimatsuya suggests that: (i) even at the bottom of a long recession children's clothing remains in demand – they need to be fed and clothed afresh as they grow, even as their parents stop buying clothes for themselves (currently, the department stores' clothing sections are empty, ditto on-the-street clothing stores); (ii) the requirements of the children's and infants' clothing market are subtle, changing constantly, much like the market in toys, making it possible for a specialist to leap ahead at the expense of traditional department stores – pricing and new ideas are crucial, as in the toy industry. Finally, the Nishimatsuya case shows that you don't need to be from Osaka/Kobe or Tokyo to launch a nationwide retail operation. There are advantages in a provincial setting: lower wage expectations for one; greater availability of staff for another; lower rents etc. Thus after a lifetime in the trade Mori-san is experiencing a halcyon age. Part of his "secret", it can be seen, is that he keeps his prices down – observant mothers know exactly what the rival department stores charge, down to the last yen.

Yoshihiro Mori / President

Stocks (¥50 par value, 1,000 shares min. trade)

Shares Issued (Nov. 1, '98) 10,363,000 shares
No. of Shareholders (Aug. 20, '98) 654

Major Holders	(%)
Yoshihiro Mori	36.5
Yuko Estate Co.	13.7
Keiko Mori	4.7
Yoshifumi Ohmura	4.5
Izumi Akashika	3.5
Michiyo Kusakabe	3.5
DKB	2.8
Foreign Owners	4.7

Earnings

Period	Sales	Operating Profit	Current Profit	Net Profit	Earnings Per Share	Dividend Per Share
Feb 96	11,287	801	751	370	39.8	5.00
Feb 97	13,514	1,132	1,078	543	57.4	5.00
Feb 98	18,188	1,297	1,229	611	60.7	10.00
**Feb 99	25,200	1,900	1,900	730	70.4	15.00
*Feb 00	30,000	2,100	2,100	800	77.2	15.00
Mid-Term						
Aug 98	11,356	725	718	263	25.5	7.50
*Aug 99	13,000	780	780	280	27.0	5.00–7.50

*Estimates; **Company estimates. Per share values in ¥, all other amounts in millions of ¥.

Balance sheet summary	1994	1995	1996	1997	1998
Current assets	3,076	2,798	3,461	3,985	6,579
Fixed assets	4,065	3,990	4,220	4,817	6,146
Total assets	7,145	6,790	7,683	8,804	12,727
Current liabilities	3,542	3,088	4,291	4,895	7,098
Fixed liabilities	1,259	1,233	599	529	535
Total liabilities	4,801	4,321	4,890	5,424	7,634
Capital Stock	618	618	618	663	1,105
Shareholders' equity	2,343	2,468	2,792	3,379	5,093
Total liabilities and equity	7,145	6,790	7,683	8,804	12,727

Note: All amounts in millions of ¥. Balance sheet, end February.

Okinawa Cellular Telephone

(Estd. 1991, listed 1997, stock code no. 9436)
Company address: 2-14-1, Kumoji, Naha City 900-8540
Tel: 81-98-869-1001 Fax: 81-98-869-2643

The company provides cellular telephone services within the prefecture of Okinawa, as the name implies. It has made a rapid entry into its field, mainly since 1993, with backing from DDI Corp., a private-sector Tokyo-based parent – and a newcomer to the telecom industry since 1984, in competition with NTT nationwide. Okinawa Cellular's market share within its territory exceeds 60% of a quickly expanding market.

Product/Sales breakdown: Cellular services accounted for 77% of income in the year to March '98, as compared with 23% for "peripheral business", mainly sales of cellular phones themselves. Sales have taken off since 1993, encouraged by rapid cuts in subscription fees and in charges, and a new way of life whereby everybody has to carry a phone, whether on the main islands or in largely rural Okinawa.

Rivals/Competitors: The competition on Okinawa is Tokyo-based NTT Mobile Communications, a bigger and more profitable company than DDI and therefore a rival not to be underestimated. On the other hand, these two are a duopoly.

History/Strategy: The firm boasts a grand total of 64 employees. It has to keep spending on equipment, to maintain its services, but the bulk of the investment needed to service its over 200,000 subscribers has been done, even if maintenance and replacement is required. With revenues rising at a rapid pace to ¥26 billion in the year to March '99, there should be a deceleration in growth and an opportunity to generate higher returns under CEO Oyadomari, a beer executive by background (Orion Breweries).

Management: Day-to-day control is in the hands of Mr. Oyadomari, who is overseen in turn by DDI Tokyo headquarters – the long-term decisions remain there, by virtue of the majority shareholding. Finance functions are controlled from Toyko.

Outlook/Hot News: The future of the company depends in part on Okinawa's economy, which is in turn dependent on tourism and on US military spending to some degree, but also on the overarching congress/competition between the parent firm DDI and NTT Mobile Communications. Some believe that DDI, which has a tie-up with Motorola to promote the latter's Iridium Plan for a global wireless telephone network, has a card to play. NTT Mobile, however, has huge resources and plans of its own. What these two potential global giants decide to do must have a bearing on Okinawa Cellular. Meanwhile, two facts stand out in Okinawa: (i) the business is expanding, if anything more rapidly than even the greatest optimists believed likely; and (ii) the increase in income will assist Okinawa Cellular in fairly rapidly paying off the ¥9.3 billion debt on its March 1998 balance sheet, incurred by capital investments.

Ichiro Oyadomari / President

Stocks (¥50,000 par value)

Shares Issued (Nov. 1, '98)	13,000 shares
No. of Shareholders (Sep. 30, '98)	811

Major Holders	(%)
DDI	51.5
Citibank (H.K.) S. Life Ins.	2.8
Okinawa Electric Power	1.7
Orion Breweries, Ltd.	1.7
Bank of The Ryukyus	1.7
Bank of Okinawa	1.7
Ryukyu Broadcasting System	1.7
Foreign Owners	6.4

Earnings

Period	Sales	Operating Profit	Current Profit	Net Profit	Earnings Per Share	Dividend Per Share
Mar 96	7,623	1,053	963	547	91,318.6	5,000,00
Mar 97	15,619	747	567	203	28,524.9	5,000.00
Mar 98	21,233	1,502	1,191	689	50,449.6	11,000.00
**Mar 99	26,000	N/A	1,400	750	64,860.7	5,000.00
*Mar 00	28,000	1,700	1,500	800	61,538.5	5,000.00
Mid-Term						
Sep 98	12,981	1,005	902	531	38,893.3	2,500.00
*Sep 99	14,000	1,050	950	550	42,307.7	2,500.00

*Estimates; **Company estimates. Per share values in ¥, all other amounts in millions of ¥.

Balance sheet summary	1994	1995	1996	1997	1998
Current assets	734	1,151	1,843	3,136	3,323
Fixed assets	2,016	2,536	5,581	12,128	14,474
Total assets	2,757	3,692	7,427	15,265	17,798
Current liabilities	612	1,385	3,423	5,202	6,992
Fixed liabilities	1,814	1,616	2,795	8,405	6,113
Total liabilities	2,426	3,002	6,219	13,607	13,106
Capital Stock	300	300	300	596	1,414
Shareholders' equity	330	689	1,207	1,657	4,691
Total liabilities and equity	2,757	3,692	7,427	15,265	17,798

Note: All amounts in millions of ¥. Balance sheet, end March.

Optex

(Estd. 1979, listed 1991, stock code no. 6914)
Company address: 4-7-5, Nionohama, Otsu City, 520-0801
Tel: 81-77-524-6990 Fax: 81-77-524-6025

A world-class specialist in sensors, a manufacturer in a million. Based in out-of-the-way Ohtsu City in Mie prefecture. Run by a founder CEO, Tohru Kobayashi, with a passion for the firm and its employees. Sensational results in terms of export performance (63% of sales), largely in infra-red sensors.

Product/Sales breakdown: Sensors for home and office protection and "crime detection" ranked high at 38% of sales in the half year to June '98. Sensors for automatic doors accounted for 22% of sales, those for consumer appliances 10% and those for industrial equipment 26%. The balance of 4% was in commodity sales.

Rivals/Competition: Optex is in a field watched over by voracious players 10 or 100 times its size. To survive against the likes of Fanuc, Kyocera and a dozen others less in the limelight it invests heavily in R & D to stay ahead. The Japanese love sensors; like robots they are a product that sets them on fire.

History/Strategy: Kobayashi-san's strategy is to keep that R & D going, even at a certain risk. With little borrowing on the balance sheet, this is an option even in the middle of the harshest credit squeeze in Japan since perhaps the late 1940s. Keeping up momentum is important, for the boss

has to keep his "family" happy – there are 230 employees. Optex literature emphasizes social values in a traditional Japanese kaisha style.

Management: The CEO, 50 years of age, has a decade ahead of him in the business, at least. All being well, the yen will be weak enough to allow handsome margins on exports and let Mr. Kobayashi keep the banks off his back. But it's always going to be a tough business. Surprises will happen in an industry that is prone to secrets.

Outlook/Hot News: The outcome for this company is in the lap of the gods, given the competition likely to emerge outside Japan in places like Taiwan. The company's James Bondian emphasis on its infra-red security sensors ("intruder detector sensors for security systems") is bound to lure competitors. Kobayashi-san has told the press (*Nikkan Kogyo Shimbun*, 12 November 1998) of two priorities: out-sourcing products as a matter of policy; and diversifying production into new fields – he mentioned digital thermometers and digital watches as possible future products. Another new field being considered by Kobayashi-san is lasers. Laser devices can be used, for example, to measure distances – a military application suggests itself ? Or perhaps for use by surveyors? This is a company to watch as it diversifies.

Torhu Kobayashi / President

Stocks (¥50 par value, 1,000 shares min. trade)

Shares Issued (Nov. 1, '98)	8,500,000 shares
No. of Shareholders (Jun. 30, '98)	731

Major Holders	(%)
Tohru Kobayashi	13.9
Tatsuya Arimoto	12.2
Katsutoshi Kurita	7.2
Bank of Tokyo-Mitsubishi	4.8
Employees' Stockholding	4.2
Suteo Oida	3.1
Kazuko Arimoto	2.4
Foreign Owners	2.3

Earnings

Period	Sales	Operating Profit	Current Profit	Net Profit	Earnings Per Share	Dividend Per Share
Dec 95	7,704	675	773	454	53.5	12.50
Dec 96	8,575	755	890	504	59.3	15.00
Dec 97	9,663	983	1,011	426	50.2	15.00
**Dec 98	10,800	1,100	1,100	520	61.2	15.00
*Dec 99	11,500	1,200	1,200	600	70.6	15.00
Mid-Term						
Jun 98	4,998	527	563	249	29.4	0
*Jun 99	5,200	570	610	280	32.9	0

*Estimates; **Company estimates. Per share values in ¥, all other amounts in millions of ¥.*

Balance sheet summary	1993	1994	1995	1996	1997
Current assets	4,828	5,124	5,786	5,981	6,475
Fixed assets	5,185	5,331	5,200	5,319	5,256
Total assets	10,014	10,455	10,986	11,300	11,731
Current liabilities	789	995	1,318	1,436	1,573
Fixed liabilities	401	396	256	67	77
Total liabilities	1,190	1,391	1,574	1,503	1,651
Capital Stock	2,633	2,633	2,633	2,633	2,633
Shareholders' equity	8,823	9,064	9,412	9,796	10,080
Total liabilities and equity	10,014	10,455	10,986	11,300	11,731

Note: All amounts in millions of ¥. Balance sheet, end December.

Origin Toshu

(Estd. 1976, listed 1997, stock code no. 7579)
Company address: 3-2-4, Sengawa-cho, Chofu City, Tokyo 182-0002
Tel: 81-3-3305-0180 Fax: 81-3-3305-0330

A restaurant chain operator offering obento – delicious take-out lunch-boxes of Japanese food. Concentrated in the Tokyo area. 175 outlets to date, growing fast. 139 employees. Hideo Anzawa, 57, is President.

Product/Sales breakdown: Mr. Anzawa's chain consists of "Origin" shops/restaurants, which offer Japanese food, including those obento (75% of sales), and "Toshu" Chinese restaurants, accounting for 17% of sales. The balance of 8% consists mainly of revenues from Mr. Anzawa's "Tenryu-Mon" restaurants. Revenues are on a steady rising curve, see figures opposite, profits likewise.

Rivals/Competitors: Throughout his working life (Anzawa-san started his business in Chofu City, outside Tokyo, in 1976) the Origin Toshu owner has watched rivals, as he disclosed at an interview in his head office. Especially arrivals from the West. McDonald's arrived in Japan in 1971, triggering the domestic-owned Skylark group into action. That was a signal to Mr. Anzawa, still then operating on a very small scale, to hone his strategy, and reflect on his options. Royal Host landed in Japan in 1976, he recalls, and made an IPO on the Fukuoka market. That was a signal to him to create his own fully fledged kabukishika kaisha (company), with a view to taking his company public once he was ready.

History/Strategy: Mr. Anzawa – a short, wiry man in a dark suit – likes to think out loud on strategy. He decided against franchising, preferring to own and operate all his outlets from his Chofu headquarters. Why, he asks? "If you franchise, you can't, if there is a recession, cut your prices – or not easily." He prefers what he sees as the McDonald's way, not to franchise. Then, if times get rough, prices can be adjusted accordingly . . . Meanwhile, to run a company in Japan, says Mr. Anzawa, is like being a monk. "You repeat the same rituals every day," to keep going. The fundamental practice must never change, only medium-term strategy. "Setting up a shop costs ¥25 million," he mentions, "the return on that, in our case, is 4-fold . . . for our competitors it's 2-fold only." His "secret", he adds, is to locate his shops at exactly the right spots, in the middle of population centres.

Management: Mr. Anzawa has not yet decided who will succeed him, he says. But he is giving the matter active consideration.

Outlook/Hot News: Anzawa-san aims to expand his chain to "1,000 shops by the year 2008", he says. "But it could be done much faster." 33 years ago he called his first company "Toshu" ("Tokyo no ichiban yushu", meaning the best company in Tokyo). "Origin" is a name he added on to his first company name in 1997. "Man must get back to fundamentals, to his origin – food," he says. That is the spirit in which he is planning for the future.

Hideo Anzawa / President

Stocks (¥50 par value, 1,000 shares min. trade)

Shares Issued (Nov. 1, '98)	5,302,000 shares
No. of Shareholders (Sep. 30, '98)	321

Major Holders	(%)
Hideo Anzawa	32.1
Kowa Co.	15.8
Employees' Stockholding	6.8
Hoyo Anzawa	5.2
Akiko Anzawa	4.6
Masakazu Tobari	3.3
DKB	2.2
Foreign Owners	0.7

Earnings

Period	Sales	Operating Profit	Current Profit	Net Profit	Earnings Per Share	Dividend Per Share
Mar 96	5,668	220	157	33	75.2	50.00
Mar 97	7,861	372	283	118	265.9	50.00
Mar 98	9,761	421	314	140	26.4	7.50
*Mar 99	11,990	426	366	161	30.4	7.50
*Mar 00	15,689	713	670	322	51.1	7.50
Mid-Term						
Sep 98	5,601	199	160	76	14.4	0
*Sep 99	7,561	360	338	159	29.9	0

*Estimates. Per share values in ¥, all other amounts in millions of ¥.

Balance sheet summary	1994	1995	1996	1997	1998
Current assets	589	528	681	932	998
Fixed assets	1,580	2,058	2,521	2,863	3,189
Total assets	2,170	2,587	3,203	3,795	4,188
Current liabilities	945	884	980	1,379	1,525
Fixed liabilities	781	1,179	1,684	1,781	1,676
Total liabilities	1,726	2,063	2,665	3,161	3,202
Capital Stock	222	277	277	277	368
Shareholders' equity	443	523	538	634	986
Total liabilities and equity	2,170	2,587	3,203	3,795	4,188

Note: All amounts in millions of ¥. Balance sheet, end March

Otsuka Kagu

(Estd. 1969, listed 1980, stock code no. 8186)
Company address: 3-1, Ariake, Koto-ku, Tokyo 135-8071
Tel: 81-3-5530-4321, Fax: 81-3-5530-5567

A highly rated furniture retailer. Family-owned and managed by the founder, Katsuhisa Otsuka, 55. Employs 1,102 staff.

Product/Sales breakdown: The company breaks down its sales – all furniture – into categories: dining (23%), living room (23%), beds (19%), storage (11%), school and office (5%), others (19%). The latter includes a small amount of rental revenue.

Rivals/Competitors: Two other Jasdaq companies active in furniture are Takarabune, also a furniture retailer, importing items from S.E. Asia and northern Europe, and Hikari Furniture, a wholesaler, each with revenues about half of Otsuka's. The first, however, has been in the red in 1996 and 1997 and is burdened with debt; the second, Hikari, sells mainly office and living-room furniture and concentrates on whole-sale of imported items. Otsuka has the stronger balance sheet.

History/Strategy: The company's history is, in brief, that it was founded by the young Katsuhisa Otsuka, then 26, in 1969, with perfect timing, just at the onset of a giant boom in home consumer items in Japan. Otsuka has kept growing, starting from its minor roots in Saitama prefecture, next door to Tokyo; then gravitating to the capital, and opening a showroom; finally, spreading into other cities, opening showrooms there, creating a members' club

for those who come to visit; and setting up a "bridal information centre" in the Ginza, perhaps to take advantage of that always promising market in Japan.

Management: Otsuka-san has indicated that the succession to him is not an issue at this time.

Outlook/Hot News: Otsuka is all but in show business. The company, since its inception at the start of the consumer boom in Japan in the late 1960s, has emphasized the importance of bringing customers into its (increasingly large) showrooms, to let the clients see a variety of items. In 1999 Otsuka is scheduled to open a 20,000 sq. metre show-room at Makuhari, Chiba, described as the largest showroom in the entire country. Otsuka's outlook must be considered fair, seeing its exemplary profits record during the 1990s. It has ridden through the recession without a blink. Otsuka Kagu has been around a long time by OTC market standards. The company went public in 1980. It is only now that it is showing its mettle, with the big showroom at Makuhari, and other facilities along the same lines, to be opened in 1999 in Osaka, Sendai and Sapporo, among other places. Otsuka-san has strengthened his company's grip on its clientele cleverly, by creating membership clubs. A lifetime of effort is paying off, recognized by a strong share price.

Katsuhisa Otsuka / President

Stocks (¥50 par value, 100 shares min. trade)

Shares Issued (Nov. 1, '98)	10,800,000 shares
No. of Shareholders (Jun. 30, '98)	405

Major Holders	(%)
Katsuhisa Otsuka	22.2
Nippon Life Ins.	8.5
Sakura Bank	5.0
Asahi Life Ins.	4.4
Haruo Otsuka	3.1
Chiyoko Otsuka	3.1
Kikyo Kikaku	2.9
Foreign Owners	9.9

Earnings

Period	Sales	Operating Profit	Current Profit	Net Profit	Earnings Per Share	Dividend Per Share
Dec 95	28,062	1,350	1,320	631	58.5	15.00
Dec 96	39,219	4,226	4,012	1,338	123.9	15.00
Dec 97	44,367	4,053	5,304	2,382	220.6	15.00
**Dec 98	54,200	5,030	5,330	2,430	225.0	15.00
*Dec 99	57,000	5,300	5,600	2,600	240.7	15.00
Mid-Term						
Jun 98	23,561	1,428	1,511	944	87.5	0
*Jun 99	25,000	1,500	1,600	800	74.1	0

*Estimates; **Company estimates. Per share values in ¥, all other amounts in millions of ¥.*

Balance sheet summary	1993	1994	1995	1996	1997
Current assets	13,545	15,224	16,216	19,506	20,638
Fixed assets	9,046	9,082	8,605	9,121	12,361
Total assets	22,592	24,307	24,821	28,628	33,000
Current liabilities	5,928	8,977	8,946	11,257	14,063
Fixed liabilities	2,196	915	992	1,329	713
Total liabilities	8,125	9,893	9,938	12,586	14,777
Capital Stock	1,020	1,020	1,020	1,020	1,020
Shareholders' equity	14,467	14,414	14,883	16,041	18,223
Total liabilities and equity	22,592	24,307	24,821	28,628	33,000

Note: All amounts in millions of ¥. Balance sheet, end December.

Paltek

(Estd. 1982, listed 1998, stock code no. 7587)
Company address: 2-3-12, Shin-Yokohama, Kohoku-ku, Yokohama 222-0033
Tel: 81-45-477-2000 Fax: 81-45-477-2010

An independent importer and seller of semi-conductors. Specializes in programmable logic devices (PLDs). 165 staff. Tadahito Takahashi, 49, is President.

Product/Sales breakdown: The PLDs accounted for 81% in the half year to June '98, according to Toyo Keizai, which singles out Altera of the US as a supplier. "Development Support Services" accounted for 8% and "networks" for 11% of revenues in the period.

Rivals/Competitors: Many, but few with a corporate culture to compare.

History/Strategy: The company "began at a table in a dingy flat in Shibuya" rented by Mr. Takahashi, according to Dave Brauer, Vice-President, an American who was there at the creation . . . In his youth Mr. Takahashi saved money to buy his morning copy of the Nikkei financial newspaper by walking between subway stations, says Mr. Brauer, a long-standing friend. The company, now established in a posh office building in Yokohama, has preserved its international atmosphere, thanks to this friendship. Roughly 10% of the staff are from overseas, including Dan Brandt of the company's finance team.

Management: Paltek has a philosophy, expressed in the phrase "Kyo Sei", or "cooperative growth" . . . more than a credo to foster team spirit and a sense of mission. A company brochure adds: "Paltek has achieved growth for itself and its Japanese customers by providing advanced semiconductors, software and design services . . . The company has continued to assist startups from around the world in the launch of their products in the Japanese market." The text continues: "The second engine of growth is emerging in telecommunications chips and software. However, Kyo Sei means reaching beyond the expectations of traditional relationships between distributor-and-customer, manufacturer-and-distributor, financial-institution-and-client. It leads Paltek into the roles of technical advisor, market research organization, and business consultant."

Outlook/Hot News: A huge photo panel of 2,000-year-old cypress trees ornaments the entrance hallway of the company's open-plan office in Yokohama. The trees are found on Yakushima, an island south of Kagoshima. That is where Takahashi-san was born. Those huge Yakushima cypresses generate an ecology of their own; they provide a habitat for other forms of life – fauna and flora. In a perfect world the visionary Takahashi-san would like to provide a habitat for his employees, where peace and harmony reign; if not for 2,000 years, then for a generation. It could work, but the first question (for the trading company in question) is the bottom line. For now the numbers are pointed upward (see tables opposite). Business is booming, thanks to a proper selection of supply sources abroad and clients at home. Paltek lists a formidable roll of clients: NEC, Sony, Sega, JVC, Mitsubishi Electric, Oki Electric, Hitachi, NTT, Ricoh – you name them.

Tadahito Takahashi / President

Stocks (¥50 par value, 1,000 shares min. trade)

Shares Issued (Nov. 1, '98)	6,590,000 shares
No. of Shareholders (Jun. 30, '98)	34

Major Holders	(%)
Tadahito Takahashi	33.6
David Wallace Brauer	12.4
Sadahiro Horiko	9.9
Endeavor Corp.	6.8
JAFCO G3 Investment Assn.	3.8
Keiko Takahashi	3.2
Employees' Stockholding	3.1
Foreign Owners	15.2

Earnings

Period	Sales	Operating Profit	Current Profit	Net Profit	Earnings Per Share	Dividend Per Share
Dec 95	6,000	919	890	519	314,893.8	10,000.00
Dec 96	8,189	1,109	1,056	379	223,525.5	10,000.00
Dec 97	10,275	1,506	1,453	707	232.9	10.00
**Dec 98	12,000	1,630	1,630	800	121.4	10.00
**Dec 99	13,200	1,750	1,850	860	130.5	10.00
Mid-Term						
Jun 98	5,553	673	707	366	62.2	0
**Jun 99	6,300	750	750	390	59.2	0

**Company estimates. Per share values in ¥, all other amounts in millions of ¥.

Balance sheet summary	1994	1995	1996	1997
Current assets	1,616	4,521	5,777	6,203
Fixed assets	106	361	360	411
Total assets	1,722	4,882	6,137	6,615
Current liabilities	789	3,249	3,970	2,944
Fixed liabilities	179	375	140	180
Total liabilities	969	3,624	4,110	3,125
Capital Stock	167	167	375	765
Shareholders' equity	753	1,257	2,027	3,489
Total liabilities and equity	1,722	4,882	6,137	6,615

Note: All amounts in millions of ¥. Balance sheet, end December.

Park24

(Estd. 1985, listed 1997, stock code no. 4666)
Company address: 1-18-9, Nishi-Gotanda, Shinagawa-ku, Tokyo 141-8524
Tel: 81-3-3491-2211 Fax: 81-3-3495-1955

A pioneer in the field of paid-for parking lots, chiefly in Tokyo. The founder, 60-year-old Mr. Nishikawa, saw an opening – the opportunity to charge people for parking on small, unattended lots – and went for it. The company grew rapidly in the midst of the recession and profits kept pace, as Park24 acquired market dominance.

Product/Sales breakdown: 88% of income is in parking fees; 11% is in sales of products, chiefly parking equipment. There is a residual 1%. This is a classic cash-flow business.

Rivals/Competitors: Mr. Nishikawa says that he has established a 50% market share, and no other firm has more than "single digit" in the market. He feels that he is in an unassailable position. Mitsui Real Estate and Itochu, a trading company, and others tried to challenge him at an earlier stage, but failed to catch up.

History/Strategy: Mr. Nishikawa started in the car parking business in the early 1970s – renting space outside hospitals and hotels, at a time (1971) when all of a sudden it was becoming respectable to charge for what had hitherto been free. He has done nothing else since, gradually perfecting his techniques. Finding that he had hit a ceiling in the early '90s he set new goals under a 6-year plan (the key aim was to enter the OTC market, he explains, as duly accomplished). Park24

now has 197 employees and rents parking spaces on 22,000 lots in all in the cities of Japan. Only 0.5% of this land is owned by his company, says Mr. Nishikawa, the rest, 99.5%, is rented. By not investing in property Mr. Nishikawa has kept his cash free and avoided losses on plunging land values. A self-confident person, he feels that "only an earthquake, an actual quake, could derail my company", and interfere with his plans for expansion, he said in an interview at his Gotanda office.

Management: This is a company run by a strong personality, an emperor in his own domain. Members of the Nishikawa family own close to 50% of the stock. The CEO mentions that he is "the only person of my generation who survives in the business – all the others have died or retired".

Outlook/Hot New: A recent downturn in the stock this year, so shortly after the IPO, has the boss wringing his hands. He hates meeting shareholders in the street, he says, because he has to apologize for something he is not in fact responsible for, the overall decline of the OTC market. Looking ahead, Nishikawa-san mentions that he would like to take Park24 abroad . . . But first of all he has business in Tokyo. He has started buying property, perhaps on the theory that real estate prices have finally bottomed out – he's not saying.

Kiyoshi Nishikawa / President

Stocks (¥50 par value, 100 shares min. trade)

Shares Issued (Oct. 31, '98)   8,350,000 shares
No. of Shareholders (Oct. 30, '98)   943

Major Holders	(%)
Kiyoshi Nishikawa	17.8
Senju Co.	16.8
Kyoko Nishikawa	7.4
Koichi Nishikawa	5.6
Isao Nishikawa	3.7
Nippon Signal	2.9
Sakura Bank	2.4
Foreign Owners	3.9

Earnings

Period	Sales	Operating Profit	Current Profit	Net Profit	Earnings Per Share	Dividend Per Share
Oct 95	10,065	471	354	150	42,958.6	5,000.00
Oct 96	14,772	1,190	1,079	462	972.8	50.00
Oct 97	18,747	1,553	1,346	679	109.4	12.00
**Oct 98	20,892	1,589	1,501	724	86.8	13.00
*Oct 99	24,035	N/A	1,674	837	100.3	N/A
Mid-Term						
Apr 98	9,934	574	517	270	32.4	N/A
**Apr 99	11,416	N/A	508	247	N/A	N/A

*Estimates; **Company estimates. Per share values in ¥, all other amounts in millions of ¥.

Balance sheet summary	1994	1995	1996	1997	1998
Current assets	2,598	3,691	3,658	3,587	3,666
Fixed assets	2,386	3,305	4,257	4,875	7,323
Total assets	4,984	6,996	7,917	8,463	10,990
Current liabilities	2,398	3,560	4,740	3,091	4,643
Fixed liabilities	1,518	2,231	1,411	205	540
Total liabilities	3,917	5,792	6,152	3,297	5,184
Capital Stock	499	499	619	1,013	1,016
Shareholders' equity	1,067	1,204	1,764	5,166	5,806
Total liabilities and equity	4,984	6,996	7,916	8,463	10,990

Note: All amounts in millions of ¥. Balance sheet, end October.

Passport

(Estd. 1969, listed 1997, stock code no. 7577)
Company address: 7-22-17, Nishi-Gotanda, Shinagawa-ku, Tokyo 141-0031
Tel: 81-3-3494-4491 Fax: 81-3-3495-0767

A home-item retail chain, running 147 shops, mainly in Tokyo, specializing in fabrics, interior lighting etc. Gen Mizuno, 67, is the founder and still runs the business. 223 employees.

Product/Sales breakdown: A large share of Passport's revenues comes from sales of textiles (28%); "goods for living", items for the home, account for another 30%; dining goods for 13%; and the remaining 29% comes from sundries and other stuff for the house.

Rivals/Competitors: The main competition comes from department stores. There, Mizuno-san has been clever, going for business in shopping centres, where people come to stroll anyway. Nobody *needs* to buy in the middle of the worst recession in retail in Japan in 40 years, as the disaster at the department stores shows – their business in home items, fabrics etc has collapsed.

History/Strategy: A glance at Gen Mizuno's numbers – gross margins of 3% on sales – suggests that his "secret" has been to get his prices down. Registering on the Jasdaq has been an accolade for a man who has seen it all come right at the end of his career, not in terms of spectacular profits, but by managing to keep expanding steadily in bad times.

Management: To have kept both profits and sales going upwards was no small achievement given that the items Passport offers are non-essentials. Gen Mizuno's ability to keep expanding suggests that (i) a lifetime in trade has taught him how to manage, (ii) the desire for imported goods – items with that extra cachet – has not diminished in Japan, and (iii) finally the recession is not as deep as some reports would have one believe, at least as regards young women – the pockets of these staunch customers, rather, are deep.

Outlook/Hot News: Mizuno-san's strategy from now on is simple. To carry on, to continue. To project an agreeable atmosphere in the shopping centres where he or his franchisees lease space; to keep expanding at a rate of 10% a year, just as if there were no recession. Bravo! On the whole, Mizuno-san prefers to run his own shops – 116 out of 147 were directly run at the last count. The business requires Mizuno-san to go head-to-head with such nitty-gritty competition as that furnished by the so-called "100 Yen Shops". Items that they fight over are such things as stationery supplies. Compare Mizuno-san to a mini-Woolworth in Britain or America.

Gen Mizuno / President

Stocks (¥50 par value, 1,000 shares min. trade)

Shares Issued (Nov. 1, '98)	5,270,000 shares
No. of Shareholders (Feb. 28, '98)	409

Major Holders	(%)
Passport Life Co.	27.4
Jun Mizuno	12.7
NED	2.9
Mutsuko Mizuno	2.9
Mikiko Ohta	2.7
Denichi Akizuki	2.5
Yokohama Capital	2.0
Foreign Owners	0.0

Earnings

Period	Sales	Operating Profit	Current Profit	Net Profit	Earnings Per Share	Dividend Per Share
Feb 96	7,641	266	231	92	340.7	50.00
Feb 97	8,448	289	253	105	277.8	50.00
Feb 98	9,588	317	268	112	22.7	7.00
**Feb 99	10,900	350	310	140	26.6	6.00
*Feb 00	11,500	380	340	170	32.3	6.00
Mid-Term						
Aug 98	5,489	210	187	81	15.5	0
*Aug 99	5,800	220	200	85	16.1	0

*Estimates; **Company estimates. Per share values in ¥, all other amounts in millions of ¥.

Balance sheet summary	1994	1995	1996	1997	1998
Current assets	1,323	1,655	1,494	1,632	1,970
Fixed assets	1,759	1,927	2,206	2,784	3,279
Total assets	3,083	3,583	3,701	4,416	5,249
Current liabilities	1,595	2,095	2,116	2,421	2,968
Fixed liabilities	897	843	854	849	951
Total liabilities	2,492	2,938	2,970	3,270	3,919
Capital Stock	138	167	167	328	369
Shareholders' equity	590	644	730	1,145	1,329
Total liabilities and equity	3,083	3,583	3,701	4,416	5,249

Note: All amounts in millions of ¥. Balance sheet, end February.

PCA

(Estd. 1980, listed 1994, stock code no. 9629)
Company address: 1-2-21, Fujimi, Chiyoda-ku, Tokyo 102-8171
Tel: 81-3-5211-2711 Fax: 81-3-5211-2743

A gem of a company. It offers software packages to an illustrious band of clients in Tokyo. PCA is debtless, a tribute to founder Masao Kawashima, 63, and colleagues at this little firm.

Product/Sales breakdown: In keeping with its private-sector mentality PCA tells you who its clients are – NEC, Ricoh, Softbank (the ubiquitous Mr. Son), Fujitsu etc – and what it does for its customers (e.g. help with the accounts). Its packages win prizes. It can charge up for its wares, within reason, hence PCA's 27% margins (see facing page for the numbers). These should be the envy of companies 10 or 100 times its size – PCA has 196 staff and annual revenues of ¥4.6 billion in the year to March 1998 on a non-consolidated basis. 19% of these are in accounting software, 11% are in sales management software, 8% in wage accounting packages and the remaining 52% in various types of software and other activities.

Rivals/Competitors: It has none in its chosen areas, judging by its margins – for all that PCA prided itself at its inception on "producing quality software at a very low cost" (see its website for that quote), the margins were destined to be huge.

History/Strategy: PCA has thought about its history – Mr. Kawashima has. That website again: "Prior to our inception (in 1980), the founders who (made) up PCA believed that computer software . . . would fulfil a need in small and medium-sized companies . . . PCA was created with the goal of becoming a leader in the development and sale of packaged business software for the small and medium-sized enterprise market. Upon their debut, our products received a great deal of attention from those (firms) which we knew carried the weight of the Japanese economy on their shoulders."

Management: Kawashima-san focuses on the future. "PCA," he says, "(sees) a number of developments in the worlds of government and finance (that) converge with those in the software industry to directly influence the software we'll be releasing."

Outlook/Hot News: "Programs utilizing Java programming will begin to appear . . . PCA Denshin Tsucho, our 'electronic bankbook' software designed to link up with the banks will (succeed) . . . Software will be designed to take more advantage . . . of Microsoft's new 'Windows 98' operating system upgrade . . .", etc. Here is a small-size firm that puts the customer first. That is what comes across. PCA started out to serve smaller firms and promptly ended up working for some of the most demanding corporations in Japan, including some big companies. Kawashima-san alluded to the fruits of these labours in an interview at his office. "If necessary, I could put ¥4 billion on this table tomorrow morning in cash," he said. A balding, bland-looking man, Kawashima-san is proud of his success, to put it mildly. Watch for him to create tie-ups with accounting firms in the UK and US in the near future.

Masao Kawashima / President

Stocks (¥50 par value, 1,000 shares min. trade)

Shares Issued (Nov. 1, '98)	6,000,000 shares
No. of Shareholders (Mar. 31, '98)	308

Major Holders	(%)
Masao Kawashima	53.4
Ctititrust & Banking	3.7
Fuji Bank	2.8
Toyo Trust	2.4
SIM Gross LP (Nenkin)	1.6

Foreign Owners	11.2

Earnings

Period	Sales	Operating Profit	Current Profit	Net Profit	Earnings Per Share	Dividend Per Share
Mar 96	3,253	743	767	399	64.4	10.00
Mar 97	4,249	1,163	1,168	577	93.1	12.50
Mar 98	4,576	1,278	1,268	623	101.2	12.50
**Mar 99	4,750	N/A	1,255	628	104.1	12.50
Mid-Term						
Sep 98	1,974	434	420	232	38.7	0

**Company estimates. Per share values in ¥, all other amounts in millions of ¥.

Balance sheet summary	1994	1995	1996	1997	1998
Current assets	4,043	1,427	1,768	2,467	2,966
Fixed assets	1,819	5,116	5,072	5,006	4,898
Total assets	5,863	6,544	6,840	7,473	7,865
Current liabilities	367	478	741	816	925
Fixed liabilities	83	391	93	100	117
Total liabilities	451	869	835	961	1,042
Capital Stock	890	890	890	890	890
Shareholders' equity	5,412	5,674	6,005	6,511	6,822
Total liabilities and equity	5,863	6,544	6,840	7,473	7,865

Note: All amounts in millions of ¥. Balance sheet, end March.

People KK

(Estd. 1977, listed 1998, stock code no. 7865)

Company address: 2-15-5 Higashi-Nihonbashi, Chuo-Ku, Tokyo 103-0004

Tel: 81-3-3862-2768 Fax: 81-3-3862-3730

A designer, maker and marketer of toys for toddlers. All the emphasis is on marketing, driven by the CEO, Chizuko Kiribuchi. Rapid increase in profits in the mid-90s led this firm to decide on its IPO in 1998.

Product/Sales breakdown: The toys are for infants, cuddly stuff. Indoor play equipment accounts for 18% of sales, educational toys for 27%, Disney-related products for 14%, toy series for toddlers for 35%, and others 6% in the year to March '98. The Disney-related share seems on the small side given the appeal of Disney in Japan.

Rivals/Competitors: Toys and electronic gadgets proliferated in Japan, leading to explosive growth (and high stock values) at big industry players Nintendo and Sega Enterprises. People KK situated itself in a niche to one side of the big electronic games mainstream, as did TOMY, an OTC rival in toys for infants.

History/Strategy: The firm has very few employees, 49 in all in Tokyo, the majority women. Almost all production is out-sourced overseas, mainly in China, where wage costs are a tiny fraction of Japanese (or Taiwanese) levels. As a result, People has almost no capital tied up in plant or investment; its fixed assets are minimal and show no tendency to grow along with sales volume. Design of new products is one key to the future, as at those bigger electronic games giants, if on a smaller stage.

Management: The original founding family, the Kiribuchis, run the firm. Family members hold 36.7% of the 3 million shares issued, the records say. CEO Chizuko Kiribuchi is a small, bright, sharp person. She wears trousers and a leopard-skin design jacket at the office, an open-plan workspace on the top floor of a building in downtown Tokyo. A rare case of a female CEO in Japan, Kiribuchi-san presides over a mainly female staff. She has the quick manner and confidence of someone who makes the most of direct contact with customers – young mothers and their kids. Finance rests in the hands of Susumu Kataoka, a director. Monthly reports, promptly readied, ensure an awareness of any downturns and risks.

Outlook/Hot News: A recent downturn in sales and profits – and a plunge in the stock price after the IPO – was caused by the credit squeeze applied in Japan as a whole in 1998, according to the CEO. She explained in an interview that the squeeze hit wholesalers and retailers, forcing them to cut back on inventories across the board. The company's immediate future depends on consumer confidence overall. "We don't expect to solve all our problems at one stroke by coming up with a single hit product like the tamagotchi," says Kiribuchi-san, in a reference to a rival's worldwide hit toy. Clearly, she has toy design in mind as a fundamental. "What we would look for is steady, incremental effort in design," she said in an interview.

Chizuko Kiribuchi / President

Stocks (¥50 par value, 1,000 shares min. trade)

Shares Issued (Nov. 1, '98)	3,000,000 shares
No. of Shareholders (Mar. 20, '98)	175

Major Holders	(%)
Shinichiro Kiribuchi	25.6
Chizuko Kiribuchi	4.1
Susumu Kataoka	4.1
Mako Yokota	3.8
Masato Kiribuchi	3.5
Hideto Kiribuchi	3.5
JAFCO	3.2
Foreign Owners	0.0

Earnings

Period	Sales	Operating Profit	Current Profit	Net Profit	Earnings Per Share	Dividend Per Share
Mar 96	3,165	386	381	143	49.6	10.00
Mar 97	3,916	558	523	268	92.7	30.00
Mar 98	4,147	692	686	373	128.8	50.00
**Mar 99	3,500	400	400	230	76.7	50.00
*Mar 00	3,700	550	550	270	90.0	50.00
Mid-Term						
Sep 98	1,389	100	90	80	26.8	0
*Sep 99	1,500	200	200	100	33.3	0

*Estimates; **Company estimates. Per share values in ¥, all other amounts in millions of ¥.

Balance sheet summary	1994	1995	1996	1997	1998
Current assets	1,350	1,553	1,549	1,945	2,505
Fixed assets	399	373	545	476	243
Total assets	1,750	1,927	2,094	2,422	2,748
Current liabilities	829	776	754	918	888
Fixed liabilities	117	65	149	82	173
Total liabilities	947	841	904	1,001	1,061
Capital Stock	87	198	198	198	198
Shareholders' equity	802	1,085	1,190	1,420	1,686
Total liabilities and equity	1,750	1,927	2,094	2,422	2,748

Note: All amounts in millions of ¥. Balance sheet, end March.

Plaza Create

(Estd. 1988, listed 1996, stock code no. 7502)
Company address: 1, Goban-cho, Chiyoda-ku, Tokyo 102-0076
Tel: 81-3-3222-3000 Fax: 81-3-3221-8780

Runs a chain of close to 1,000 film and camera shops, where film is processed – claimed to be the largest operator of its kind, processing film, in Japan. Founder Yasuhiro Oshima is still only 35. He has 247 employees.

Product/Sales breakdown: The near-1,000 outlet network was built up at speed. The company repeatedly lapped itself, adding 100 new shops a year on average for 10 years! Film (it sells Fuji film at its "Fujicolor Palette Plaza" shops) and cameras constitute the bulk of its business – 35% of sales (gross revenues were ¥34.1 billion on a consolidated basis in the year to March '98; on a non-consolidated basis the number was ¥14.5 billion). Photographic paper accounted for 28% of sales; other equipment and appliances for 20%; and actual photo developing for 9%, with a residual 8% coming in from franchise income.

Rivals/Competition: Plaza Create works closely with Fuji Photo Film, as the supplier of its film and supplies. Their great rival is Kodak of the US. Competition between Fuji and Kodak has been bitter in the extreme in recent years, with distribution networks such as Plaza Create at the forefront of the struggle.

History/Strategy: Wisely, Mr. Oshima consolidates his accounts. Consolidation brought to light some fierce losses at a Hong Kong subsidiary – losses that wiped out the earnings, however modest, in purely dom-estic operations in Japan in the year to March '98. Plaza Create's loss in that year shows that the company marched into a stone wall in Hong Kong with its subsidiary there. Meanwhile borrowings – these came from Fuji Bank and from the IBJ, both of which opted to become shareholders at an earlier stage – rose to ¥2 billion by the late 1990s.

Management: Oshima-san could not go on like this. He will have had his bankers all over him. Management steadied in the year to March 1999. All being well – see numbers opposite – Plaza Create will have recorded a non-consolidated profit, perhaps even a record on this basis, with sales going up.

Outlook/Hot News: Plaza Create may have established a record for collapsing a share price. Following its IPO in 1996 – Nomura and Daiwa were the lead underwriters – the stock price, initially ¥19,200, plummeted all the way down to ¥980 in the autumn of 1998. It picked up a bit thereafter but still . . . Oshima-san's ability to bounce back suggests (i) that he has gone back to basics, i.e. selling film and supplies in Japan; (ii) that he is receiving strong support from Fuji, still in the midst of its war with Kodak; and (iii) that his bankers like his business, which generates good cash flow. Out of Plaza Create's 934 shops in action, as of September 1998 only 94 were directly run, the rest being franchises, thus tying up little of Plaza Create's capital.

Yasuhiro Oshima / President

Stocks (¥50 par value, 100 shares min. trade)

Shares Issued (Sep. 30, '98)	6,082,000 shares
No. of Shareholders (Sep. 30, '98)	1,171

Major Holders	(%)
Chubu Shahin	34.1
Yasuhiro Ohshima	31.4
Fuji Bank	2.0
Employees' Stockholding	1.2
IBJ	1.0
Foreign Owners	0.4

Earnings

Period	Sales	Operating Profit	Current Profit	Net Profit	Earnings Per Share	Dividend Per Share
Mar 96	10,768	470	574	253	155.7	5.00
Mar 97	13,656	774	751	412	71.3	15.00
Mar 98	14,450	804	1,061	152	25.1	20.00
**Mar 99	14,800	980	1,070	500	82.2	10.00
*Mar 00	16,500	990	1,150	520	85.5	10.00
Mid-Term						
Sep 97	7,214	452	560	268	44.2	5.00
**Sep 98	7,109	480	535	130	21.4	5.00

*Estimates; **Company estimates. Per share values in ¥, all other amounts in millions of ¥.

Balance sheet summary	1994	1995	1996	1997	1998
Current assets	1,971	1,880	3,639	4,811	9,153
Fixed assets	1,691	2,543	3,328	8,663	10,658
Total assets	3,662	4,424	6,968	13,474	19,825
Current liabilities	1,674	2,040	3,749	3,795	8,380
Fixed liabilities	1,484	1,614	1,833	2,537	4,300
Total liabilities	3,158	3,655	5,582	6,332	12,680
Capital Stock	146	186	391	997	997
Shareholders' equity	503	786	1,305	7,142	7,144
Total liabilities and equity	3,662	1,305	6,968	13,474	19,825

Note: All amounts in millions of ¥. Balance sheet, end March.

Q'sai

(Estd. 1965, listed 1997, stock code no. 2596)
Company address: 1-7-16, Kusagae, Chuo-ku, Fukuoka 810-8606
Tel: 81-92-724-0179 Fax: 81-92-724-0189

A firm that built its reputation on a health-giving proprietary cabbage juice, known as aojiru. Based in Fukuoka, in northern Kyushu, Q'sai is the creation of the current owner, President Tsuneo Hasegawa, aged 65. Q'sai is known for its witty TV ads. It is highly profitable, however small. 400 employees.

Product/Sales breakdown: Product recognition is important. Q'sai has achieved this through a well-known TV ad. A veteran actor, known for his roles as a villain in films – a Vincent Price-type character – downs a small bottle of Q'sai's green liquid and grimaces. "Ugh! Horrible! (pause) Give me another!" The majority (61%) of Q'sai's sales consists of this "kell juice", kell being a cabbage with a luxuriant leaf. Other major lines are: frozen egg-related food products (18%); frozen confectionery items (9%); other frozen foodstuffs (11%); purchased products (1%), for the half year to August 1998.

Rivals/Competitors: Q'sai has no direct rivals in its kell juice specialty. Otherwise, it must compete with everybody, a plethora of players in the food industry, supplying supermarkets etc. Sensitive to his margins, Mr. Hasegawa practises a direct sales strategy. His juice – ¥150 a 90cc bottle – is packed up and shipped direct to the customer. The produce is not in the shops.

History/Strategy: Hasegawa-san was a sarari-man until the age of 30. He opened his own business at that time, not knowing what lay ahead. In time – in 1981 – he developed his green juice, never looking back thereafter . . . he likes to boast (i) that there are no artificial additives and (ii) that his "horrible" juice is good for people who, like him, suffer from high blood pressure on occasion. "Q'sai" is a play on words in Japanese; it implies that "help is coming".

Management: Mr. Hasegawa's intention is to keep going forward, to keep expanding. He is shy on one subject: profit margins. "Analysts are always asking me that question, I never have anything to say," he responds.

Outlook/Hot News: The company says that it is opening a research facility. Like the energetic Mr. Mizuno of Hokuto, the mushroom grower in Nagano, also a recent arrival on the OTC market in Tokyo, Mr. Hasegawa prizes R & D. Neither man wants to leave it all to nature. Hasegawa-san is extending his production facilities in April in response to demand for his "horrible" juice. The company is his – he owns "Capital Egg", listed as the largest shareholder – and he decides everything. The key to his success would appear to be Q'sai's marketing. Hasegawa-san and his staff have built up a miniature army of some 10,000 distribution "outlets", actually people who call on their neighbours to discuss such matters as the alleged anti-cancer properties of aojiru juice. Hiroaki Ohishi, a Q'sai director, explained in an interview that distribution is the "secret" of Q'sai's great performance. Thus Hasegawa-san broke through after a 30-year struggle.

Tsuneo Hasegawa / President

Stocks (¥50 par value, 1,000 shares min. trade)

Shares Issued (Nov. 1, '98)   21,494,000 shares
No. of Shareholders (Aug. 31, '98)   1,126

Major Holders	(%)
Capital Egg	27.2
Tsuneo Hasegawa	10.9
Kazuko Hasegawa	8.6
Hiroshi Hasegawa	8.1
Mika Hasegawa	8.1

Foreign Owners   3.0

Earnings

Period	Sales	Operating Profit	Current Profit	Net Profit	Earnings Per Share	Dividend Per Share
Feb 96	11,934	1,799	1,575	751	12,529.2	500.00
Feb 97	13,670	2,907	2,870	1,356	73.5	10.00
Feb 98	16,572	3,861	3,742	1,824	88.9	15.00
**Feb 99	18,000	4,200	4,250	2,130	99.1	17.00
*Feb 00	19,500	4,600	4,800	2,400	111.7	15.00
Mid-Term						
Aug 98	8,563	2,060	2,065	987	46.0	7.50
*Aug 99	9,000	2,150	2,150	1,100	51.2	7.50

*Estimates; **Company estimates. Per share values in ¥, all other amounts in millions of ¥.

Balance sheet summary	1994	1995	1996	1997	1998
Current assets	1,564	1,853	3,678	8,512	10,716
Fixed assets	2,956	3,119	5,338	4,999	6,902
Total assets	4,521	4,973	9,017	13,512	17,619
Current liabilities	2,396	2,632	3,844	4,653	4,040
Fixed liabilities	1,700	1,865	2,993	2,020	1,354
Total liabilities	4,097	4,497	6,838	6,674	5,395
Capital Stock	15	15	30	1,705	3,186
Shareholders' equity	424	476	2,178	6,837	12,223
Total liabilities and equity	4,521	4,973	9,017	13,512	17,619

Note: All amounts in millions of ¥. Balance sheet, end February.

Ralse

(Estd. 1961, listed 1993, stock code no. 9948)
Company address: 1-9-6, Hiragishi-Ichijo, Toyohira-ku, Sapporo 062-8611
Tel: 81-11-813-2525 Fax: 81-11-814-0123

A Sapporo, Hokkaido, supermarket chain, comparable to Tairaya, the Saitama-based supermarket operator, as a regional operation with strength in its roots. A family-owned and managed business. The 63-year-old CEO, Mr. Yokoyama, is the largest shareholder. 862 employees.

Product/Sales breakdown: The chain concentrates on foodstuffs (75%) including a high proportion of fresh and perishable produce. Ralse also sells clothing (11% of sales), sundry goods (10%) and other items (4%). These figures are for the half year to August 1998.

Rivals/Competitors: Mr. Yokoyama says that historically the firm regarded the big Tokyo-based department stores as rivals on Hokkaido turf. Ralse had to close down its first ever store when Tokyu, a Tokyo store, opened up close by. Today, the shoe is on the other foot.

History/Strategy: The CEO says that he is re-opening on the spot where, 37 years ago, his firm had to close down that first shop. This was located, Mr. Yokoyama recalls, at Yamabana Chiku. The intention is to compete with Tokyu. Ralse is expanding elsewhere; the company opened 5 new supermarkets in 1998, all in Hokkaido, Japan's northernmost main island. Last year, the CEO observes, the regional economy was hit by the failure of a bank, Hokkaido Takushoku Bank; this was the largest bank failure in Japan to date – the collapse of the best-known institution in Hokkaido depressed the local economy, which was already in recession. However, Ralse – the company name is based on an English-language slogan (Rising Affluent Life Service) – is prospering. Like Tairaya, it is building up what it calls its "wholesale division" to enhance its internal supply lines.

Management: Is very much in the hands of Mr. Yokoyama, whose family started the business in 1961.

Outlook/Hot News: The firm will celebrate its 40th anniversary in 2001. Mr. Yokoyama aims to launch Ralse on the Tokyo stock exchange (second section), preferably by then. Sales and profits look set to keep growing, as planned. Ralse's stock is healthy despite the worst retail climate in 40 years, nowhere in Japan worse than in Hokkaido. Sales and profits look set to keep marching upward. This is being achieved by expanding, by creating new outlets – 3 large new supermarkets in 1999, adding to a total of 40 already established by late 1998. The company has invested in a new distribution centre near Sapporo, mainly to process its fresh vegetables. The company continues to recruit new staff despite the bleak climate in Hokkaido.

Kiyoshi Yokoyama / President

Stocks (¥50 par value, 1,000 shares min. trade)

Shares Issued (Nov. 1, '98)	15,138,000 shares
No. of Shareholders (Aug. 31, '98)	799

Major Holders	(%)
Kiyoshi Yokoyama	12.1
Masao Kato	5.9
Hokkaido Bank	4.1
Employees' Stockholding	3.0
Hokuyo Bank	3.0
Naokiyo Satooka	2.8
Toyo Trust	2.2
Foreign Owners	7.7

Earnings

Period	Sales	Operating Profit	Current Profit	Net Profit	Earnings Per Share	Dividend Per Share
Feb 96	61,517	1,401	1,589	709	65.4	12.50
Feb 97	67,367	2,082	2,198	1,015	86.5	13.50
Feb 98	72,805	2,585	2,767	1,304	87.2	16.50
**Feb 99	80,700	2,875	2,950	1,400	92.5	16.50
*Feb 00	88,000	3,100	3,150	1,500	99.1	16.50
Mid-Term						
Aug 98	39,943	1,400	1,514	668	44.4	0
*Aug 99	42,000	1,500	1,600	700	46.2	0

*Estimates; **Company estimates. Per share values in ¥, all other amounts in millions of ¥.

Balance sheet summary	1994	1995	1996	1997	1998
Current assets	4,487	5,068	3,496	3,988	5,305
Fixed assets	12,195	12,546	14,440	17,085	19,752
Total assets	16,683	17,614	17,936	21,074	25,057
Current liabilities	10,387	8,680	8,971	8,838	12,907
Fixed liabilities	2,009	4,118	3,191	2,756	962
Total liabilities	12,397	12,799	12,162	11,594	13,869
Capital Stock	1,238	1,303	1,475	2,895	3,187
Shareholders' equity	4,285	4,815	5,773	9,479	11,187
Total liabilities and equity	16,683	17,614	17,936	21,074	25,057

Note: All amounts in millions of ¥. Balance sheet, end February.

Right On

(Estd. 1980, listed 1995, stock code no. 7445)
Company address: 37-1, Higashi-Arai, Tsukuba City, Ibaraki Pref. 305-0033
Tel: 81-298-58-0321 Fax: 81-298-58-0331

A leisurewear retail chain – specializing in blue jeans – concentrated in the Tokyo region. President is Masaharu Fujiwara, 52. 335 employees.

Product/Sales breakdown: Right On evaluates its sales items according to which part of the anatomy is covered – 34% bottoms, 39% tops and knits and 15% in outdoor shirts and wear. Other items accounted for 12% of sales totalling ¥28.7 billion in the year to August '98.

Rivals/Competition: Sometime around the "oil shokku" of 1979 jeans became acceptable wear in Japanese cities, the formalities ceased. Dozens of retailers sprang into action, some importing from the US, more from Korea, Taiwan and Hong Kong. The survivors of the blue jean wars of that era were few, but they included Right On, thanks to its management – the products on offer were basically the same.

History/Strategy: Right On has expanded its sales by cutting prices and thereby its own margins – these were 2–3% in recent years, compared with a much higher 7–8% at competitors Jeans Mate, a Tokyo-based firm (family-owned, like Right On) that concentrated its efforts in the middle of the city. Right On has favoured suburban outlets, while Jeans Mate went for shops near the railway stations. Price cutting put pressure on Right On's finances, as witness the balance sheet. The company carries debt approximating ¥5.5 billion, according to the *Japan Company Handbook*, equivalent to a decade of net profits averaged over the last 3 years. By contrast, Jeans Mate is debtless.

Management: The owning Fujiwara family took the decision to go on the Jasdaq in 1995, thereby motivating those staff who hold stock – equivalent to 4.5% of issued capital.

Outlook/Hot News: Right On is not the most conventionally minded retail chain operation in Japan, basing itself at Tsukuba City outside Tokyo. Yet it has made a success of locating itself in what is still considered one of the less attractive regions near Tokyo. Tsukuba and fashion? They shouldn't mix! Right On defied the stereotype and is accelerating sales of its items. The credit goes to President Fujiwara. He has borrowed from the banks (e.g. Tokai Bank) to build his expansion. The banks have judged that he knows what he's doing; despite the credit squeeze they have not called the loans in . . . An outdoor-wear boom caught on in Japan, as witness the clothes young people wear in the streets of Tokyo, and Fujiwara-san managed to take advantage of that. By the end of 1998, Right On ran a total of 137 shops, including 21 added during 1998. New outlets include shops at Shibuya and in Ikebukuro, two parts of Tokyo that teem with youth. Right On plans to set up in Hakata – in northern Kyushu – in spring 1999; it looks as if it's going for a nationwide campaign.

Masahiro Fujiwara / President

Stocks (¥50 par value, 1,000 shares min. trade)

Shares Issued (Nov. 1, '98)	6,046,560 shares
No. of Shareholders (Aug. 20, '98)	285

Major Holders	(%)
Masahiro Fujiwara	22.6
Fujiwara Kosan	15.7
Yusuke Fujiwara.	5.4
Employees' Stockholding	4.5
Tama Chuo Shinkin Bank	4.0
Ryosei Fujiwara	3.7
Sumitomo Trust	3.6
Foreign Owners	3.3

Earnings

Period	Sales	Operating Profit	Current Profit	Net Profit	Earnings Per Share	Dividend Per Share
Aug 96	20,097	557	430	196	48.8	12.00
Aug 97	25,160	874	719	240	59.6	12.00
Aug 98	28,674	2,021	1,801	621	154.1	12.00
**Aug 99	34,400	2,373	2,143	1,023	169.2	12.00
*Aug 00	35,500	2,350	2,200	730	120.7	12.00
Mid-Term						
Feb 98	14,609	978	906	347	86.3	0
**Feb 99	17,055	1,350	1,232	597	78.7	0

*Estimates; **Company estimates. Per share values in ¥, all other amounts in millions of ¥.*

Balance sheet summary	1994	1995	1996	1997	1998
Current assets	4,320	6,804	7,299	7,913	8,203
Fixed assets	4,129	4,946	6,500	7,674	8,949
Total assets	8,450	11,751	13,799	15,588	17,152
Current liabilities	4,582	6,964	7,609	8,787	9,485
Fixed liabilities	2,256	2,041	3,303	3,722	4,022
Total liabilities	6,839	9,005	10,912	12,509	13,507
Capital Stock	557	791	791	791	791
Shareholders' equity	1,610	2,745	2,886	3,078	3,644
Total liabilities and equity	8,450	11,751	13,799	15,588	171,52

Note: All amounts in millions of ¥. Balance sheet, end August.

Ryohin Keikaku

(Estd. 1989, listed 1995, stock code no. 7453)
Company address: 4-26-3, Higashi-Ikebukuro, Toshima-ku, Tokyo 170-8424
Tel: 81-3-3989-4403 Fax: 81-3-5954-7022

One of the strongest companies on the Jasdaq. Active in design, retail, wholesale. CEO is Kaoru Ariga, 53. Has 508 employees. Part of the Seiyu group formed by Seiji Tsutsumi originally.

Product/Sales breakdown: Sales are leaping up at the company's Muji stores – including 65 outlets in Japan, shops in Hong Kong and Singapore and eight shops in the UK. Overall, clothing amounted to 35% of ¥45 billion in sales in the half year to August '98. Household goods were 53% of sales, counting many hundreds of products. Foodstuffs – including health foods of many varieties – accounted for 12% of turnover.

Rivals/Competitors: The retail trade is intensely competitive in Japan as the fate of the Seiyu parent company – Ryohin Keikaku spun off from Seiyu supermarket chain in 1989 – has shown. Seiyu is in hideous financial shape, while Ryohin, staffed originally by design experts from Seiyu, has shot up.

History/Strategy: The decision to spin off Seiyu experts into this new firm was made by Seiji Tsutsumi, then chairman of Saison group, owner of Seibu department stores and of Seiyu. Tsutsumi's idea was to deploy the design talent within Seiyu to greater advantage. That goal was accomplished at a heavy cost to Seiyu, thereby gutted of key talent. The supermarket giant has never been the same; it is today one of two desperately sick retail mammoths in Japan, the other being Daiei.

Management: The moral is once you fall off the design curve in Japan, you risk failure. More good people leave and the downward spiral repeats itself. Seiji Tsutsumi, as the largest individual shareholder in Ryohin, has benefited on that side (but lost on his Seiyu holdings). He stepped down as Chairman of the Saison group in 1991.

Outlook/Hot News: Making goods in China, designing them in Japan – that's what everyone in retail does. Only they do it a shade better at Ryohin, judging by results and by actions. The company is expanding overseas, and has chosen the UK as its main target, opening seven shops in central London under the Muji name, and two more outlets in autumn 1998 outside London, one at Kingston-upon-Thames, the other in the Manchester area at Trafford. Ryohin opened a first shop in Paris at St. Sulpice on the Left Bank. This looks like just the beginning of Ryohin's drive overseas. The Japanese excel at design, and no one has done a better job of letting Tokyo designers go to work on household goods design than Ryohin Keikaku. In five years' time Ryohin Keikaku will have opened a total of 50 shops in Europe, trade sources say. To be sure, the Muji storefronts – you can see one in the King's Road in London, another in the Fulham Road – have something different (a touch of austerity, of minimalism).

Kaoru Ariga / President

Stocks (¥50 par value, 100 shares min. trade)

Shares Issued (Nov. 1, '98)	14,039,000 shares
No. of Shareholders (Aug. 31, '98)	3,475

Major Holders	(%)
Seiyu, Ltd.	36.2
Chase Manhattan Bank (London)	3.9
Mitsubishi Trust	3.3
Toyo Trust	2.0
State Street Bank & Trust	2.0
Sumitomo Trust	1.9
Family Mart Co.	1.8
Foreign Owners	27.9

Earnings

Period	Sales	Operating Profit	Current Profit	Net Profit	Earnings Per Share	Dividend Per Share
Feb 96	47,862	3,897	3,614	1,714	170.9	15.00
Feb 97	60,786	5,160	5,334	2,722	199.5	24.00
Feb 98	73,047	6,729	7,025	3,454	246.1	35.00
**Feb 99	89,709	N/A	8,708	4,204	299.5	44.00
*Feb 00	105,000	10,300	10,500	5,100	363.3	44.00
Mid-Term						
Aug 98	45,508	4,234	4,418	2,133	152.0	22.00
*Aug 99	52,000	5,100	5,200	2,500	178.1	22.00

*Estimates; **Company estimates. Per share values in ¥, all other amounts in millions of ¥.*

Balance sheet summary	1994	1995	1996	1997	1998
Current assets	3,406	5,625	7,959	18,917	18,807
Fixed assets	6,992	8,369	9,584	11,645	19,497
Total assets	10,398	13,995	17,543	30,562	38,305
Current liabilities	6,564	10,604	6,750	7,946	12,655
Fixed liabilities	1,977	696	138	203	209
Total liabilities	8,541	11,301	6,888	8,149	12,865
Capital Stock	621	621	2,099	6,766	6,766
Shareholders' equity	1,857	2,693	10,654	22,413	25,440
Total liabilities and equity	10,398	13,995	17,543	30,562	38,305

Note: All amounts in millions of ¥. Balance sheet, end February.

Ryomo Systems

(Estd. 1970, listed 1990, stock code no. 9691)
Company address: 3-4025, Hirosawa-cho, Kiryu City, Gunma Pref. 376-8502
Tel: 81-277-53-3131 Fax: 81-277-52-0188

A systems development/data communications company serving the local authorities in Gumma prefecture, an hour north of Tokyo. Ryomo Systems is itself a spin-off from Mitsuba, a well-known post-World War Two manufacturer of small motors, e.g. wiper motors for cars. Both firms were created by the late Sadao Hino.

Product/Sales breakdown: Ryomo's 1997/8 ¥10.2 billion turnover was 65% systems development, 32% data processing and 3% software development, the company says.

Rivals/Competitors: It is doubtful whether Ryomo *has* much competition in its sleepy world up in Gumma. Staff contacted up there by phone seem to be on another planet (to be fair, they are not permitted to speak to outsiders very much; such constraints apply to most Japanese firms that do business with government; they have to gag themselves) . . . A cosy relationship with the local authorities in effect secures business for Ryomo. Revenues and profits were moving up in the year ending March '99 (see table on facing page).

History/Strategy: The story goes back to 1946, the year in which Mr. Hino, a young engineer with a sense of mission, set up Mitsuba in the provincial Gumma city of Kiryu. Starting there – at a time of great penury after World War Two – Hino-san went on to create, with others, an industrial company employing 2,750 staff today, a large enterprise for an out-of-the way spot, starting from scratch . . . Mitsuba prospered

thanks to a relationship with Honda Motor, a client for its motors, and thanks to orders from other famous Japanese car companies. How it became necessary to do what was eventually done – to spin off the company's systems development division as a separate entity – is a tale one would probably have to go to Gumma to pin down. Hino-san, the dominant personality up there, the man who secured financing for the two firms, was the driving force behind creating the new firm, Ryomo Systems. Hino took the post of Chairman in 1976.

Management: Mr. Hino's death in July 1998 at the age of 90 came at a time when the company was picking up additional business, and starting to prosper under President Hisao Kidokoro, despite the recession, by stitching itself into the community, involving itself in many fields, including education. Still connected to Mitsuba, which is its majority shareholder, Ryomo is nonetheless run as an independent operation, staffed by Mitsuba OBs such as Kidokoro. The older firm has "jobs for the boys" at Ryomo Systems during a time when the recession is biting into Mitsuba's long-established business in Japan.

Outlook/Hot News: In time the now not so little spin-off company Ryomo Systems, already employing 510 people may come to dwarf the old-established rust belt firm, its parent Mitsuba. It is possible. It appears to have been the instinct of the late Mr. Hino. He liked to do new things. And so say all of us.

Hisao Kidokoro / President

Stocks (¥50 par value, 1,000 shares min. trade)

Shares Issued (Nov. 1, '98)	3,510,000 shares
No. of Shareholders (Sep. 30, '98)	323

Major Holders	(%)
Mitsuba Corp.	51.1
Bank of Yokohama	5.0
Wako Securities	3.7
Dai-ichi Life Ins.	1.9
IBJ	1.8
Secom Toyo General Ins.	1.8
Daihyaku Life	1.6
Foreign Owners	0.1

Earnings

Period	Sales	Operating Profit	Current Profit	Net Profit	Earnings Per Share	Dividend Per Share
Mar 96	7,878	252	134	36	10.4	6.00
Mar 97	8,723	322	183	103	29.6	6.00
Mar 98	10,212	599	485	133	38.2	8.00
**Mar 99	10,600	680	560	160	45.6	8.00
*Mar 00	11,000	700	600	280	79.8	8.00
Mid-Term						
Sep 97	4,585	116	75	34	9.9	0
**Sep 98	5,261	126	85	46	13.3	0

*Estimates; **Company estimates. Per share values in ¥, all other amounts in millions of ¥.

Balance sheet summary	*1994*	*1995*	*1996*	*1997*	*1998*
Current assets	5,717	5,525	6,053	5,195	5,782
Fixed assets	3,653	3,527	3,495	3,367	3,151
Total assets	9,374	9,054	9,548	8,563	8,934
Current liabilities	1,460	1,349	4,185	1,537	1,936
Fixed liabilities	2,898	2,684	329	1,911	1,772
Total liabilities	4,358	4,033	4,515	3,449	3,709
Capital Stock	1,966	1,966	1,966	1,966	1,966
Shareholders' equity	5,016	5,020	5,033	5,114	5,224
Total liabilities and equity	9,374	9,054	9,548	8,563	8,934

Note: All amounts in millions of ¥. Balance sheet, end March.

Saint Marc

(Estd. 1989, listed 1995, stock code no. 7479)
Company address: 173-104, Hirata, Okayama City, 700-0952
Tel: 81-86-246-0309 Fax: 81-86-246-1339

A quality bakery/restaurant chain with its roots in western Honshu at Okayama City, spreading throughout Japan. A newcomer, driven by CEO and chief shareholder Naoyuki Katayama, 40, who uses franchises. A spin-off from a local confectionery business, by origin.

Product/Sales breakdown: The little restaurants with the Saint Marc name – company staff say the name needed to be crisp and gallic-sounding but has no other meaning – account for 33% of sales in items consumed on the spot or shopped for and taken away. Sales to franchises of supplies like sugar and flour account for 38% of revenues, and royalties for 19%, with "member store fees" standing for an additional 10% in the year to March 1998.

Rivals/Competitors: Spreading the net wide, to include all chain competitors, Saint Marc stands out by its high margins – these were well over 20% of sales in recent years – and high net profits. It bears comparison to Doutor Coffee Co. Ltd. of Tokyo in terms of its attraction to a younger crowd looking for quick service and quality. Saint Marc is differentiated by its emphasis on fresh-baked items, a draw in today's Japan.

History/Strategy: Saint Marc lists very few staff employees, only 54. Katayama-san runs his show out of his computer at the office in Okayama City – well to the west of Osaka, an unusually distant spot from which to spread out a restaurant franchise chain nationwide. This strategy – office costs are lower than in Tokyo – contrasts with Doutor's, the latter spreading out from Tokyo on a bigger scale, having started years earlier.

Management: An owner shacho (president) with years ahead in the business, Mr. Katayama has maintained control of his operations, notably financial management. He is a numbers-oriented manager, who is highly regarded by investors. A credit check reveals no borrowings. Shareholder value is increasing rapidly as the name "Saint Marc" – with a cosmopolitan flavour aimed at young women – catches on.

Outlook/Hot News: Katayama-san has built a chain from scratch in 10 years, using others' efforts. Out of his 171 restaurants in March 1998, only 12 were directly run, the remaining 159 being franchise operations. He offers up-market, light French meals to young ladies – the richest of the cash-rich in today's Japan. Katayama takes in a large proportion of his revenues in royalties. This, too, suggests he is being clever – selling a name he created for nothing. Expect him to keep coming up with variations of his theme. For instance, he has come up with a "bakery kiln" brand of restaurant, still harping on the baking aspect, all very homely.

Naoyuki Katayama / President

Stocks (¥50 par value, 100 shares min. trade)

Shares Issued (Nov. 1, '98)   7,289,040 shares
No. of Shareholders (Sep. 30, '98)   1,810

Major Holders	(%)
Naoyuki Katayama	15.4
Dekoru Co.	13.7
Rep. Noriko Shintani	12.1
Creo Co., Ltd.	4.8
Venture Link	4.8
Daiwa Bank Tokyo	4.4
Toyo Trust	3.9
Foreign Owners	3.9

Earnings

Period	Sales	Operating Profit	Current Profit	Net Profit	Earnings Per Share	Dividend Per Share
Mar 96	4,048	992	882	459	89.9	10.00
Mar 97	5,326	1,399	1,405	674	101.8	12.00
Mar 98	6,411	1,683	1,704	873	131.8	15.00
**Mar 99	6,560	1,881	1,901	995	136.6	15.00
*Mar 00	7,600	2,150	2,250	1,100	150.9	15.00
Mid-Term						
Sep 98	3,237	918	925	462	63.5	7.50
*Sep 99	3,500	930	950	480	65.9	7.50

*Estimates; **Company estimates. Per share values in ¥, all other amounts in millions of ¥.

Balance sheet summary	1994	1995	1996	1997	1998
Current assets	448	866	2,517	3,070	3,879
Fixed assets	1,203	1,450	1,642	2,132	2,224
Total assets	1,651	2,316	4,160	5,206	6,106
Current liabilities	558	748	670	991	1,113
Fixed liabilities	830	661	143	293	306
Total liabilities	1,389	1,410	814	1,284	1,419
Capital Stock	76	341	625	625	625
Shareholders' equity	262	905	3,346	3,922	4,686
Total liabilities and equity	1,651	2,316	4,160	5,206	6,106

Note: All amounts in millions of ¥. Balance sheet, end March.

Saizeriya

(Estd. 1973, listed 1998, stock code no. 7581)
Company address: 2-5, Asahi, Yoshikawa City, Saitama Pref. 342-0008
Tel: 81-489-91-9611 Fax: 81-489-91-9637

A fast-developing Italian restaurant chain. Started by Yasuhiko Shogaki, 52, still the President of this family-owned business after 25 years. Had 664 employees as of the end of August 1998.

Product/Sales breakdown: Pizza, pasta, snacks (36%); fish and meat dishes (27%); beverages, desserts (19%); appetizers, salads, soups (17%); others (1%).

Rivals/Competitors: Chain restaurants are expanding at great speed in Japan. Saizeriya expects to have 225 outlets by August 1999, adding 47 during the year. Competition is hotting up.

History/Strategy: Sometime about 130 years ago, someone must have opened Japan's first Italian restaurant. Many followed – the Japanese have a taste for pasta. Who they were, when they packed it in, the records do not say. However, one sharp-eyed person – Yasuhiko Shogaki – succeeded in establishing Japan's first nationwide chain of Italian restaurants. The name, Saizeriya (which derives from the name of a flower: gardenia), is likely to survive, given the success of the chain in taking root all over the country in, be it noted, directly run operations, not franchised ones. But is the food delicious? Brokers ING Baring comment: "While we would not want to argue that Saizeriya provides great cuisine, the fare is basic but tasty . . . Crucial ingredients, e.g. olive oil, pasta, wine, tomato paste etc. are imported directly from Italy."

Management: Someone in Italy is going to make a lot of money? Perhaps, but Saizeriya management evidently knows a trick or two about driving down costs after a quarter of a century in the trade. Success did not come easily. The same British broker adds: "Vegetables are procured daily . . . shipped to a central processing plant . . . The plant (in Chiba) has the capacity to service 300 restaurants and, as Saizeriya's chain expands, further economies of scale should drive down unit processing costs."

Outlook/Hot News: Given the trend at mass eateries in Japan, which is to price down in the recession – with Saizeriya way at the low end, offering food at prices close to those at Skylark group restaurant chains Bamiyan and Jonathan's (not far from McDonald's) – Mr. Shogaki is going to have to keep pressing those suppliers in Italy. A restaurant-chain war is stepping up in Japan. The owner's strategy is to boost the size of his chain, thus far concentrated in the Tokyo area. His aim is to build up to a level of 1,000 little restaurants, increasingly in shopping centres and malls. Shogaki-san comments: "The Japanese economy is in a recession, companies are not growing . . . but the restaurant industry is not doing so badly, apart from large, gorgeous places." Compared with the US, the Japanese chain-restaurant industry is behind, notes Mr. Shogaki. A battle, he says, is going on between chains like his and combini ("convenience stores"), with their ready supplies of processed foods.

Yasuhiko Shogaki / President

Stocks (¥50 par value, 1,000 shares min. trade)

Shares Issued (Nov. 1, '98)	12,540,000 shares
No. of Shareholders (Aug. 31, '98)	865

Major Holders	(%)
Yasuhiko Shogaki	46.6
Babetto Co.	9.6
Employees' Stockholding	4.6
Goldman Sachs International	2.7
Kunio Shagaki	2.5
Asahi Bank	2.4
Toyo Trust	1.4
Foreign Owners	10.5

Earnings

Period	Sales	Operating Profit	Current Profit	Net Profit	Earnings Per Share	Dividend Per Share
Aug 96	16,165	1,264	1,232	626	764.5	100.00
Aug 97	19,415	2,029	2,001	929	1,066.1	100.00
Aug 98	23,870	2,611	2,571	1,236	106.8	10.00
**Aug 99	30,596	N/A	3,339	1,736	106.5	10.00
*Aug 00	36,000	3,850	3,800	1,900	116.6	10.00
Mid-Term						
Feb 98	10,768	1,042	1,030	501	45.5	0
**Feb 99	13,690	N/A	1,282	666	N/A	0

*Estimates; **Company estimates. Per share values in ¥, all other amounts in millions of ¥.*

Balance sheet summary	1994	1995	1996	1997	1998
Current assets	2,233	2,946	3,082	4,890	7,090
Fixed assets	3,303	3,870	4,364	6,961	9,613
Total assets	5,537	6,817	7,446	11,851	16,703
Current liabilities	2,582	2,406	2,453	3,551	4,264
Fixed liabilities	346	454	508	2,593	3,050
Total liabilities	2,928	2,861	2,961	6,145	7,315
Capital Stock	120	563	563	748	1,640
Shareholders' equity	2,609	3,955	4,484	5,705	9,388
Total liabilities and equity	5,537	6,817	7,446	11,851	16,703

Note: All amounts in millions of ¥. Balance sheet, end August.

Sawako

(Estd. 1990, listed 1995, stock code no. 1784)
Company address: 2-15-8, Nakata, Chikusa-ku, Nagoya 464-0074
Tel: 81-52-732-3850 Fax: 81-52-732-6066

A new-fangled, no-nonsense building con-
tractor. Sawako specializes in low-cost,
small-scale apartment buildings, putting
them up on land owned by customers who
want to tear down their old homes and
rebuild, to secure a new place to live plus
apartments to rent. Founder Junichi Ohira,
52, has come up with standarized designs
for buildings that are quick to erect.

Product/Sales breakdown: Some 94% of
Sawako's business is in the construction of
apartment blocks. Single-family houses
account for 2%, offices for 3% and other
construction for another 1%. The work is
spread out between the Tokyo area, the Kansai and Sawako's Nagoya homeground. The
latter accounted for most of an order book
of ¥36.5 billion at the end of August 1998.
Orders slowed thereafter as the recession
continued and the banks squeezed credit.

Rivals/Competitors: Mr. Ohira is a
redoubtable relative newcomer to an industry long dominated – for decades in fact –
by such firms as Daiwa House and Sekisui
House. The construction industry has been
in a major slump in Japan for years; some
of the largest firms were threatened with
bankruptcy – despite strong backing from
politicians – and numerous medium or small
outfits merged or went under. For Sawako
to have been able to brush aside this trend,
when others had so much at stake, is most
impressive.

History/Strategy: How has Sawako prospered? The Nagoya region – Toyota is

centred there – somehow fosters a flinty attitude in business. Sawako, unlike many in its
industry, has refrained from speculation in
property; the firm has concentrated on its
specialty, putting up standard units. Meanwhile, for a small company boss Mr. Ohira
adopted the extremely unusual strategy of
complete transparency; he registered
Sawako on the Nasdaq in New York. Company spokesmen explain that he took that
step to ensure that everything about the firm
is laid out in accordance with Nasdaq regu-
lations in black and white. Sawako was the
first Japanese OTC firm to seek a Nasdaq
listing for a very long time indeed – since
1975.

Outlook/Hot News: Sawako may well
continue to expand despite the dull trend in
housing construction in Japan, in sales and
in earnings. The company's forecasts are less
optimistic, however, than those of brokers
in Tokyo, where Sawako has numerous fans.
To expand, Ohira-san obviously has to
spread out beyond the Nagoya region much
more. To assist his growth strategy he purchased Fuji Construction, a small-medium
builder . . . The scope for expansion on current lines seems very great. Japanese people
who own old homes are faced with problems:
(i) their mostly wooden houses become
decreasingly inhabitable after 30 years – they
rot; and (ii) as the population ages, the
number of those who want convenient flats,
as opposed to rambling mansions, for their
declining years, increases very quickly.

Junichi Ohira / President

Stocks (¥50 par value, 100 shares min. trade)

Shares Issued (Nov. 1, '98)   15,979,595 shares
No. of Shareholders (Jul. 31, '98)   2,301

Major Holders	(%)
Junichi Ohira	11.3
Office Ohira	10.6
Employees' Stockholding	4.4
Shuichi Kondo	4.0
Masayuki Sumiya	3.8
Hero & Co.	3.1
Mitsui Trust	2.7
Foreign Owners	17.0

Earnings

Period	Sales	Operating Profit	Current Profit	Net Profit	Earnings Per Share	Dividend Per Share
Jul 96	15,742	1,444	1,223	658	75.8	20.00
Jul 97	21,151	1,576	1,551	800	65.9	15.00
Jul 98	22,448	1,775	1,654	876	57.4	15.00
**Jul 99	22,550	1,899	1,729	882	55.2	15.00
*Jul 00	23,500	2,000	1,850	950	59.5	15.00
Mid-Term						
Jan 98	11,285	814	711	402	27.1	0
**Jan 99	10,250	755	647	330	20.7	0

*Estimates; **Company estimates. Per share values in ¥, all other amounts in millions of ¥.

Balance sheet summary	1994	1995	1996	1997	1998
Current assets	4,379	6,563	11,712	13,157	16,303
Fixed assets	386	629	740	725	1,786
Total assets	4,765	7,192	12,453	13,900	18,099
Current liabilities	1,979	2,752	4,270	4,586	5,082
Fixed liabilities	31	36	58	582	3,265
Total liabilities	2,011	2,788	4,328	5,168	8,348
Capital Stock	1,479	2,629	5,821	5,821	5,987
Shareholders' equity	2,754	4,403	8,124	8,731	9,751
Total liabilities and equity	4,765	7,192	12,453	13,900	18,099

Note: All amounts in millions of ¥. Balance sheet, end July.

Sazaby

(Estd. 1972, listed 1997, stock code no. 7553)
Company address: 2-11-1, Sendagaya, Shibuya-ku, Tokyo 151-0051
Tel: 81-3-5412-1820 Fax: 81-3-5411-3001

A retail/fashion/restaurant life-force in today's Tokyo. Created when he was 29 by self-described former "beach bum" Rikuzo Suzuki, now 55, a controversial man-about-town/businessman. 1,722 employees in September 1998.

Product/Sales breakdown: Leather goods including handbags account for the lion's share (48%) of Sazaby's ¥48.7 billion annual sales. Its restaurant (Kihachi) and coffee bar (Starbucks) outlets and other food outlets add up to 23% of revenues; household goods to another 18%, other purchased products 6% and others 5%.

Rivals/Competition: "Half a step ahead" has become the company motto; stay just a fraction ahead of the crowd – with your clients.

History/Strategy: As a young man Suzuki-san first attracted attention by serving on the staff of Shintaro Ishihara, a novelist turned right-wing politician. Thereafter, he struck out on his own and started importing used 1950s furniture from Europe. From such humble beginnings he branched out into women's handbags, eventually doing his own designs in his own workshops; he latched on to Agnès B, the French fashion designer, importing from Paris . . . Rikuzo Suzuki's crowning achievement has been to create an entrepreneurial style. The company ministers to its clients. Suzuki-san and staff aim at "satisfying the desires of people who want to inject a dash of creativitry, style and individuality into their lives". This is the air that his new coffee bars project – Suzuki created a joint venture with Starbucks Coffee International of the US, starting in 1996 – of just lifting things up a bit. Meanwhile, he has expanded the company yearly. Profits declined in the 1997/8 year, but were back on an uptrend in the current year to March '99. The former "beach bum" has made good. By September 1998 he had opened a formidable 299 shops, restaurants and tea houses, all directly run.

Management: Sazaby Inc. is being sued by Sotheby's, the international auction house, for alleged borrowing of the latter's name – admitted to by Suzuki-san in a celebrated 1992 interview with the magazine *Tokyo Journal*. This contentious matter had dragged on for years and had not been settled at the time of writing. "Sotheby" and "Sazaby" are written in the same phonetic kana letters, making the two indistinguishable in Japanese script.

Outlook/Hot News: Suzuki-san, the CEO, delegates the running of the business to others, while he dashes about the world. Masatoku Mori, the COO, is in charge when the restless founder is away, as he is much of the year. Sazaby looks to be set on a steep upward path. It is doing brilliantly but *must* resolve that legal stew if it wants to have a good name abroad.

Rikuzo Suzuki / President

Stocks (¥50 par value, 1,000 shares min. trade)

Shares Issued (Nov. 1, '98)   20,939,000 shares
No. of Shareholders (Mar. 31, '98)   1,501

Major Holders	(%)
Rikuzo Suzuki	25.2
Masatoku Mori	11.8
Yuji Tsunoda	6.5
Masaki Mori	4.8
Las International Ltd.	4.8
Hiroshi Nakamura	3.2
Bank of Tokyo-Mitsubishi	2.8
Foreign Owners	6.6

Earnings

Period	Sales	Operating Profit	Current Profit	Net Profit	Earnings Per Share	Dividend Per Share
Mar 96	1,644	204	233	160	N/A	10,000.00
Mar 97	1,979	317	315	207	70,545.5	12,500.00
Mar 98	3,063	506	502	342	105,112.9	12,500.00
*Mar 99	4,140	900	850	500	125,000.0	12,500.00
*Mar 00	4,600	1,000	1,000	590	147,500.0	12,500.00
Mid-Term						
Sep 98	1,957	304	225	158	39,003.7	0
*Sep 99	2,100	350	350	180	45,000.0	0

*Estimates. Per share values in ¥, all other amounts in millions of ¥.

Balance sheet summary	1995	1996	1997	1998
Current assets	11,853	16,807	15,792	22,660
Fixed assets	7,629	9,900	12,486	14,788
Total assets	19,485	26,710	28,279	37,448
Current liabilities	7,622	10,459	10,020	11,422
Fixed liabilities	4,436	4,309	2,966	2,176
Total liabilities	12,059	14,768	12,987	13,599
Capital Stock	918	1,862	2,089	4,593
Shareholders' equity	7,426	11,942	15,291	23,848
Total liabilities and equity	19,485	26,710	28,279	37,448

Note: All amounts in millions of ¥. Balance sheet, end March.

Shinki

(Estd. 1954, listed 1995, stock code no. 8568)
Company address: 1-6-1, Nishi-Shinjuku, Shinjuki-ku, Tokyo 163-1528
Tel: 81-3-3345-9331 Fax 81-3-3345-9349

Trust a moneylender to tell you the truth. "Looking at Japan's sluggish economy," says 38-year-old President Naoyoshi Maeda of Shinki, "we think that it will take at least one year for a recovery to materialize . . . the financial system through which money, the economy's lifeblood, is allocated, is badly hurt."

Product/Sales breakdown: Shinki breaks down its business 55%:40% as between commercial and consumer loans, with 5% on other business. Whichever side of the line he looks, however, Maeda-san is cautious: "finance for small and medium-sized companies and consumer finance, Shinki's business areas, will see increasing levels of risk exposure in line with a rise in corporate and personal bankruptcies and in unemployment."

Rivals/Competitors: Shinki is a small player relative to some in its field, notably Takefuji, Japan's largest consumer loan company – the latter jumped from the OTC market straight to the Tokyo Stock Exchange, first section, in late 1998. Takefuji's loan portfolio is 10 times the size of Shinki's, its net profits were 15 or 20 times as large in recent years. Part of the explanation for the disparity appears to lie in the payrolls. Shinki lists 1,313 staff (with an astonishingly young average age of 25) as against 4,030 at Takefuji. The concern is that Shinki has too many staff relative to business volume. Still, profits and revenues are climbing year-by-year.

History/Strategy: Shinki, like other finance companies, attracts foreign investors (if not to the same degree as Takefuji). The company has very close ties with foreign banks as a source of funds – "our lifeblood" says Maeda-san, using that image again in the company's 1998 annual report. Bloomberg has reported that Shinki's foreign fund sources include Credit Lyonnais, Citibank and ABN Amro Bank. But there were others in Japan . . . including Orix Corp., the respected leader in the non-banking financial industry.

Management: Its "NOLOAN" product – loans that are "interest-free" for the first week – is an innovation dating to 1996 that Shinki likes to boast about as "the first genuinely novel product in the industry".

Outlook/Hot News: As long as Japan's traditional banks are unwilling (or unable) to offer "unsecured" loans to small/medium-sized companies and/or to individuals such non-bank finance companies will flourish, furnishing the "lifeblood" of the big cities of Japan, to a great extent. The ongoing credit squeeze in Japan is expanding the opportunities of finance companies such as Shinki. The company, however, has failed to grasp its opportunities to anything like the degree of Takefuji, as mentioned above. The relative failure suggests a lack of management. Shinki is said to be trying to follow in the steps of Takefuji by setting up ATM cash dispensers nationwide, but the latter has leaped ahead, opening 18,857 ATMs by end December 1998. A figure for Shinki was not found.

Naoyoshi Maeda / President

Stocks (¥50 par value, 100 shares min. trade)

Shares Issued (Nov. 1, '98)   22,680,000 shares
No. of Shareholders (Sep. 30, '98)   3,367

Major Holders	(%)
Naofumi Maeda	24.4
Think Data Co.	15.0
Himeji Jujikai Foundation	12.5
Setsu Maeda	4.7
Naoyoshi Maeda	3.9
Ryuko Sakamoto	3.1
Michiko Maeda	3.1
Foreign Owners	11.2

Earnings

Period	Sales	Operating Profit	Current Profit	Net Profit	Earnings Per Share	Dividend Per Share
Mar 96	24,863	6,533	6,000	2,710	245.1	15.50
Mar 97	34,074	8,551	7,718	3,815	207.1	17.50
Mar 98	41,056	10,243	9,476	4,002	176.5	23.00
**Mar 99	39,362	10,026	10,026	4,826	212.7	23.00
*Mar 00	39,000	10,400	10,130	4,880	215.2	23.00
Mid-Term						
Sep 98	19,154	5,104	4,819	2,519	111.1	0
*Sep 99	18,900	5,510	4,830	2,530	111.6	0

*Estimates; **Company estimates. Per share values in ¥, all other amounts in millions of ¥.

Balance sheet summary	1994	1995	1996	1997	1998
Current assets	65,786	82,095	118,311	154,558	153,353
Fixed assets	6,197	6,092	9,386	13,150	14,605
Total assets	71,984	88,187	127,698	167,708	167,958
Current liabilities	42,180	52,197	66,397	76,033	80,640
Fixed liabilities	20,133	24,788	72,910	65,670	57,667
Total liabilities	62,313	76,986	109,307	141,703	138,307
Capital Stock	1,040	1,040	2,916	5,016	5,016
Shareholders' equity	9,671	11,200	18,390	26,005	29,651
Total liabilities and equity	71,984	88,187	127,698	167,708	167,958

Note: All amounts in millions of ¥. Balance sheet, end March.

Shinwa

(Estd. 1959, listed 1997, stock code no. 6880)
Company address: 4-12-17, Yaoi-cho, Nakano-ku, Tokyo 164-0013
Tel: 81-3-3381-8131 Fax: 81-3-3381-4588

A firm active in the car audio field – manufacturing in China and exporting the products to Asia and to Europe – whose future depends on the intriguing personality in charge there, Yoshifumi Naito, Shinwa's President and main shareholder, aged 44.

Product/Sales breakdown: This is very much a single-product firm. Some 93% of its turnover is concentrated in cassette-player decks for cars, and the rest of the sales consist of related parts and royalties. The eggs are in one basket.

Rivals/Competitors: You name them – Sony, Matsushita, Sharp etc – they can all be there in a flash, if the going is worth it. But is it? Given that assembling the devices is labour-intensive, which means going to China in practice?

History/Strategy: Mr. Naito, a forthright man, tall and open, says that the future of his firm can be understood in the light of (i) its short history of just under 40 years and (ii) its manufacturing investments in China – all that he has to run in Japan is a head office with many of his 99 staff working out of a low-slung building in a Tokyo suburb that has the atmosphere of a private house. Relaxing at a table there Mr. Naito explained how the firm was created by his uncle, how that uncle, Kyohei Naito, invented a cassette deck that turns itself around automatically "from A to B", and how this invention led to investment in a manufacturing operation in the Canton region, where Shinwa now has two plants;

one a joint venture employing 4,500 people, the other a wholly owned Shinwa plant, a subsidiary with 1,000 on the payroll.

Management: To get to where he is now three things had to happen, Mr. Naito continued. First, his uncle invited him into the business in 1979, adopting him as his heir, and sent him to Hong Kong to represent Shinwa, dealing with Chinese business partners; next, sadly, his uncle died at an early age, and the business then came under the control of one of his staff in Tokyo; finally, Mr. Naito, finding that all was not well, came back from Hong Kong and displaced the interim President in favour of himself in 1990. Having cleared away the mess he found at head office, Mr. Naito believes that he has put the company on a sound footing also as regards China and operations there. "Japanese companies like to put in a hierarchy of Japanese managers, all Japanese only, in plants in China," he notes, "and they like to remit earnings back to Japan at once – I do it differently, the senior positions are all taken by Chinese, trust is needed."

Outlook/Hot News: Will it work? "Everything depends," Mr. Naito said, flashing a look, "on knowing whom you can trust." Of course, he is right. Of late the cassette decks, which are exported from China to elsewhere in Asia and to Europe, and are installed in GM cars and other cars, have won quality awards. All Mr. Naito has to do – he considers – is to keep it up. In April 1999 he is due to open a manufacturing plant in Hungary.

Yoshifumi Naito / President

Stocks (¥50 par value, 100 shares min. trade)

Shares Issued (Nov. 1, '98) 6,466,000 shares
No. of Shareholders (Mar. 31, '98) 637

Major Holders	(%)
Shinward Co.	35.5
Yoshifumi Naito	15.3
Fumiko Naito	9.3
Sayoko Naito	4.0
Sumitomo Bank	3.2
DKB	2.5
Mitsui Trust	1.8
Foreign Owners	3.5

Earnings

Period	Sales	Operating Profit	Current Profit	Net Profit	Earnings Per Share	Dividend Per Share
Mar 96	10,624	16	456	169	1,062.4	200.00
Mar 97	10,028	299	780	411	2,577.4	300.00
Mar 98	9,678	215	1,033	502	100.0	40.00
**Mar 99	9,900	450	1,200	650	101.0	45.00
*Mar 00	12,500	400	1,450	850	131.5	45.00
Mid-Term						
Sep 97	4,214	141	263	193	40.3	0
Sep 98	5,401	272	498	348	60.1	0

*Estimates; **Company estimates. Per share values in ¥, all other amounts in millions of ¥.*

Balance sheet summary	1995	1996	1997	1998
Current assets	7,912	7,496	6,957	6,006
Fixed assets	3,649	4,482	3,992	5,797
Total assets	11,561	11,979	10,949	11,803
Current liabilities	5,114	4,719	4,378	4,024
Fixed liabilities	1,652	2,319	1,259	941
Total liabilities	6,767	7,039	5,638	4,965
Capital Stock	313	313	313	855
Shareholders' equity	4,794	4,940	5,311	6,837
Total liabilities and equity	11,561	11,979	10,949	11,803

Note: All amounts in millions of ¥. Balance sheet, end March.

Step

(Estd. 1979, listed 1995, stock code no. 9795)
Company address: 2-1-19, Shonandai, Fujisawa City, Kanagawa Pref. 252-0804
Tel: 81-466-45-5500 Fax: 81-466-43-4095

A "crammer" with some 64 schools, mostly small, staffed by 304 teachers and admin staff. Based in prosperous Kanagawa Prefecture outside Tokyo, to the south-west. Run by the founder, Kyoji Tatsui, 49, who is also the chief shareholder.

Product/Sales Breakdown: The company divides its activities between primary school students (6%), middle school students (85%) and high school students (8%). It is a juku in Japanese terminology, meaning a crammer for students younger than those seeking university entrance.

Rivals/Competitors: The field is big, including both juku and yobiko (crammers for university entrance exams). Not all of these, by any means, have chosen to go public. Among those who have opted for an IPO, one that closely resembles Step is Meiko Network Japan, based in Tokyo. Step's performance (and stock price) is superior, as between these two.

History/Strategy: Mr. Tatsui says that the decision to register his business on the OTC market was taken to enhance the image of his institution. As such, it succeeded, he also says. The company has borrowed substantially long-term – Step reported total long-term debt of ¥1.347 billion in early 1998, mostly not due for repayment until 2010, secured against property. The length of the loans suggests that the banks concerned took a positive view of the company's future. Step's margins – at close to or over 20% of revenues in recent years – look impressive.

Management: Tatsui-san has impressed his personality on his institution and on the market, to judge by results. Half a dozen crammers have registered on the OTC market – other successful ones are found in Shizuoka and in Kyushu – and Step counts as a leader judged by its stock price. The best-run crammer of the bunch?

Outlook/Hot News: Education is a priority for parents in Japan, not least in regions like Kanagawa. A little lift in the economy – out of recession – could further consolidate Step's position. Tatsui-san's main thought is to branch out into teaching entrants for university entrance exams, *the* big hurdle in Japanese education. One's university determines one's station in life. There is huge pressure on children in their teens to do well in university exams. Preparing pupils for university entrance – such crammers are the yobiko mentioned above – is a more formidable (and potentially more profitable) task than preparing them for middle or high school entrance. Step has a strong balance sheet, those excellent margins and a formidable roll-call of shareholders for such a small company. Tatsui-san is young enough to tackle a new strategy.

Stocks (¥50 par value, 1,000 shares min. trade)

Shares Issued (Nov. 1, '98)	3,830,000 shares
No. of Shareholders (Sep. 30, '98)	434

Major Holders	(%)
K Planning	17.0
Kyoji Tatsui	15.4
Kikue Tatsui	12.4
Employees' Stockholding	4.8
Sumitomo Trust	4.5
Daiwa Bank Tokyo	4.1
Toyo Trust	3.7
Foreign Owners	3.9

Kyoji Tatsui / President

Earnings

Period	Sales	Operating Profit	Current Profit	Net Profit	Earnings Per Share	Dividend Per Share
Mar 96	3,386	716	659	330	92.9	53.00
Mar 97	3,734	749	702	346	90.5	46.00
Mar 98	4,246	835	781	400	104.5	53.00
**Mar 99	4,340	N/A	710	400	104.4	53.00
Mid-Term						
Sep 98	1,985	375	346	180	47.2	0
**Sep 99	2,090	N/A	330	190	49.6	0

**Company estimates. Per share values in ¥, all other amounts in millions of ¥.

Balance sheet summary	1994	1995	1996	1997	1998
Current assets	709	1,146	1,865	823	983
Fixed assets	3,329	3,625	4,671	5,228	5,401
Total assets	4,038	4,771	6,537	6,051	6,385
Current liabilities	1,257	613	1,331	732	819
Fixed liabilities	1,234	1,848	1,048	1,025	1,046
Total liabilities	2,491	2,461	2,379	1,757	1,866
Capital Stock	323	499	1,329	1,329	1,329
Shareholders' equity	1,546	2,310	4,157	4,294	4,518
Total liabilities and equity	4,038	4,771	6,537	6,051	6,385

Note: All amounts in millions of ¥. Balance sheet, end March.

Sun-Wa Technos

(Estd. 1949, listed 1982, stock code no. 8137)
Company address: 2-8-7, Yaesu, Chuo-ku, Tokyo 104-0028
Tel: 81-3-5202-4011 Fax: 81-3-5202-4054

A specialized trading company, handling electrical/electronic equipment for big-time Japanese manufacturers. History of half a century. Run by Masujiro Yamada, 69, one of the family that created the business in 1949. Has 320 staff.

Product/Sales breakdown: The company divides its revenue sources between electronic machinery (60%), which is basically what it does for a living, for people like Yaskawa Electric and Omron; electric machinery (27%), the less interesting part of the business; and general machinery (13%), covering a variety of stuff.

Rivals/Competitors: A trading house, lacking technology of its own, exists by virtue of its ability to sell. The Japanese have a saying that "the moment you leave your house you have 7 enemies ready to pounce on you". Masujiro Yamada's predecessors and he did well to survive this far, during the recession of the 90s, with hardly more than a scratch or two.

History/Strategy: To locate a head office at Yaesu, on that side of the tracks at Tokyo Station, is a strategy for a medium-small trading company. Okyakusan – "clients" – get off the train and walk straight into your arms, in theory. In practice that worked, roughly until 1993, when the company's profits dipped towards zero. At that point the company changed its name from "Yamada Kogyo", the old-established name, to the lively moniker it bears today. "Sun" signifying the sun, the deity; "Wa" suggesting harmony, in a direct translation of one reading in Japanese; and "Technos", taken from the Greek, signifying a high-tech intention or dream. Yamada-san, a member of the founding family, remained CEO, but an attempt was made to refurbish the image of a firm that risked going downhill in a recession that would last for no one knew how long. The strategy worked; the results picked up in subsequent years; both sales and net profits rose for 4 out of 5 successive years. The rather grand shareholders – 2 large manufacturers, 2 life-insurance companies, 2 banks – were no doubt pleased.

Management: Now that the profits are expected to dip a bit (see earnings estimate opposite for year to March '99), with sales off by a few per cent, is there a crisis? Not on the basis of these numbers. Not with the fairly OK balance sheet that Sun-Wa Technos presents – borrowing amounted to ¥3 billion in the end March 1998 balance sheet.

Outlook/Hot News: Given the support of major institutions and manufacturers, and ongoing revenues at close to the record level of 1997/8, Sun-Wa Technos has every reason to plough on. How long will the recession last? That is the question. Some say another 4–5 years. That will test almost everyone, including Sun-Wa Technos. The company is, however, strongly supported by shareholders – top-ranked institutions. Their function, as such, is to furnish credit, an indispensable need for a trading company. For the future, Sun-Wa Technos plans to upgrade internal communications by joining its 11 sales offices all over Japan through a new LAN (local area network) system at a reported cost of several hundred million yen.

Masujiro Yamada / President

Stocks (¥50 par value, 1,000 shares min. trade)

Shares Issued (Nov. 1, '98)	8,845,000 shares
No. of Shareholders (Sep. 30, '98)	1,245

Major Holders	(%)
Yaskawa Electric	6.7
Dai-ichi Life Ins.	6.1
Tokai Bank	5.0
Asahi Bank	4.9
Sanwa Bank	4.6
Origin Electric	3.7
Yasuda F. & M. Ins.	3.3
Foreign Owners	0.0

Earnings

Period	Sales	Operating Profit	Current Profit	Net Profit	Earnings Per Share	Dividend Per Share
Mar 96	34,621	599	623	217	24.2	8.00
Mar 97	40,784	759	779	203	22.6	8.00
Mar 98	43,558	854	898	275	30.6	9.00
**Mar 99	41,000	N/A	400	200	22.4	11.00
Mid-Term						
Sep 98	20,474	170	216	135	15.1	5.00

**Company estimates. Per share values in ¥, all other amounts in millions of ¥.

Balance sheet summary	1994	1995	1996	1997	1998
Current assets	10,986	12,393	14,139	15,570	17,729
Fixed assets	3,804	5,107	5,550	6,161	6,603
Total assets	14,791	17,501	19,690	21,731	24,332
Current liabilities	10,723	13,342	15,406	17,328	17,333
Fixed liabilities	127	143	140	148	2,560
Total liabilities	10,851	13,486	15,546	17,477	19,894
Capital Stock	1,266	1,266	1,266	1,266	1,266
Shareholders' equity	3,940	4,014	4,143	4,254	4,438
Total liabilities and equity	14,791	17,501	19,690	21,731	24,332

Note: All amounts in millions of ¥. Balance sheet, end March.

Tairaya

(Estd. 1984, listed 1996, stock code no. 7520)
Company address: 1160-1, Nakagami-cho, Akishima City, Tokyo 196-0022
Tel: 81-42-546-3711 Fax: 81-42-546-3714

Operates a food supermarket chain in Tokyo and in neighbouring Saitama prefecture. An owner-managed business run by President Tomio Taira, a veteran in his field who made his mark in recent years, expanding the company and opening new stores, emphasizing fresh food.

Product/Sales breakdown: The company breaks down turnover as between perishable foodstuffs (37.2%), groceries (45%), its drug division (1.4%) and wholesale division (16.4%) for the year to February '98. It operates 29 supermarkets (11 in Tokyo, 17 in Saitama and 1 in Chiba).

Rivals/Competition: Tairaya's is a crowded field. The acknowledged industry leader nationwide is the giant Ito-Yokado Co., with its affiliates. Tairiya has found a niche and a way of operating in its region, that took it ahead of competitors at a time when the recession has brought difficulty to retailers at the top of the profession (Daiei, Seiyu) and at the Mom & Pop store level. Other players, including the biggest ones, have barely kept sales and current profits stable in recent years. Tairaya, which traces its local roots back to 1934, with eventual incorporation in 1984, has by contrast been able to increase sales and earnings at a steady pace, year after year in the 1990s.

History/Strategy: Mr. Taira, 59, employed 563 staff as of August 1998 plus numerous part-timers. His programme is to keep opening stores and to keep up the momentum of expansion at a local level, mainly. "Competition will greatly increase in the market," he says. "Anxiety over employment will remain. However, we will not let these tough conditions (and) price decreases cut into our sales. What's important for us is to offer well-balanced supermarkets where customers (shop) for fresh, high-quality, reasonably priced products."

Outlook/Hot News: Taira-san believes that "our business environment will continue to be quite a challenging one. With the relaxation of the large-scale retail stores law (protecting small shops from big ones) we plan to further improve our operating efficiency through streamlining distribution channels, developing on-line systems etc." His owner's philosophy is to keep expanding, using economies of scale to keep prices down and increase profits. During 1998 Taira-san stepped up his commitment in Saitama prefecture, north of Tokyo, opening 5 new supermarkets. His basic strategy is to expand by using M & A, not only by building new outlets – for a businessman of his generation in Japan he has an unusually open attitude towards merging others. As a key move, Taira-san plans to open a "wholesale distribution centre" at Tokorozawa in southern Saitama, to supply up to 150 retail outlets in due course.

Tomio Taira / President

Stocks (¥50 par value, 1,000 min. trade)

Shares Issued (Nov. 1, '98)　　4,419,000 shares

No. of Shareholders (Aug. 31, '98)　422

Major Holders	(%)
Takuma Co.	21.0
Tomio Taira	15.6
Employees' Stockholding	5.5
Hisato Miyoshi	4.5
Asahi Bank	3.0
Jewel	2.7
Tsuyoshi Kishida	2.3
Foreign Owners	6.0

Earnings

Period	Sales	Operating Profit	Current Profit	Net Profit	Earnings Per Share	Dividend Per Share
Feb 96	27,560	592	513	241	61.7	12.50
Feb 97	33,328	715	601	289	70.6	15.00
Feb 98	42,658	831	740	340	77.1	15.00
**Feb 99	50,000	N/A	805	380	86.0	15.00
*Feb 00	53,000	950	850	400	90.5	15.00
Mid-Term						
Aug 98	25,368	487	401	200	45.3	0
*Aug 99	26,500	500	420	210	47.5	0

*Estimates; **Company estimates. Per share values in ¥, all other amounts in millions of ¥.*

Balance sheet summary	1994	1995	1996	1997	1998
Current assets	3,063	2,747	2,446	2,963	4,024
Fixed assets	4,894	4,838	5,219	5,840	6,476
Total assets	7,957	7,585	7,666	8,803	10,501
Current liabilities	3,288	3,216	3,175	3,727	4,662
Fixed liabilities	3,220	2,894	2,012	1,490	1,996
Total liabilities	6,508	6,110	5,188	5,218	6,658
Capital Stock	438	438	837	1,147	1,147
Shareholders' equity	1,448	1,475	2,478	3,585	3,842
Total liabilities and equity	7,957	7,585	7,666	8,803	10,501

Note: All amounts in millions of ¥. Balance sheet, end February.

Taiyo Ink Mfg.

(Estd. 1953, listed 1990, stock code no. 4626)
Company address: 2-7-1, Hazawa, Nerima-ku, Tokyo 176-8508
Tel: 81-3-5999-1511 Fax: 81-3-5999-1501

A world-class manufacturer of "resist inks" used in the manufacture of printing circuit boards. Mitsuo Kawahara, 61, is main shareholder and Chief Executive of Taiyo Ink. 259 employees.

Product/Sales breakdown: The company divides its "resist ink" sales between those for "general machinery" usage (9% of all sales) and "high performance machinery" usage (60% of sales). So-called "auxiliary agents", including "plasma disks", account for another 28% of sales. A very high proportion of the company's business is overseas – exports accounted for 53% of revenues in the year to March '98.

Rivals/Competitors: The company's 20% profit margins testify to its strong market position and dominance within Japan itself. Taiyo Ink claims a 50% market share in Japan in "resist inks", a 20% market share in the US, and dominant market shares in Korea and Taiwan.

History/Strategy: Set up 46 years ago in Tokyo's Nerima ward, the company took nearly 20 years to achieve its technical breakthrough in 1972 – the invention of "resist inks" used in the preparation of printed circuit boards, a process that requires etching and other technologies right at the cutting edge of scientific knowledge in the field. Another 16–18 years passed before Taiyo Ink moved forward to exploit its patented knowhow by setting up offices overseas, first in Korea, then in the US. Taiyo America was set up in 1990 as a sales company in the US. In 1995 the company commenced manufacturing there.

Management: When a company has depended on one person as much as Taiyo Ink has, then people want to know what his plans are. For now Kawahara-san continues to run the company, as he has done ever since his appointment as president in 1975.

Outlook/Hot News: Mr. Kawahara's Taiyo Ink is a world leader in its field of "resist inks". Highly specialized, driven by one man, the company climbed to prominence in 1990, with its accession to Jasdaq. Kawahara-san owes his success in part to organizing ability but chiefly to his own electro-chemical skills in an area that very few people in the world have pursued. No one could have foreseen the emergence of the company as a high-flyer until its advance in "resist inks" in 1972. Just so, no one can say for certain what lies ahead. Yet with its patent in place, and plentiful acceptance in the workplace, what Taiyo Ink chiefly requires is continued managerial competence as much as anything. For now its performance is superb. Taiyo Ink is, however, expecting a downturn in sales and profits in 1998/9. This should be no surprise given Taiyo's huge dependence on exports and the strength of the yen against the dollar.

Mitsuo Kawahara / President

Stocks (¥50 par value, 1,000 shares min. trade)

Shares Issued (Nov. 1, '98)	9,300,000 shares
No. of Shareholders (Sep. 30, '98)	250

Major Holders	(%)
Mitsuo Kawahara	26.6
Kowa Co.	8.4
Employees' Stockholding	5.0
Shikoku Chemicals	4.8
Sakura Bank	4.1
Mitsui Life Ins.	2.9
Toyo Trust	2.4
Foreign Owners	7.0

Earnings

Period	Sales	Operating Profit	Current Profit	Net Profit	Earnings Per Share	Dividend Per Share
Mar 96	10,456	1,436	1,487	540	58.2	19.50
Mar 97	12,299	2,436	2,405	1,277	137.4	42.00
Mar 98	15,963	3,890	4,034	2,260	243.1	73.00
**Mar 99	14,625	N/A	3,861	2,170	233.3	25.00
Mid-Term						
Sep 98	7,753	2,045	2,438	1,305	140.4	12.50

**Company estimates. Per share values in ¥, all other amounts in millions of ¥.

Balance sheet summary	1994	1995	1996	1997	1998
Current assets	6,391	6,896	7,771	8,973	11,985
Fixed assets	7,594	8,074	7,897	8,244	9,743
Total assets	13,986	14,971	15,669	17,217	21,728
Current liabilities	2,432	3,023	3,510	4,015	5,378
Fixed liabilities	2,371	2,329	2,217	2,235	3,597
Total liabilities	4,804	5,352	5,728	6,251	8,976
Capital Stock	2,420	2,420	2,420	2,420	2,420
Shareholders' equity	9,181	9,618	9,941	10,966	12,752
Total liabilities and equity	13,986	14,971	15,669	17,217	21,728

Note: All amounts in millions of ¥. Balance sheet, end March.

TDC Software Engineering

(Estd. 1963, listed 1997, stock code no. 4687)
Company address: 5-33-6, Sendagaya, Shibuya-ku, Tokyo 151-0051
Tel: 81-3-3350-8111 Fax: 81-3-3350-8155

A medium-sized sofware development company, based in Tokyo, with 699 employees. Connected to NTT Data Corp., and largely serving NTT, the partly privatised telecom giant. President Kazuyoshi Funai, 62, runs the firm under the control of Chairman Katsui Nozaki, the chief stockholder of TDC Software Engineering.

Product/Sales breakdown: TDC releases few data – despite having registered on the OTC. The *Japan Company Handbook*, published by Toyo Keizai, states that "systems development" accounts for 98% of the company's revenues (¥77 billion in 1997/8); there is *no* breakdown. Part of the problem is that the state, broadly defined, acts both as the company's major client *and* as a source of finance (see below). The whole thing's cosy.

Rivals/Competitors: How to understand the docility of private sector software companies? Best to keep in mind the culture of attentive obedience found around such firms as NTT and NTT Data. The latter is 100 times the size of little TDC Software. NTT Data makes lots of money; TDC Software, by contrast, in common with others in its industry (e.g. ISB Corp.), experienced falling turnover and collapsing profits in the mid-1990s, only to be rescued by orders from NTT Data and others. In theory the shoals of software development companies compete like mad. In practice, many of them kowtow to the authorities, waiting for the officials to divide up the pie.

History/Strategy: Literature put out by President Funai on the web underlines the psychology of dependence existing between software development companies like TDC and the State. "We have received many letters of appreciation over the years from satisfied customers because of our advanced systems development," states the company. "NTT has designated us as a business partner etc." Note the tone of pride . . . Decades ago the Japanese Government, seeing the software industry lagging behind America, opted for a counter-strategy, setting up universities and institutions in the Tsukuba area, north of Tokyo, as Japan's answer to Silicon Valley and pumping subsidies into software players, large and small. Not much happened. Just pumping money does not make for creativity.

Management: The key to TDC's future may lie in the dexterity of Funai-san, who was hand-picked from NTT – he held a senior post at NTT Systems Technology – by chairman Nozaki in 1995, and appointed president of TDC in the following year.

Outlook/Hot News: The software industry eagerly awaits details of the government's plans for a ¥7 trillion-funded Super Highway in telecoms, administered by the MPT (Ministry of Posts and Telecommunications). Talk of this has lifted hopes in the software world – and stock prices. TDC was one of the many boats lifted by this tide during 1998. There is little doubt that morale is recovering under Funai-san, with the steady growth in both sales and profits since he took over. TDC is hiring approximately 100 graduates a year – a sure sign of confidence and not untypical of software firms with close ties to government and long-term relations with NTT, Fujitsu and other clients.

Kazuyoshi Funai / President

Stocks (¥50 par value, 1,000 shares min. trade)

Shares Issued (Nov. 1, '98)	4,790,000 shares
No. of Shareholders (Mar. 31, '98)	245

Major Holders	(%)
Katsumi Nozaki	20.4
Employees' Stockholding	20.0
Nozaki Office Co.	13.1
Yoshifumi Fujii	4.5
Masakazu Mitani	3.8
Fuji Bank	2.5
Mitsubishi Trust	2.4
Foreign Owners	5.1

Earnings

Period	Sales	Operating Profit	Current Profit	Net Profit	Earnings Per Share	Dividend Per Share
Mar 96	5,168	156	104	11	29.8	50.00
Mar 97	6,418	494	460	162	379.9	50.00
Mar 98	7,731	707	635	241	53.4	8.00
**Mar 99	9,100	N/A	870	370	77.2	10.00
Mid-Term						
Sep 98	4,113	346	338	116	24.3	0

**Company estimates. Per share values in ¥, all other amounts in millions of ¥.*

Balance sheet summary	1994	1995	1996	1997	1998
Current assets	3,936	3,730	4,047	4,052	4,364
Fixed assets	973	875	890	873	979
Total assets	4,909	4,606	4,937	4,926	5,343
Current liabilities	2,630	2,300	2,340	2,303	2,259
Fixed liabilities	1,157	1,234	1,357	1,240	1,138
Total liabilities	3,788	3,535	3,698	3,543	3,398
Capital Stock	337	337	424	424	579
Shareholders' equity	1,121	1,070	1,239	1,382	1,945
Total liabilities and equity	4,909	4,606	4,937	4,926	5,343

Note: All amounts in millions of ¥. Balance sheet, end March.

Terashima

(Estd. 1971, listed 1998, stock code no. 7586)
Company address: 2-17-5, Amakubo, Tsukuba City, Ibaraki Pref. 305-0005
Tel: 81-298-56-8888 Fax: 81-298-56-7828

Japan has the fastest-ageing population in the world. There are plentiful personal savings. These two factors resulted in a growing opportunity for drugstore chain services, as seen in the rise of regional chains, for instance Tsuruha in Hokkaido – and Terashima, also a family-owned chain, in southern Ibaraki, just north of Tokyo.

Product/Sales Breakdown: The pattern of life is pretty similar all over Japan. Sales at Tsuruha stores and at Terashima ones – both chains started up in the early 1970s – follow similar trends. Cosmetics and beauty-care items, for example, account for 17% of sales at both chains. Health-care items accounted for one third of sales in each case (36% at Terashima). Identical items are on offer, obtained from the same sources of supply, nationwide. Home-care items accounted for 19% of sales at Terashima, "convenience items" for 24%, and others for 3%, in the half year to August 1998.

Rivals/Competition: This augurs competition. Which is stronger, Tsuruha, which has ambitions to create a nationwide chain, Terashima, or a Tokyo chain of drugstores such as Sundrug, based in Fuchu City?

History/Strategy: Terashima has unique strengths. The owner, Takao Terashima, 51, implanted the company in the historic Tsukuba region in 1971, just at the moment when a full-scale government programme for developing the area as the home of a new university took effect, expanding the local community. Nearly three decades later the large drugstores favoured by Terashima-san

– with floorspace of 500 sq. metres or more – have become landmarks in the region. The firm has roots. Terashima has made his mark in other ways. In recent years he launched an aggressive campaign of expansion, pushing up sales by 50% in the 1996–9 period.

Management: The role that families play in the often family-owned drugstore chain business is watched with interest. Members of the Terashima family own by far the largest blocks of shares in the firm, making the chain all but invulnerable to any hostile takeover bid.

Outlook/Hot News: The Terashimas face an interesting future. Are they in fact on a collision path with rival interests? It is hard to imagine that Tsuruha and its ally, the Jusco supermarket chain, which is based in Chiba, next door to Ibaraki, have not considered their options as regards Terashima. Tsuruha and Jusco have linked hands, expanding side by side in new locations, as there is no direct competition between them, rather there is a complementarity. Terashima-san, watch out! Not that the Ibaraki businessman is inactive. Terashima-san has (i) reduced his personal holding in the company from 42.4% to 32.3%, thereby getting some cash; (ii) embarked on a strategy of opening more outlets (he had 68 stores at the end of 1998, and planned to open 10 more in 1999); (iii) increased the emphasis on beauty care and cosmetic items; and (iv) created a new tie-up with another drugstore chain operation called Iijima in neighbouring Gumma prefecture.

Takao Terashima / President

Stocks (¥50 par value, 1,000 shares min. trade)

Shares Issued (Nov. 1, '98)	5,435,000 shares
No. of Shareholders (Aug. 31, '98)	104

Major Holders	(%)
Takao Terashima	32.3
Satoko Terashima	12.7
Systemhouse Co.	7.0
Nikko Securities	3.7
Employees' Stockholding	3.6
Fumio Terashima	3.3
Mito Shinkin Bank	2.5
Foreign Owners	0.0

Earnings

Period	Sales	Operating Profit	Current Profit	Net Profit	Earnings Per Share	Dividend Per Share
Feb 96	18,766	490	413	72	157.5	40.00
Feb 97	21,547	500	417	72	157.9	40.00
Feb 98	24,786	901	800	429	92.3	7.50
*Feb 99	29,500	1,300	1,170	540	99.4	10.00
*Feb 00	33,000	1,500	1,400	700	128.8	10.00
Mid-Term						
Aug 98	14,281	569	494	267	55.7	0
*Aug 99	15,500	600	550	280	51.5	0

*Estimates. Per share values in ¥, all other amounts in millions of ¥.

Balance sheet summary	1994	1995	1996	1997	1998
Current assets	1,721	2,733	3,187	3,648	4,596
Fixed assets	3,615	3,875	4,145	5,478	5,907
Total assets	5,336	6,609	7,333	9,127	10,504
Current liabilities	1,965	2,906	3,347	4,389	5,462
Fixed liabilities	2,878	2,847	2,661	3,356	3,169
Total liabilities	4,844	5,754	6,009	7,746	8,631
Capital Stock	32	192	393	393	433
Shareholders' equity	491	854	1,324	1,381	1,872
Total liabilities and equity	5,336	6,609	7,333	9,127	10,504

Note: All amounts in millions of ¥. Balance sheet, end February.

Tiemco

(Estd. 1969, listed 1996, stock code no. 7501)
Company address: 3-1-11, Kikukawa, Sumida-ku, Tokyo 130-8555
Tel: 81-3-5600-0122 Fax: 81-3-5600-0302

A profitable family-owned trading firm specializing in sports items for fishermen – lures, flies and outdoor clothing. A marketing operation which imports and outsources, the leading firm in its speciality in Japan. Run by the owner, Sadahiko Sakai, with his son.

Product/Sales breakdown: Tiemco, located in downtown Tokyo in the Sumida-Ku section, divided its ¥5.1 billion 1996/7 turnover between lure-fishing items (36%), fly-fishing items (35%), clothing (25%) and other items (4%).

Rivals/Competitors: Sakai-san, who meets visitors dressed casually, without a necktie, mentions Shimano Inc. (a TSE first-section company) and Daiwa Seiko Inc. (also on the first section) as rivals selling comparable items to himself, but also marketing sports and recreation products of other types, not only fishing kit. As such Tiemco is in a class by itself, according to Mr. Sakai.

History/Strategy: The company has reported 20% margins on its sales in recent years. Its performance is attributable to the person in charge. Sakai-san, the founder, warns however that the retailing climate has turned for the worse. He describes current conditions as "the worst I've seen in the 29 years since we started the business". To meet this challenge he proposes (i) to introduce new items at a faster pace and (ii) to go in for "re-education" of his 97 staff.

Management: The family business will in due course be run by Seiichi Sakai, the son of the founder. He has been trained on the job for the last half dozen years after an initial spell working at Fuji Xerox. The CEO has thus secured the indispensable, a successor. Sakai Sr. is 61, his son is in his late twenties.

Outlook/Hot News: Both sales and profits are on the way down. The company must now prepare to meet those "worst" conditions described by Sakai-san. He expects the current downturn to prolong itself for a matter of years, he says. The much tougher atmosphere is seen in Tiemco's 1997/8 results. The company's fat 20% trading margins have been cut and net profits all but halved. However, Tiemco has a strong balance sheet. Borrowings amounted to only a few per cent of assets as of May 1998. Foreign investors have lately cut their shareholdings in Tiemco, however the shares thereupon began to look cheap, at least to Japanese investor Takefuji (see table opposite). Tiemco is well implanted in its specialty, and should be able to take advantage of an upturn, when it comes. Sakai-san and his son, interviewed at their office, came across as a refreshing, determined pair – both speaking impeccable English.

Sadahiko Sakai / President

Stocks (¥50 par value, 1,00 shares min. trade)

Shares Issued (Nov. 30, '98)   3,339,995 shares
No. of Shareholders (Nov. 30, '98)   1,312

Major Holders	(%)
Sadahiko Sakai	19.0
Masami Kanai	12.1
Toshinori Shimoda	7.0
JAFCO	7.8
Seiichi Sakai	3.9
Sumitomo Trust	3.0
Takefuji Corp	1.8
Yaeko Sakai	1.8
Foreign Owners	2.7

Earnings

Period	Sales	Operating Profit	Current Profit	Net Profit	Earnings Per Share	Dividend Per Share
Nov 95	3,467	707	627	353	143.3	12.50
Nov 96	4,755	1,085	857	456	145.7	22.50
Nov 97	5,105	988	958	425	127.5	22.50
Nov 98	4,357	623	588	230	69.0	22.50
**Nov 99	4,520	661	684	279	83.7	22.50
Mid-Term						
May 98	2,549	472	440	202	60.8	0
**May 99	2,590	434	426	163	49.1	0

**Company estimates. Per share values in ¥, all other amounts in millions of ¥.

Balance sheet summary	1993	1994	1995	1996	1997
Current assets	1,469	1,633	2,002	6,459	5,893
Fixed assets	2,232	2,212	2,216	2,302	3,388
Total assets	3,701	3,846	4,219	8,762	9,282
Current liabilities	996	1,023	974	1,128	2,234
Fixed liabilities	1,252	1,147	1,016	1,020	103
Total liabilities	2,248	2,170	1,990	2,148	2,338
Capital Stock	393	393	513	1,079	1,079
Shareholders' equity	1,453	1,675	2,228	6,613	6,944
Total liabilities and equity	3,701	3,846	4,219	8,762	9,282

Note: All amounts in millions of ¥. Balance sheet, end November.

Tocalo

(Estd. 1951, listed 1996, stock code no. 5961)
Company address: 4-13-4, Fukae-Kitamachi, Higashi-Nadaku, Kobe 658-0013
Tel: 81-78-411-5561 Fax: 81-78-452-8178

Many years ago (in 1970) two Japanese steel firms united to create the world's largest integrated steelmaker – Nippon Steel Corp. Tocalo is a Kobe-based offshot of Nittetsu Shoji, a trading house subsidiary of Nippon Steel, the child of a child. Tiny Tocalo is sufficiently far from the capital to have escaped being drawn in to the drama of being big for bigness' sake. The CEO is Akira Nakahira, an engineer of 67. He has 350 employees.

Product/Sales breakdown: Tocalo – called Toyo Calorizing Industry until 1981 – has built up some first-class heat-spraying techniques, used for surfacing boilers, semiconductors – can be big, can be small – or whatever materials there are that must be surfaced to protect them against extreme heat, corrosion etc. Mr. Nakahira and his predecessors over decades have kept Tocalo going as world-class specialists in their field, toiling away quietly in their workshops down in Kobe – this is the kind of work that requires meticulous care and safety checks, the stuff the Japanese excel at. An overall breakdown of sales (¥9 billion in 1997/8) is: flame-spray processing (82%), Toyada-diffusion processing (10%), "ZAC" coating (3%), and plasma-transferred arc processing (5%).

Rivals/Competitors: This company is number one, perhaps, in the west of Japan in flame-spray processing. It does only 5% of its business with Nippon Steel; the bulk is done with Kobe Seiko and with Mitsubishi Heavy Industries, both firms having big workshops in Kobe. This business is done on tough margins of under 10%, thereby keeping out rivals and strengthening long-standing relationships with these clients.

History/Strategy: Comparing Tocalo with its parent and grandparent, Tocalo has been around for a lot longer – since 1951, as compared with Nittetsu Shoji, its parent (1971) and Nippon Steel (1970). The other big difference is financial: the two giant steel firms – the integrated maker and its sales company – have accumulated gigantic debts on their balance sheets. A major increase in interest rates, for all that it is not on the cards in the immediate future, would put both companies in jeopardy . . . Little Tocalo has borrowed only ¥1.7 billion, according to its March 1998 balance sheet.

Management: The decision to go on Jasdaq has brought public attention to Tocalo for the first time in its history. It now ranks as a public entity, its employees, who hold stock in the company, watch the share price go up and down etc.

Outlook/Hot News: The joys of being small! All Tocalo has to do is to carry on with what it has been doing so well for nearly 50 years – staying ahead as a world leader in its field. The company survived a very major earthquake in Kobe in 1995 . . . Its case suggests: (i) its technology is so specialized – and understood by so few outside Tocalo – that Nippon Steel has thought it best to leave well alone; (ii) independence has suited the engineers and scientists down in Kobe, key staff who have in turn beeen defended from outside interference by their senior executives; (iii) excellence in technology will continue to be the company's driving force; notably its flame-spray processing. The one obvious concern about Tocalo is its relationships with ailing parent and grandparent companies. The outlook is uncertain for the Japanese steel industry, which was embroiled in a trade dispute in early 1999 with the US over exports to America.

Akira Nakahira / President

Stocks (¥50 par value, 1,000 shares min. trade)

Shares Issued (Nov. 1, '98)	6,041,000 shares
No. of Shareholders (Sep. 30, '98)	549

Major Holders	(%)
Nittetsu Shoji	60.4
Employees' Stockholding	4.2
Akira Nakahira	2.5
Mariko Hirose	2.3
Shinto Ind. Co.	1.6
Kaoru Saijo	1.4
Hachiro Yamamoto	1.0
Foreign Owners	1.2

Earnings

Period	Sales	Operating Profit	Current Profit	Net Profit	Earnings Per Share	Dividend Per Share
Mar 96	7,493	420	400	171	33.1	12.50
Mar 97	8,412	652	577	261	46.9	12.50
Mar 98	9,044	688	677	303	50.2	12.50
**Mar 99	9,200	730	700	330	54.6	12.50
Mid-Term						
Sep 98	4,547	386	367	158	26.3	0

**Company estimates. Per share values in ¥, all other amounts in millions of ¥.

Balance sheet summary	1994	1995	1996	1997	1998
Current assets	2,952	4,012	4,486	4,411	4,917
Fixed assets	2,626	2,491	2,625	2,814	3,583
Total assets	5,578	6,503	7,112	7,225	8,500
Current liabilities	2,509	3,310	4,007	3,202	3,894
Fixed liabilities	845	990	796	528	910
Total liabilities	3,355	4,301	4,803	3,731	4,804
Capital Stock	425	425	425	795	795
Shareholders' equity	2,223	2,202	2,309	3,493	3,696
Total liabilities and equity	5,578	6,503	7,112	7,225	8,500

Note: All amounts in millions of ¥. Balance sheet, end March.

Tokyo Lithmatic

(Estd. 1972, listed 1998, stock code no. 7861)
Company address: 2-19-20, Higashi-Sakashita, Itabashi-ku, Tokyo 174-0042
Tel: 81-3-5970-7031 Fax: 81-3-5392-7763

A family-owned DTP (desk-top publishing) outfit. You walk in to one of their "service bureaux" with your sketch and they help turn it into an ad or design, using their expensive computers. Run by President Ryuichi Suzuki, 31. Has 603 staff.

Product/Sales breakdown: Suzuki-san divides up his revenues as between DTP-related (69%) and the rest, including "analog processing services" (23%), printing (5%), real estate leasing (2%) and others (1%). Originally, Tokyo Lithmatic was a printer, offering off-set services at 20% below anyone else to get started in the early 1970s; the company has branched out into a much broader field now.

Rivals/Competitors: In the big league there is Dentsu TEC, a first section company on the Tokyo Stock Exchange, roughly 10 times the size of Tokyo Lithmatic. How much the two choose to compete is the question; they can concentrate on different areas. This is a matter for the young shacho (president) of Tokyo Lithmatic. As head of the nimbler firm, he can go many different ways.

History/Strategy: Ryuichi Suzuki is the youngest of the CEOs in this directory of small cap companies (next to him comes Shigeta-san of Hikari Tsushin, who is 32). Suzuki-san, however, inherited the job in late 1995 (he graduated from Waseda University in Tokyo, then spent a few months at Nomura Securities before joining his father in the business). He is the boss's son, he has not had to fight for his turf; as the eldest boy of the owner – father Takao remains Chairman - he has to prove himself. Currently, the company is committed, having spent a lot of money on computers, to a strategy that requires a hugely competitive spirit, great knowledge and an ability to lead. The "service bureaux" it has set up to greet customers off the street need to be run – like those of Kinko's, the American stationers and copiers – in a freewheeling way that suits today's Japan, putting customers first.

Management: In other words, the business has to have a creative atmosphere. This is easier said than done in a Japan where, for all the lip service paid to creativity, most companies operate on stereotyped lines, with decks of senior management pressing down on those below, and resisting initiative. Tokyo Lithmatic has a chance of success, because it is different; Takao Suzuki expanded the company to its present size by repeatedly reinventing it.

Outlook/Hot News: Tokyo Lithmatic's variety of customers – publishers, design offices, advertisement agencies, printers – means that Ryuichi Suzuki has a number of different directions he can take the company. Venture businesses, including game software, have attracted him; he has created a new subsidiary, Seitron & Art, with 23 staff. With some 18 outlets (those "service bureaux") established by late summer 1998 – 15 in Tokyo, 3 in Osaka – the question is: what comes next? Suzuki Jr. faces a tabula rasa (a "blank sheet").

Ryuichi Suzuki / President

Stocks (¥50 par value, 1,000 shares min. trade)

Shares Issued (Nov. 1, '98)	4,970,000 shares
No. of Shareholders (Jun. 30, '98)	28

Major Holders	(%)
Takao Suzuki	50.4
Ryuichi Suzuki	21.7
JAFCO	4.0
Shizue Suzuki	2.5
JAFCO Gı(A) Investment Assn.	1.4
JAFCO Gı(B) Investment Assn.	1.4
JAFCO Properties	1.4
Foreign Owners	4.4

Earnings

Period	Sales	Operating Profit	Current Profit	Net Profit	Earnings Per Share	Dividend Per Share
Dec 95	6,667	632	426	212	775.1	100.00
Dec 96	8,430	632	523	235	857.7	100.00
Dec 97	10,060	991	878	297	833.9	100.00
**Dec 98	10,600	1,150	920	520	104.6	15.00
**Dec 99	11,200	1,300	1,150	650	130.8	14–15.00
Mid-Term						
Jun 98	5,292	739	618	327	74.9	0
**Jun 99	5,700	730	650	350	70.4	6.5

**Company estimates. Per share values in ¥, all other amounts in millions of ¥.

Balance sheet summary	1993	1994	1995	1996	1997
Current assets	2,318	2,343	2,835	3,142	3,600
Fixed assets	6,629	6,566	5,671	5,827	6,709
Total assets	8,950	8,911	8,507	8,970	10,310
Current liabilities	2,349	3,332	3,805	3,487	3,372
Fixed liabilities	3,877	2,755	1,694	2,265	2,319
Total liabilities	6,227	6,087	5,499	5,753	5,692
Capital Stock	457	457	457	459	1,027
Shareholders' equity	2,722	2,823	3,008	3,216	4,618
Total liabilities and equity	8,950	8,911	8,507	8,970	10,310

Note: All amounts in millions of ¥. Balance sheet, end December.

Tomy

(Estd. 1953, listed 1997, stock code no. 7867)
Company address: 7-9-10, Tateishi, Katsushika-ku, Tokyo 124-8511
Tel: 81-3-3693-8721 Fax: 81-3-5698-2463

A toy company with a great logo. Located on the far edge of Tokyo in a provincial setting that smacks of neighbouring Chiba prefecture. CEO Kantaro Tomiyama, 44, is from the third generation in his family to own and run Tomy (315 employees).

Product/Sales breakdown: The firm caters to small children. It breaks down its annual sales of ¥57 billion (or ¥93 billion on consolidated account in the last full year) as between cuddly stuff for babies and infants (25%), toys for boys (27%) and for girls (14%), and then other bits and pieces (31%). A final 3% is in royalties.

Rivals/Competitors: Tomy is the kingpin in its field in Japan, 10 times the size of People Co. Ltd., the other largely-for-small-kids toy company. These two face Sega Enterprises and Nintendo – both listed on the stock exchange's first section; these much bigger firms specialize in electronic toys and video games but also do other toys. As a world-class company Tomy keeps an eye on the US stalwarts – Fisher-Price, Mattel and Hasbro – and watches the shelves at Toys "R" Us, now active in Japan, to see what's new from America.

History/Strategy: There is a bust of the founder, Kantaro's grandfather, Eichiro, in the lobby of the head office. This *is* a family business. It has the frills of internationalism; Tomiyama-san travels a lot and turns out a glossy annual report in English. He has concluded a marketing agreement with Hasbro of late to handle that firm's toys in Japan. In the end it is Japan that counts. Tomy's surge in performance in recent years was related to its success with Pokemon ("pocket monsters"), small furry creatures that transformed Tomy's sales and balance sheet. When the firm registered on the OTC and made its IPO, Tomiyama-san used the money to pay off ¥7 billion in bank borrowing and added ¥1.7 billion to reserves.

Management: Stays in the hands of the owner, a graduate of Hull University in the UK. Tomiyama-san bemoans what he calls "the worst retail business climate (in Japan) in more than 40 years", but takes pride in Tomy's record results in the midst of the recession.

Outlook/Hot News: Results will dip in the current year to end-March '99 in terms of sales and earnings . . . A hunt for new toy designs will continue with added vim . . . Tomy executives say it is too early for "conservative" Japanese consumers to accept new-fangled marketing via the Internet from America. The problem, according to Tomy's executive director, Masaharu Sato, is that Japanese consumers are not yet ready to entrust strangers with confidential data – their credit card numbers – as people do in America. He acknowledged the success of e.toys, a net-using toy operation in America, in an interview at the Chiba head office. He questioned whether such a development will occur in Japan in the near future.

Kantaro Tomiyama / President

Stocks (¥50 par value, 100 shares min. trade)

Shares Issued (Nov. 1, '98)   11,100,000 shares
No. of Shareholders (Sep. 30, '98)   1,399

Major Holders	(%)
Tomy Insurance	11.3
Kantaro Tomiyama	9.8
Chojiro Tomiyama	9.3
Tokyo Small Bus. Invest't	4.9
Employees' Stockholding	4.1
Masaru Tomiyama	2.4
Foreign Owners	11.7

Earnings

Period	Sales	Operating Profit	Current Profit	Net Profit	Earnings Per Share	Dividend Per Share
Mar 96	26,852	700	564	−998	−123.3	0
Mar 97	33,427	2,071	1,831	836	103.3	10.00
Mar 98	57,399	5,302	4,972	1,617	187.3	25.00
**Mar 99	47,000	N/A	3,400	1,700	153.2	25.00
Mid-Term						
Sep 98	22,496	1,783	1,747	978	90.9	12.50

**Company estimates. Per share values in ¥, all other amounts in millions of ¥.*

Balance sheet summary	1995	1996	1997	1998
Current assets	14,228	15,980	15,669	21,886
Fixed assets	10,054	9,745	10,319	10,334
Total assets	24,282	25,725	25,989	32,220
Current liabilities	11,173	13,653	13,120	15,487
Fixed liabilities	6,020	6,023	5,984	6,672
Total liabilities	17,193	19,677	19,104	22,159
Capital Stock	405	405	405	1,230
Shareholders' equity	7,088	6,048	6,884	10,060
Total liabilities and equity	24,282	25,725	25,989	32,220

Note: All amounts in millions of ¥. Balance sheet, end March.

Traveler

(Estd. 1964, listed 1989, stock code no. 9838)
Company address: 1-10, Kojimachi, Chiyoda-ku, Tokyo 102-0083
Tel: 81-3-3234-7911 Fax: 81-3-3238-7540

A retailer of souvenirs to Japanese travellers outside their country. Founder Itsushi Kamiyama, 57, still runs the business he created in 1964, just before Japan burst open to the outside world. He has 592 staff.

Product/Sales breakdown: Foodstuffs (chocolates, biscuits) account for 50% of the company's revenues; sundries (trinkets, miniature replicas of the Statue of Liberty etc) for another 18%; liquor for 16%. Domestic souvenirs account for only 2%, personal goods for 9%, business support 4% and others for 1%. The business is concentrated on travellers overseas.

Rivals/Competitors: The challenge for Traveler Corp. staff has been to get the public in Japan to know of its existence rather than to fight off violent competition. To this end, Traveler has prepared lavish catalogues in colour, with photos of all the souvenirs you can collect in Tokyo, Osaka or elsewhere – Traveler set up offices nationwide; also some shops overseas – rather than lugging them back to Japan from abroad (see below).

History/Strategy: "Traveler"? What's in a name? . . . The intention of the founder, Itsushi Kamiyama, was to catch in a single noun – recognizable to a majority of Japanese, most of whom know some English – the essence of his business. The company is a glorified omiyagesan (a firm that provides omiyage or "travel souvenirs"). Unique? No, probably not. But Traveler Corp. got into its field very early on, in the days before

foreign travel was possible for more than a handful of businessmen, officials and academics. With a head start, Traveler has prospered.

Management: The key idea, seized upon by Kamiyama-san 35 years ago, was that carrying those omiyage back home from overseas – numerous omiyage had to be bought for everyone at the office – was mendokusai (troublesome). Getting in and out of planes with bags full of stuff really took the joy out of travelling. So why not make arrangements to do otherwise? Furnish the travellers with catalogues so that they could chose the chocolates or biscuits or cognac – or some little trinkets – and take delivery back in Tokyo (or elsewhere in Japan), ready to hand over there. This was the core idea. It worked, and is increasingly workable, to judge by the steady rise in Traveler's revenues, powered by a flow of Japanese overseas, even in these recession times, on a scale that hardly anybody imagined back in 1964 – Kamiyama-san was on to something.

Outlook/Hot News: Kamiyama-san has stuck by a particular way of working over decades . . . He earns 5% on his sales. He has accumulated little debt on his balance sheet. By far the largest individual stockholder, serving as the CEO, he has to ask himself how the succession is to be provided for. Meanwhile, faced by a disappointing first half in 1998/9, the company is said to be teaming up with a US duty-free chain – Duty Free Shopppers of California – to beef up its business.

Itsushi Kamiyama / President

Stocks (¥50 par value, 1,000 shares, min. trade)

Shares Issued (Nov. 1, '98) 6,930,000 shares
No. of Shareholders (Mar. 30, '98) 966

Major Holders	(%)
Itsushi Kamiyama	22.2
Asahi Life Ins.	7.1
World Wide	5.6
DKB	4.9
Employees' Stockholding	3.9
Toyo Trust	3.6
Chuo Trust	3.5
Foreign Owners	0.9

Earnings

Period	Sales	Operating Profit	Current Profit	Net Profit	Earnings Per Share	Dividend Per Share
Mar 96	19,882	887	868	327	47.2	10.00
Mar 97	21,976	1,067	980	380	54.9	11.00
Mar 98	23,577	1,248	1,170	412	59.6	11.00
**Mar 99	24,380	N/A	1,180	530	76.5	11.00
Mid-Term						
Sep 98	11,925	549	441	176	25.5	0

**Company estimates. Per share values in ¥, all other amounts in millions of ¥.

Balance sheet summary	1994	1995	1996	1997	1998
Current assets	2,951	3,016	3,219	3,387	4,166
Fixed assets	3,887	3,485	3,720	3,797	3,780
Total assets	6,838	6,502	6,940	7,185	7,946
Current liabilities	3,264	2,851	3,136	3,147	3,713
Fixed liabilities	401	333	277	256	175
Total liabilities	3,665	3,184	3,413	3,404	3,888
Capital Stock	807	807	807	807	807
Shareholders' equity	3,173	3,317	3,526	3,781	4,058
Total liabilities and equity	6,838	6,502	6,940	7,185	7,946

Note: All amounts in millions of ¥. Balance sheet, end March.

Trend Micro

(Estd. 1989, listed 1998, stock code no. 4704)
Company address: 2-2-1, Yoyogi, Shibuya-ku, Tokyo 151-8583
Tel: 81-3-5334-3600 Fax: 81-3-5334-3653

A Japanese core firm of an international group of companies created by Steve Chang, a Taiwan citizen, to offer anti-virus software to computer companies and users. A world authority in his field, Mr. Chang, 44, moved Trend Micro's group head office from Taiwan to Tokyo in 1996, to prepare for the company's IPO in 1998.

Product/Sales Breakdown: These are early days, the company having launched its IPO in August 1998. It divides its services between "PC client software" (49%), "LAN Server and Other Software Products" (28%) and "Royalties and Others" (23%) – the last percentage being an exceptionally high number.

Rivals/Competitors: Trend Micro claims a market share in Japan of over 50% ("59% of the package (retail) market . . . and 54% of the market for enterprise solutions"). The company identifies Network Associates as an actual competitor in Japan. It is the world stage, America, that counts most, however. Trend Micro distributes material from Forrester Research Inc. of the US that names 7 companies active in the anti-computer-virus field in America. That report gives Trend Micro alone a top 4-star grade.

History/Strategy: The shareholder register lists Softbank Holdings Inc. as the largest stockholder, meaning that Softbank owner Masayoshi Son, a well-known businessman of Korean ancestry, has a whip hand. All shareholders are listed as being from overseas, mainly Taiwan. Such a purely foreign-owned operation is becoming less unusual in Japan. Mr. Chang's decision to base himself in Tokyo, meanwhile, suggests that he sees huge potential in the market in Japan, where the market is less mature by far than in the US. He founded Trend Micro in the USA in 1983 before setting it up in Japan in 1989.

Management: Mr. Chang's strategy is to beat a drum, warning of dangers ahead. "Originally, viruses were primarily written in assembly languages," he states in his 1997 annual report. "By 1996 . . . so-called second-generation viruses had begun making their appearance. And now we need to defend against the third generation, known as malicious Java/ActiveX code." He adds: "The number of known viruses has increased from 183 in 1990 to more than 13,000 in 1997, with 5 or 6 new viruses emerging every day."

Outlook/Hot News: Forecasts call for steep sales and earnings growth and high returns of 30% going through the current year to Dec. 1999 and beyond. Watch for sparks to fly, as others enter this business in Japan. For a small foreign-owned firm – Trend Micro has 107 staff at its Yoyogi HQ – to maintain a 50% market share, however strong its technology, would be a miracle. Meanwhile, a spokesman for Trend Micro said, in a telephone interview, that the company/group is relatively less prominent in other countries. In the US, the largest and most competitive market, Trend Micro has "less than 10%" of the market in anti-computer-virus software. The company is working with Hewlett-Packard of the US to develop sales there.

Steve M. J. Chang / President

Stocks (¥50 par value, 500 shares min. trade)

Shares Issued (Nov. 1, '98)	20,750,000 shares
No. of Shareholders (Jun. 30, '98)	14

Major Holders	(%)
Softbank Holdings Inc.	35.0
Trueway Co.	24.5
Gainway Enterprises Ltd.	12.6
Lin, Wei Yao	5.7
Chang, Ming-Jang	5.0
Chen, Mei-Hua	3.6
Foreign Owners	100.0

Earnings

Period	Sales	Operating Profit	Current Profit	Net Profit	Earnings Per Share	Dividend Per Share
Dec 95	627	16	5	3	N/A	0
Dec 96	1,769	390	378	166	141,218.4	0
Dec 97	4,842	1,682	1,666	704	39,135.1	0
**Dec 98	6,942	N/A	1,848	905	47.8	0
*Dec 99	10,000	3,000	3,000	1,500	72.3	0
Mid-Term						
Jun 98	2,708	650	719	423	23.5	0
*Jun 99	3,800	1,100	1,100	550	26.5	0

*Estimates; **Company estimates. Per share values in ¥, all other amounts in millions of ¥.*

Balance sheet summary	1995	1996	1997
Current assets	324	999	2,895
Fixed assets	17	2,178	2,106
Total assets	342	3,177	5,002
Current liabilities	307	1,638	2,756
Fixed liabilities	0	2	4
Total liabilities	307	1,641	2,760
Capital Stock	30	697	900
Shareholders' equity	34	1,536	2,241
Total liabilities and equity	342	3,177	5,002

Note: All amounts in millions of ¥. Balance sheet, end December.

Tsuchiya Twoby Home

(Estd. 1986, listed 1998, stock code no. 1753)
Company address: 13-9-1, Nishi, Kita-Nanajo, Chuo-ku, Sapporo 060-0007
Tel: 81-11-261-0466 Fax: 81-11-261-0678

Subsidiary of Tsuchiya Home; a Sapporo, Hokkaido, builder of residences, like the parent company. President is Tamotsu Nakanishi, 52. Has 190 employees.

Product/Sales breakdown: The firm divides its activities between "custom-built housing", using steel frames for the structure (61%); "pre-planned housing", including imported homes, ready to put up (28%); real estate (5%); others (6%).

Rivals/Competition: Direct competitors in pricey Western-style homes of the kind the company ideally likes to build are not that numerous, the market being small. However, elsewhere in Japan, as in Hokkaido, economic home-builders are having success. Higashi Nihon Home, for example, based in Morioka, Iwate – northern Honshu – is doing well with conventional, built-to-order wooden homes. The existence of alternative, cheaper homes puts downward pressure on the prices of everyone in a recession.

History/Strategy: As a "frontier" part of the Japanese archipelago, Hokkaido benefited from a benign regulatory atmosphere. Financial oversight from Tokyo was relaxed to the point of permitting banks, for example, to finance housing construction without the clients having to put up part of the purchase price as upfront money; repayment schedules were easygoing. The central government strategy contributed to the development of Hokkaido but, in harder times, paved the way for the collapse of Hokkaido's largest bank, the Hokkaido

Development Bank, in 1997. This is the tough atmosphere in which Tsuchiya Twoby Home – "Twoby" is pronounced "2-by" – has to struggle to survive. Sales and earnings dipped in 1998.

Management: Strategic decisions are in the hands of Mr. Kozo Tsuchiya, 57, the founder of Tsuchiya Home, and major shareholder therein. When the company went public in 1998, President Nakanishi bravely announced that Tsuchiya Twoby Home was pressing on with its strategy – building those steel-structure homes.

Outlook/Hot News: It is hard to know how much of a market there will be for upmarket housing, and how much for standardized, barrack-like structures of the kind offered homeowners by another company, Sawako, in another part of Japan. As long as the recession prevails in Japan, notably in construction, entrepreneurs will look to home-building as one area that will keep going. But there is ¥2.7 billion of debt on Tsuchiya Twoby Home's non-consolidated balance sheet, enough to give grounds for concern. The sudden deterioration of business conditions in Hokkaido, following the collapse of the Hokkaido Development Bank two years ago, creates a grave situation for this company. With sales down by a quarter in the year to October 1998, and a sudden plunge into the red on operations, owner Mr. Tsuchiya has to look lively. Can he manage? Brokers in Tokyo ask whether his management style is too old-fashioned – too "Japanese" – to be appropriate.

Tamotsu Nakanishi / President

Stocks (¥50 par value, 1,000 shares min. trade)

Shares Issued (Nov. 1, '98)	5,000 shares
No. of Shareholders (Oct. 31, '97)	27

Major Holders	(%)
Tsuchiya Home	88.9
Tsuchiya Sogo Kenkyujo	2.7
Employees' Stockholding	1.4
North Pacific Bank	0.8
Takugin	0.6
Fuji Bank	0.6
Hokkaido Bank	0.6
Foreign Owners	0.0

Earnings

Period	Sales	Operating Profit	Current Profit	Net Profit	Earnings Per Share	Dividend Per Share
Oct 95	6,714	205	173	72	14,550.2	5,000.00
Oct 96	8,168	344	329	116	22,211.2	10,000.00
Oct 97	9,031	391	373	201	36,967.5	10,000.00
Oct 98	6,666	−215	−265	−306	−53,680.1	15,000.00
**Oct 99	8,155	N/A	225	100	16,806.7	10,000.00
Mid-Term						
Apr 98	1,416	−84	−113	−139	−254,98.6	0
**Apr 99	2,257	N/A	4	2	N/A	0

**Company estimates. Per share values in ¥, all other amounts in millions of ¥.

Balance sheet summary	1994	1995	1996	1997	1998
Current assets	2,992	3,297	3,758	2,951	5,820
Fixed assets	385	341	680	907	864
Total assets	3,378	3,639	4,438	3,859	6,684
Current liabilities	2,812	3,028	3,592	2,848	5,936
Fixed liabilities	94	113	130	152	165
Total liabilities	2,906	3,141	3,723	3,000	6,102
Capital Stock	250	250	315	315	346
Shareholders' equity	471	497	715	858	581
Total liabilities and equity	3,378	3,639	4,438	3,859	6,684

Note: All amounts in millions of ¥. Balance sheet, end October.

Tsuruha

(Estd. 1975, listed 1998, stock code no. 7573)
Company address: 20-1-24, Higashi, Kita-Nijuyonjo, Higashi-Ku, Sapporo 065-0024
Tel: 81-11-783-2755 Fax 81-11-783-2981

A family-owned drug supermarket chain based in Hokkaido, now seeking to spread its network nationwide, but still concentrated almost entirely in Japan's northern island. Tsuruha has brushed aside the recession under the leadership of two brothers – Hajime (Chairman), 66, and Tatsuru (President), 56, – themselves the largest shareholders in the business. 994 employees.

Products/Sales breakdown: The company analyses its sales under these heads – pharmaceuticals (22%), cosmetics (17%), sundries (35%), infant items (11%), other items (14%) and sales to other outlets (1%).

Rivals/Competitors: Like the Hokkaido food chain Ralse – also a regional supermarket chain with a registration on the OTC – Tsuruha has driven forward into a marketing niche that apparently no one else was sure was there. Lots of others sell drugs and cosmetic items in Hokkaido, but no one else had the panache and push of the Tsuruha brothers, and built up a momentum.

History/Strategy: The family traces its start in business to 1929, and only incorporated their firm in 1975. Having built a foundation in Hokkaido with lowish but steady margins of a little under 5% on sales (turnover is now over ¥50 billion a year), the Tsuruhas have opened stores in northern Honshu and are spreading further south. They see their current chain of 175 shops growing to a total of 1,000 stores – a Boots of Japan – by the year 2010.

Management: One of the keys to Tsuruha's success, the owners say, has been their affiliation with JUSCO, one of the great general-item supermarket chains in Japan, a hard-headed, well-run company based in Chiba prefecture outside Tokyo (JUSCO has annual sales of ¥2,420 billion, many times those of Tsuruha). Little Tsuruha has fostered the relationship, and it could be crucial to their plans for nationwide expansion, the two being complementary in many ways.

Outlook/Hot News: Tsuruha's stock price took off after its IPO in 1998, all but doubling in its first few months on the OTC market (the opposite happened at other companies, caught up in the recession). This auspicious start augurs well for the Tsuruhas. Sales and earnings should continue to rise, touching new records yearly. The company remains very much a family-run affair, with the Tsuruha brothers owning stock directly and through Crane Shoji, a Tsuruha family concern. Several considerations lead one to expect Tsuruha to prosper: (i) the company has little debt on its balance sheet and should be able to borrow to finance a nationwide expansion; (ii) JUSCO is committed to supporting Tsuruha – JUSCO chairman Takuya Okada actually serves on Tsuruha's board. Still, for now Tsuruha is thoroughly oriented towards Hokkaido. 162 of its 175 shops are there. Look for JUSCO and Tsuhura to make joint investments in other companies as they expand.

Tatsuru Tsuruha / President

Stocks (¥50 par value, 1,000 shares min. trade)

Shares Issued (Nov. 1, '98)	8,416,000 shares
No. of Shareholders (May. 15, '98)	32

Major Holders	(%)
Crane Shoji	23.8
Hajime Tsuruha	17.2
Jusco Co.	16.8
Hiroko Tsuruha	9.2
Tatsuru Tsuruha	7.7
Employees' Stockholding	6.6
Hirokatsu Kamata	4.2
Foreign Owners	0.0

Earnings

Period	Sales	Operating Profit	Current Profit	Net Profit	Earnings Per Share	Dividend Per Share
May 96	34,307	1,093	1,144	503	2,646.2	150.00
May 97	42,616	1,636	1,748	809	4,249.2	150.00
May 98	49,548	1,892	2,121	1,040	136.7	15.00
**May 99	57,866	N/A	2,690	1,398	166.1	15.00
*May 00	63,000	2,300	2,500	1,300	154.5	15.00
Mid-Term						
Nov 97	23,713	918	1,069	591	77.7	0
Nov 98	28,376	1,170	1,312	713	86.6	0

*Estimates; **Company estimates. Per share values in ¥, all other amounts in millions of ¥.*

Balance sheet summary	1995	1996	1997	1998
Current assets	5,099	5,847	6,589	6,791
Fixed assets	4,341	4,961	5,613	6,781
Total assets	9,440	10,808	12,203	13,573
Current liabilities	4,385	5,082	5,981	6,886
Fixed liabilities	1,840	2,071	1,809	1,298
Total liabilities	6,226	7,154	7,791	8,185
Capital Stock	802	802	802	802
Shareholders' equity	3,214	3,654	4,411	5,388
Total liabilities and equity	9,440	10,808	12,203	13,573

Note: All amounts in millions of ¥. Balance sheet, end May.

UHT

(Estd. 1967, listed 1990, stock code no. 6148)
Company address: 446-268, Aza-Shimo-Kagamidar, Oaza-Haruki, Togo-cho,
Aichi County, Aichi Pref. 470-0162
Tel: 81-5613-8-2101 Fax: 81-5613-8-2383

A tool maker – ranked as Japan's number 2 maker of piercing mills (instruments for boring tiny holes in printed circuit boards) – and highly esteemed. CEO is Masakazu Kakimoto, 64, one of two brothers who devoted their lives to the enterprise; the older one having now retired. Has 106 staff.

Product/Sales breakdown: UHT's ultra high-speed piercing drills account for 40% of the business; pneumatic tools add up to another 26%; and those piercing drills for PCBs (the boards that carry little decks of semiconductors, to constitute the brain of a device) account for a vital 17% of the business – UHT being ranked second to Japan Steel Works, a large company, in this speciality. Equipment and others account for 17%.

Rivals/Competitors: UHT's margins – 20% in a good year – suggest that the Nagoya engineering community holds the firm in high regard, esteeming quality work. Not too many can compete at this level, or the margins would be lower. Decent margins have allowed the brothers Kakimoto to keep their books free of debt.

History/Strategy: It's likely that it takes at least as much vim to run a small machinery company in the Nakoya region – the heart of Japan's engineering world – as a big one. The little companies are the salt of the earth; *they* are the fast-movers; the tiddlers that dart about, keeping as quiet as possible. UHT (formerly Ushio Corp.) is one of those minnows that make the Nagoya area, collectively, the most exciting engineering culture in Asia (and home to Toyota Motor and its group). Somehow, the UHT's contrive to make money, even with the yen far above levels anticipated up to the Plaza Accord of 1985 ... UHT, for its part, set up a new research facility in autumn 1998, investing ¥200 million in the project.

Management: Masakazu Kakimoto is a genial, but shrewd, person, an organizer and an engineer by training, who also knows how to sell. "What I seek to convey to customers," he said, on taking over the running of the business in 1993, "is that it is the customer who benefits from buying a product from us, not (primarily) we who make a profit – that way the customer may come back to buy again, believing that it's in his own interest."

Outlook/Hot News: The current shacho (president) took over from his elder brother Yasuo in 1993, the latter having decreed that he "would retire at 65, without fail". He kept his promise. Not every boss knows when to step down, nor keeps a promise to do so. On such decisions – on good faith – a company can rise or fall ... Masakazu Kakimoto mentions that his hobby is playing with PCs. He likes to fool around for hours, he says. That is how he gets his ideas for new products – the computer itself constitutes, he observes, a "paper of infinity", matter that goes on forever. "On a clear day you can see forever," etc. Not a shacho to underestimate. For all that, in the current year to April 1999 sales and earnings are down. The company exported 29% of output in the half year to October 1998, and is being squeezed by the higher yen.

Masakazu Kakimoto / President

Stocks (¥50 par value, 1,000 shares min. trade)

Shares Issued (Nov. 1, '98)   4,854,000 shares
No. of Shareholders (Apr. 30, '98)   553

Major Holders	(%)
Yasuo Kakimoto	20.1
Masakazu Kakimoto	18.0
Yasumitsu Kakimoto	10.2
Koichi Endo	3.3
Fumiaki Matsumoto	2.6
Tokai Bank	2.4
Mieko Senda	1.9
Foreign Owners	0.0

Earnings

Period	Sales	Operating Profit	Current Profit	Net Profit	Earnings Per Share	Dividend Per Share
Apr 96	1,807	334	382	191	38.0	10.00
Apr 97	2,105	416	510	256	51.0	15.00
Apr 98	3,131	750	847	407	81.5	21.00
**Apr 99	2,700	N/A	673	343	70.7	15.00
*Apr 00	3,000	650	720	370	76.2	15.00
Mid-Term						
Oct 97	1,754	506	550	255	50.8	0
Oct 98	1,258	271	318	178	36.7	0

*Estimates; **Company estimates. Per share values in ¥, all other amounts in millions of ¥.

Balance sheet summary	1994	1995	1996	1997	1998
Current assets	3,528	3,593	3,745	3,664	4,086
Fixed assets	1,908	1,796	1,863	1,900	1,908
Total assets	5,438	5,390	5,609	5,564	5,995
Current liabilities	347	269	612	399	670
Fixed liabilities	846	705	461	443	423
Total liabilities	1,193	975	1,073	842	1,093
Capital Stock	1,077	1,077	1,077	1,077	1,077
Shareholders' equity	4,245	4,415	4,536	4,721	4,901
Total liabilities and equity	5,438	5,390	5,609	5,564	5,995

Note: All amounts in millions of ¥. Balance sheet, end April.

Unipulse

(Estd. 1970, listed 1998, stock code no. 6842)
Company address: 1-3, Sengendai-Nishi, Koshigaya City, Saitama Pref. 343-0041
Tel: 81-489-77-1111 Fax: 81-489-76-5200

Takami Yoshimoto – founder, owner and President of Unipulse, an electronic engineering firm – is disturbed. The 15–20% gross returns his company was making have fallen away to 5% perhaps, he is not yet sure about the outcome. "Still, we are waiting for the economy to pick up," he says.

Product/Sales breakdown: Engineering – finding solutions and then designing specific answers to problems – is what Yoshimoto-san does. The day before he met our team he had gathered with another of our subjects, Junichi Ohira, president of the builder-contractor Sawako, to discuss how Unipulse could assist Ohira-san on a problem. The work is piecemeal. One project after another faces the 40 skilled R & D engineers at Yoshimoto-san's works in Saitama, outside Tokyo. Measuring control equipment accounts for 40% of sales, computer/communications equipment for 17%, amplifying equipment for measuring for 10% and others for 33% – it's a regular smorgasbord of electronic stuff.

Rivals/Competitors: To get ahead in a crowded field – Japan is home to hundreds of thousands of small engineering firms – Yoshimoto, 57, uses PR. He carries with him a collection of recent articles about him and his company. Some 28 years after he created his firm Yoshimoto-san decided to register Unipulse on the OTC market. He did so to broaden the image of his firm as an acknowledged outfit specializing in custom-made control devices. "I didn't go on the OTC to raise money or to distribute shares among relatives," he said, "the idea was to make ourselves known as a solid firm,

thereby attracting good engineers to work with us." This indicates that warding off competition is not the least of this man's concerns.

History/Strategy: What enabled Yoshimoto to push ahead from a standing start in 1970 to build up a firm with 121 staff and sales of ¥3 billion a year? His Saitama-based company has in fact attracted a bright nucleus of engineers. Yoshimoto-san has achieved this by personal example. He is an exquisitely polite, balding man with stocky shoulders, and yet something of the brisk darting manner of a sparrow. "As a boy I loved to make things – messing about with radios was a big thing for me – I always wanted to move my hands," he says.

Management: In the depths of Japan's worst recession/slowdown in 40 years Mr. Yoshimoto says that he is sure that half of the work currently in hand at his firm will continue. However, work on a joint project with Sony – on a play-station – abruptly came to a halt. Yoshimoto-san doesn't know why. Half of his current activity may be discontinued. At the worst.

Outlook/Hot News: Much, if not everything, depends on the overall economy. Yoshimoto does not know when the recession will end. "Honestly, I have no idea, though I do have a sense that the government is finally getting its act together," he says. Every day is a battle for small–medium size company owners in work like Yoshimoto's, a bit linked to construction. The best of the firms will survive. Unipulse has a strong balance sheet and has just moved into a new head office.

Takami Yoshimoto / President

Stocks (¥50 par value, 1,000 shares min. trade)

Shares Issued (Sep. 30, '98)	4,747,000 shares
No. of Shareholders (Sep. 30, '98)	755

Major Holders	(%)
Takami Yoshimoto	32.1
Employees' Stockholding	7.3
JAFCO	5.5
Takeo Hoshi	3.5
Sakura Bank	2.6
Fuji Bank	2.6
Asahi Bank	2.6
Foreign Owners	0.6

Earnings

Period	Sales	Operating Profit	Current Profit	Net Profit	Earnings Per Share	Dividend Per Share
Sep 95	2,403	308	290	103	309.6	50.00
Sep 96	2,746	449	456	253	761.5	50.00
Sep 97	3,136	545	500	272	705.6	50.00
Sep 98	3,276	634	519	391	89.4	14.00
**Sep 99	3,422	680	601	335	70.6	12.00
Mid-Term						
Mar 98	1,679	313	286	156	36.0	0
**Mar 99	1,667	352	296	165	34.8	0

**Company estimates. Per share values in ¥, all other amounts in millions of ¥.

Balance sheet summary	1994	1995	1996	1997	1998
Current assets	2,041	2,281	2,546	2,598	3,211
Fixed assets	1,330	1,270	1,292	1,957	2,545
Total assets	3,372	3,552	3,839	4,555	5,756
Current liabilities	685	927	1,076	1,284	1,301
Fixed liabilities	1,152	1,011	926	813	1,364
Total liabilities	1,838	1,939	2,002	2,097	2,665
Capital Stock	521	521	521	714	825
Shareholders' equity	1,533	1,613	1,836	2,457	3,090
Total liabilities and equity	3,372	3,552	3,839	4,555	5,756

Note: All amounts in millions of ¥. Balance sheet, end September.

Vitec

(Estd. 1987, listed 1993, stock code no. 9957)
Company address: 1-31-5, Higashi-Shinagawa, Shinagawa-Ku, Tokyo 140-0002
Tel: 81-3-3458-4611 Fax 81-3-3458-4757

A little firm that trades semiconductors on behalf of Sony. Operates out of the Shinagawa section as an integral, if little-observed, part of the world's largest audio and video manufacturer. Run by Syunichi Shirai, himself a shareholder – he owns 2.4% of the stock, the records show.

Product/Sales breakdown: The company divides its sales into two main lines – the chips account for 70% of turnover and "electronic parts" for 26%, with a residual 4% in other activities. The semiconductors and parts are mainly for video and audio use, according to Vitec. It is diversifying into CD-ROM drives. It designs semiconductor circuits.

Rivals/Competitors: Sony's annual sales of close to ¥7 trillion make it a giant alongside this affiliate with just 163 staff and 1997/8 consolidated turnover of ¥89.5 billion. Vitec is roughly 1% the size of Sony, which furnishes Vitec with business at tough 1–2% margins. This arrangement buttresses Vitec against the many other companies it contends with in semiconductor trading and in chip design; some of these rivals are giant first section companies in the same league as Sony. So Vitec is Sony by another name, the parent company owning 46.9% of the stock.

History/Strategy: Vitec hit a bad patch in the mid-90s, all but losing money in its 1994/5 year. Since then it has gained ground each year, the figures show. It remains out of the limelight, attracts little attention from the press and the investment community (foreign shareholding is minimal, compared with Sony's whacking 44%), getting on with its job of furnishing Sony's manufacturing arms with those chips and parts.

Management: Shirai-san takes a low posture to one side of the glittering big carnival in Shinagawa that Sony represents. Now 57, he has run Vitec for two years.

Outlook/Hot News: The prospect is that margins will be maintained and sales will continue to grow. Having increased sales by 50% in the latter half of the 1990s – a brilliant time for Sony, which roared ahead of the competition during the period – Vitec has consolidated its role as a fetcher and carrier for its illustrious shareholder. In an interview at his head office, Shirai-san said that he expects Vitec to surpass ¥100 billion in consolidated sales in the current year and to go on growing to exceed ¥150 billion in the year ending March 2001. The Vitec executive – a brisk, silver-haired salesman, not an engineer – judges his company's progress relative to rivals. These are Mitsubishi Electric's chip-trader Ryoyo Electro (annual sales in the ¥120–130 billion range) and NEC's chip-merchandising affiliate Ryosan, with annual sales of ¥250+ billion a year. Neither Ryosan nor Ryoyo have managed to increase sales in recent years; their profits have sunk. Vitec is doing well, expanding into China as its latest strategy.

Syunichi Shirai / President

Stocks (¥50 par value, 1,000 shares min. trade)

Shares Issued (Nov. 1, '98)	10,177,000 shares
No. of Shareholders (Mar. 31, '98)	978

Major Holders	(%)
KMF Co.	33.8
Sony	13.1
Kunihiro Imano	4.0
Tokai Bank	2.6
DKB	2.6
Bank of Tokyo-Mitsubishi	2.6
Employees' Stockholding	2.5
Foreign Owners	0.6

Earnings

Period	Sales	Operating Profit	Current Profit	Net Profit	Earnings Per Share	Dividend Per Share
Mar 96	40,812	316	727	295	30.7	7.50
Mar 97	46,922	792	850	434	43.9	10.00
Mar 98	59,668	1,016	1,256	634	62.8	15.00
**Mar 99	57,700	1,310	1,300	560	55.0	15.00
**Mar 00	65,000	1,450	1,500	700	68.8	15.00
Mid-Term						
Sep 98	27,249	571	549	159	15.7	0
**Sep 99	31,000	680	700	330	32.4	0

**Company estimates. Per share values in ¥, all other amounts in millions of ¥.*

Balance sheet summary	1994	1995	1996	1997	1998
Current assets	14,955	15,874	15,864	21,214	26,867
Fixed assets	2,605	3,956	4,633	5,361	4,594
Total assets	17,560	19,830	20,498	26,575	31,461
Current liabilities	10,605	12,611	12,282	14,498	19,663
Fixed liabilities	0	286	1,059	4,077	2,982
Total liabilities	10,605	12,897	13,341	18,575	22,645
Capital Stock	2,120	2,120	2,120	2,360	2,500
Shareholders' equity	6,955	6,933	7,156	7,999	8,815
Total liabilities and equity	17,560	19,830	20,498	26,575	31,461

Note: All amounts in millions of ¥. Balance sheet, end March.

Yahoo! Japan

(Estd. 1996, listed 1997, stock code no. 4689)
Company address: 24-1, Nihonbashi-Hakozakicho, Chuo-ku, Tokyo 103-0015
Tel: 81-3-5642-8028 Fax: 81-3-5641-3680

A joint venture company between Yahoo! Inc. of the US and Softbank Corp. of Japan. Sells advertising space on the Internet. Universally (or almost universally) forecast to have no chance of succeeding in Japan. Confounding the critics, so far. 65 employees. President is Masahiro Inoue, 41.

Product/Sales breakdown: Yahoo! Japan's results dipped over and down in the first two quarters of calendar year 1998, checking its advance. Advertising sales (71% of revenues in the first quarter) fell to 69% of revenues in the second quarter, with other sources accounting for 31%, mostly Internet guide books. Boasts 500,000 subscribers at end 1998, having introduced members-only services in July 1998. Results for the half year were net sales up from ¥538 million in Jan–June '97 to ¥735 million in first half 1998, a 37% increase; net profits were up by 34% in the same period.

Rivals/Competitors: Within Japan the company is the pioneer. Others are struggling to catch up, but for now are behind.

History/Strategy: JVs (joint ventures) have a way of failing in Japan, historically and inevitably. Mr. Inoue says that that is because Japanese trading companies shoehorn their way into deals, and get in the way. His JV will work . . . As an illustration of how he manages Yahoo! Japan: when it became clear that the first half of 1998 was not going according to plan, Inoue-san says he introduced two changes in the way Yahoo! Japan goes about its business. Firstly, he initiated a practice whereby his staff make direct calls on clients, in addition to those made by the advertising agency he uses. These direct calls are "to explain Internet advertising", he says. The agency still gets a commission. The other initiative has been to join with "all Yahoo! international properties" in selling ads, making "global sales", e.g. to IBM and Hewlett-Packard. On this business the local agency gets no commission. These two changes put Yahoo! Japan back on track, says Mr. Inoue.

Management: Chairman Masayoshi Son works out of the same building, in the downtown Hakozaki section, as Mr. Inoue. Son-san is a force to reckon with as the owner of Softbank Corp., the main shareholder, and one of the most prominent younger-generation businessmen in Japan.

Outlook/Hot News: Yahoo! Japan's President Inoue is changing the way business is done in Japan. To be sure, the changes he is making are small, incremental steps, not revolutionary moves. But a determined person can move mountains in Japan by taking such steps. The Japanese monitor tiny alterations of procedure with almost obsessive interest . . . Inoue-san is focussing on the bottom line, see the page opposite for earnings forecasts (by Toyo Keizai, not by Yahoo! Japan). Therein lies an illustration of how Inoue is changing things. He has informed Jasdaq that he wishes Yahoo! Japan not to have to report earnings forecasts. In exchange, Yahoo! Japan is furnishing Jasdaq with its quarterly results, American-style. "No one can promise (what will happen in) the future," says Mr. Inoue, "especially in this (economic) situation." Therefore, no forecasts!

Masahiro Inoue / President

Stocks (¥50,000 par value)

Shares Issued (Nov. 1, '98)	6,775 shares
No. of Shareholders (Mar. 31, '98)	255

Major Holders	(%)
Softbank Corp.	51.3
Yahoo! Inc.	34.2
Goldman Sachs Int'l	2.8
Fiji	1.1
Sumitomo Trust	0.8
Northern Trust (A VFC) Authority	0.6
Foreign Owners	40.6

Earnings

Period	Sales	Operating Profit	Current Profit	Net Profit	Earnings Per Share	Dividend Per Share
Mar 96	N/A	−3	−5	−5	−1322.5	0
Mar 97	413	49	49	23	5,988.7	0
Mar 98	1,269	146	131	64	11,895.6	0
*Mar 99	1,700	190	190	90	15,000.0	0
*Mar 00	2,500	270	270	120	20,000.0	0
Mid-Term						
Sep 98	735	81	82	42	6,344.9	0
*Sep 99	1,000	130	130	60	10,000.0	0

Estimates. Per share values in ¥, all other amounts in millions of ¥.

Balance sheet summary	1996	1997	1998
Current assets	200	296	981
Fixed assets	5	79	266
Total assets	205	375	1,247
Current liabilities	10	157	229
Fixed liabilities	0	0	0
Total liabilities	10	157	229
Capital Stock	200	200	434
Shareholders' equity	194	218	1,018
Total liabilities and equity	205	375	1,247

Note: All amounts in millions of ¥. Balance sheet, end March.

Zensho

(Estd. 1982, listed 1997, stock code no. 7550)
Company address: 2-15-10, Kita-Saiwai, Nishi-ku, Yokohama 220-0004
Tel: 81-45-316-6996 Fax: 81-45-321-6614

A fast-food chain. Little restaurants operating under the name of Sukiya, offering gyudon – rice topped with beef– as the staple item. The company, only 17 years old, has spread out from the Tokyo-Yokohama area, where it began. 146 employees. The President and chief shareholder, with his family members, is Kentaro Ogawa, 50.

Product/Sales breakdown: Gyudon "says it all", accounting for 81% of sales (revenues in the year to March '98 were ¥13.5 billion). Ogawa-san is diversifying into curry, another staple in Japan, and curry dishes already account for 7% of sales, with other items accounting for 12%. The basic gyudon dish costs ¥400 and the "curry-raisu" ¥480. Hardly anyone can compete with these prices – McDonald's, with similar prices, perhaps a shade below, does not offer the items in question. Ogawa-san located his shops on roadside sites where possible, not in the big cities. A "family atmosphere" is sought.

Rivals/Competitors: There are many rivals. In a recession verging on a breakdown of the economy, people want to eat out for as little as possible. 1996 was a bad year, it coincided with outbreaks of "mad cow" disease abroad. But from February 1997, business perked up again. The company was in the black for 19 months in a row thereafter, according to Ogawa-san.

History/Strategy: "Food is fundamen-tal," says Mr. Ogawa, seeking to account for his success. "Look around you, though, and you will see the industry is still growing. It is not 'mature'. So I decided to go into it. 'Best quality at a low price' is my slogan." To get prices down, costs must be pushed down. Zensho owns farms and grows cattle on them. The company transports the beef to the shops, handling that part of the "production line" itself, and then prepares the gyudon dishes for the public. Ogawa-san's strategy has been to cover all 4 main stages of the process, he says.

Management: The company aims to open 30 more shops by the year 2000, and to spread throughout Japan.

Outlook/Hot News: Japan isn't quite in an economic state where it needs soup-kitchens as in the middle of a depression but it is heading in that direction. Zensho has hit the fast-food restaurant market at a level that works, price-wise, as its numbers show (see opposite page). Dishes priced in the ¥400 range are what the public seeks – as at McDonald's. Not that everything is perfect. Bigger rivals in the gyudon trade – Yoshinoya D & C, Matsuya Foods – benefit from economies of scale and, in Yoshinoya's case, long experience. Ogawa-san built up a chain of 201 outlets by autumn 1998. But he also accumulated borrowings of over ¥7 billion, equivalent to many years of net profits. Costs have to be watched.

Kentaro Ogawa / President

Stocks (¥50 par value, 1,000 shares min. trade)

Shares Issued (Nov. 1, '98)	4,578,000 shares
No. of Shareholders (Mar. 31, '98)	580

Major Holders	(%)
Nihon Create Co.	31.2
Kentaro Ogawa	16.9
Kazumasa Ogawa	3.8
Yohei Ogawa	3.8
Asahi Bank	3.5
Employees' Stockholding	2.2
Yokohama Capital	2.1
Foreign Owners	0.6

Earnings

Period	Sales	Operating Profit	Current Profit	Net Profit	Earnings Per Share	Dividend Per Share
Mar 96	11,205	712	476	222	546.0	100.00
Mar 97	11,736	746	515	231	56.8	10.00
Mar 98	13,523	945	720	243	55.6	12.00
**Mar 99	15,287	927	851	256	55.9	10.00
Mid-Term						
Sep 98	7,282	347	316	20	4.5	0

**Company estimates. Per share values in ¥, all other amounts in millions of ¥.

Balance sheet summary	1994	1995	1996	1997	1998
Current assets	1,054	1,346	2,213	2,545	2,370
Fixed assets	6,989	7,942	7,759	8,035	8,570
Total assets	8,043	9,288	9,972	10,580	10,940
Current liabilities	2,961	3,670	3,981	4,324	3,995
Fixed liabilities	4,133	4,588	4,762	4,843	4,945
Total liabilities	7,095	8,258	8,743	9,168	8,941
Capital Stock	418	418	418	418	598
Shareholders' equity	947	1,029	1,228	1,412	1,999
Total liabilities and equity	8,043	9,288	9,972	10,580	10,940

Note: All amounts in millions of ¥. Balance sheet, end March.

Appendix 1
JASDAQ Registered Companies

Name	Code No.	SIC Industry Name	Financial Year	Market	Date
A&CMOS INC.	6888	electrical	07/31		
ABLE INC.	8872	real estat	03/31		
ACCESS CO., LTD	4700	service	03/31		
ACE KOEKI CO. LTD	8749	sec/ commod	03/31		
ADO ELECTRONIC IND. CO. LTD	8073	wholesale	03/31		
ADTEC CORP.	6840	electrical	03/31		
ADVAN CO. LTD	7463	wholesale	03/31		
AGRO-KANESHO CO. LTD	4955	chemicals	12/31		
AIKO CORP.	9909	wholesale	03/20		
AIKOH CO. LTD	4988	chemicals	03/31		
AIN PHARMACIEZ INC.	9627	service	04/30		
AIREX INC.	6944	electrical	01/31		
AISAN TECHNOLOGY CO. LTD	4667	service	03/31		
AJIS CO. LTD	4659	service	03/31		
AKAGI SUISAN CO. LTD	2878	foods	03/31		
AKATSUKI PRINTING CO. LTD	7918	other prot	03/31		
AKIKAWA FOODS & FARMS CO LTD	1380	fishery/ag	03/31		
ALOKA CO. LTD	7704	precision	03/31		
ALTECH CORP.	4641	service	12/31		
AM JAPAN CO. LTD	8047	wholesale	03/31		
AMSC CO. LTD	7468	wholesale	03/31		
AMWAY JAPAN LTD	9821	wholesale	08/31		
ANDO CHEMICAL WORKS CO. LTD	7528	wholesale	03/31		
ANDOR CO. LTD	4640	service	03/31		
ANRAKUTEI CO. LTD	7562	retailsale	03/31		
AOKI SUPER CO. LTD	9977	retailsale	02/20		
ARC LAND SAKAMOTO CO. LTD	9842	retailsale	02/20		
ARGO GRAPHICS INC.	7595	wholesale	03/31		
ARGOTECHNOS 21 CORP.	4692	service	03/31		
ARRK CORP.	7873	other prot	03/31		
ART VIVANT CO. LTD	7523	retailsale	03/31		
ARUZE CORP.	6425	machinery	03/31		
ASAHI HOMES CO. LTD	1913	constructn	03/31		
ASAHI INTELLIGENCE SERVICE CO. LTD	9799	service	03/31		

Name	SIC Code No.	Industry Name	Financial Year	Market	Date
ASAHI KAGAKU KOGYO CO. LTD	7928	chemicals	08/31		
ASAHI PRINTING AND PACKAGING CO. LTD	3951	pulp/paper	03/31		
ASAHI RUBBER INC.	5162	rubber	03/31		
ASAHIDANKE CO. LTD	5281	glass/cera	03/31		
ASCII CORP.	9473	other prot	03/31		
ASEED CO. LTD	9959	retailsale	03/31		
ASK PLANNING CENTER INC.	9756	service	12/31		
ATHENA KOGYO CO. LTD	7890	chemicals	09/30		
ATL SYSTEMS INC.	4663	service	04/30		
ATLUS CO. LTD	7866	other prot	03/31		
ATOMIX CO. LTD	4625	chemicals	03/31		
ATSUGI NYLON SHOJI CO. LTD	8284	wholesale	03/31		
AUCNET INC.	9669	service	12/31		
AUTO HELLOES CO. LTD	7547	retailsale	03/31		
AVAL DATA CORP.	6918	electrical	03/31		
AVELCO CO. LTD	7539	wholesale	03/31		
AVEX INC.	7860	other prot	03/31		
AVON PRODUCTS CO. LTD	4915	chemicals	12/31		
BAMIYAN CO. LTD	7546	retailsale	12/31		
BANDAI LOGIPAL INC.	9089	land trans	02/28		
BELC CO. LTD	9974	retailsale	02/28		
BELTECNO CORP	7926	other prot	03/31		
BELX CO. LTD	4672	service	12/31		
BISACAYE CO. LTD	7542	wholesale	12/31		
BLUE GRASS CO. LTD	7478	retailsale	02/20		
BODYSONIC CO. LTD	6819	electrical	03/31		
B-R31 ICE CREAM CO. LTD	2268	foods	12/31		
BROADCASTING SYSTEM OF NIIGATA INC.	9408	service	03/31		
BUNKAHOSO BRAIN CO. LTD	9653	service	03/31		
BUNKYODO CO. LTD	9978	retailsale	03/31		
BUSINESS BRAIN SHOWA-OTA INC.	9658	service	03/31		
C TWO-NETWORK CO. LTD	7588	retailsale	03/31		
CABIN INDUSTRIAL CO. LTD	7737	precision	12/31		
CANARE ELECTRIC CO. LTD	5819	non-fer ml	03/31		
CANON CHEMICALS INC.	6422	machinery	03/31		
CANON COMPONENTS INC.	6906	electrical	12/31		
CANON COPYER SALES CO. LTD	8295	wholesale	12/31		
CANON SOFTWARE INC.	9623	service	12/31		
CAR MATE MDFG. CO. LTD	7297	trans eqp	03/31		
CGI CORP.	4959	chemicals	03/31		
CENTRAL UNI CO. LTD	7706	precision	03/31		
CERESPO CO. LTD	9625	service	03/31		
CHACOTT CO. LTD	3603	textile	03/31		

Name	SIC Code No.	Industry Name	Financial Year	Market	Date
CHARLE CO. LTD	*9885	wholesale	03/31	OSE 2nd	1998/11/30
CHICHIBU RAILWAY CO. LTD	9012	land trans	03/31		
CHIYODA INTEGRE CO. LTD	6915	electrical	08/31		
CHIYODA UTE CO. LTD	5387	glass/cera	03/31		
CHOYA CORP.	3592	textile	01/31		
CHUKYO IYAKUHIN CO. LTD	4558	pharmacy	03/31		
CHUO BUSSAN CORP.	9852	wholesale	03/31		
CHUO KAGAKU CO. LTD	7895	chemicals	12/31		
CHUO SJOJI CO. LTD	5382	glass/cera	03/31		
CHUOKEIZAI-SHA INC.	9476	other prot	09/30		
CHUOMUSEN CO. LTD	6716	electrical	03/31		
CHUONYU CO. LTD	9053	land trans	09/30		
CITIZEN ELECTRONICS CO. LTD	6892	electrical	03/31		
CLIP CORP.	4705	service	03/31		
COCO'S JAPAN CO LTD	9943	retailsale	02/38		
CO-COS NOBUOKA CO. LTD	3599	textile	03/31		
COLIN CORP.	6872	electrical	11/30		
COMBI CORP.	7935	other prot	03/31		
COMO CO. LTD	2224	foods	03/31		
COMTEC INC.	9657	service	03/31		
CONSEC CORP.	9895	wholesale	03/31		
COPAL ELECTRONICS CO. LTD	6883	electrical	03/31		
COSEL CO. LTD	6905	electrical	05/20		
COWBOY CO. LTD	9971	retailsale	09/30		
COX CO. LTD	9876	retailsale	02/20		
COYO CORP. CO.	8866	real estat	03/31		
CRC RESEARCH INSTITUTE INC.	9660	service	03/31		
CREATE MEDIC CO. LTD	5187	rubber	12/31		
CREO CO. LTD	9698	service	03/31		
CRESCO LTD	4674	service	03/31		
DAIDENSHA CO. LTD	9907	wholesale	03/31		
DAIICHI COMMODITIES CO. LTD	8746	sec/ commod	03/31		
DAIICHI FORGING CO. LTD	5645	iron/steel	03/31		
DAIICHI KENSETSU CORP.	1799	constructn	03/31		
DAIICHIKOSHO CO. LTD	7458	wholesale	03/31		
DAIKA CORP.	9926	wholesale	07/31		
DAIKEN CO. LTD	5900	metal pro	02/28		
DAIMON CO. LTD	7497	retailsale	03/31		
DAIOHS CORP.	4653	service	03/31		
DAISEKI CO LTD	9793	service	02/28		
DAISHIN CHEMICAL CO. LTD	4629	chemicals	03/31		
DAISHINTO INC.	9785	service	03/31		
DAISHO CO. LTD	2816	foods	03/31		
DAITEC CO. LTD	9796	service	09/30		

Name	Code No.	SIC Industry Name	Financial Year	Market	Date
DAITO KOUN CO. LTD	9367	trans servs	03/31		
DAITO MECHATRONICS CO. LTD	9923	wholesale	04/30		
DAIWA DENSETSU CORP.	1985	constructn	09/30		
DAIWA FUTURES CO. LTD	8743	sec/ commod	03/31		
DAIWA KOHTAI CO. LTD	5694	iron/steel	03/31		
DAIWA LOGISTICS CO. LTD	9054	land trans	03/31		
DAIWA SYSTEM CONSTRUCTION CO. LTD	1749	constructn	09/30		
DAIYA TSUSHO CO. LTD	7462	retailsale	03/31		
DALTON CORP.	7432	wholesale	03/31		
DAYTONA CORP.	7228	trans eqp	12/31		
DENKODO CO. LTD	8290	retailsale	03/31		
DENTSU TEC INC.	4682	service	03/31		
DIGICUBE CO. LTD	7589	wholesale	03/31		
DIGITAL ELECTRONICS CORP.	6884	electrical	03/31		
DIO CHEMICALS LTD	3533	textile	11/30		
DISCO CORP.	6146	machinery	03/31		
DMS INC.	9782	service	03/31		
DOUTOR COFFEE CO. LTD	9952	wholesale	03/31		
DRAKE BEAM MORIN-JAPAN INC.	4688	service	03/31		
EASTON CO. LTD	9995	wholesale	03/31		
EAZIMA CO. LTD	1997	constructn	08/31		
EBARA JITSUGYO CO. LTD	6328	machinery	03/31		
EBATA CORP.	5278	glass/cera	03/31		
EIDAI KAKO CO. LTD	7877	chemicals	03/31		
EIKEN INDUSTRIES CO. LTD	7265	trans eqp	10/31		
EITARO CO. LTD	9985	retailsale	03/31		
EIWA CO. LTD	9811	wholesale	03/31		
ELECTRONIC AND IND. ENTERPRISES INC.	8049	wholesale	12/31		
EMORI & CO. LTD	9963	wholesale	03/31		
EMOTO INDUSTRY CO. LTD	7948	other prot	03/31		
ENCHO CO. LTD	8208	retailsale	03/31		
ENIX CORP.	9684	service	03/31		
ENOMOTO CO. LTD	6928	electrical	03/31		
ENSHU TRUCK CO. LTD	9057	land trans	03/31		
ENVIRONMENTAL CONTROL CENTER CO. LTD	4657	service	03/31		
ESCOM, INC.	9472	other prot	03/31		
ESTELLE CO. LTD	7872	other prot	03/31		
ETA ELECTRIC INDUSTRY CO. LTD	6891	electrical	03/31		
EXCEL CO. LTD	7591	wholesale	09/30		
EYEFUL HOME TECHNOLOGY INC.	9662	service	03/31		
F.C.C. CO. LTD	7296	trans eqp	03/31		

Name	Code No.	SIC Industry Name	Financial Year	Market	Date
FAMILY INC.	8298	retailsale	03/31		
FANCL CORP.	4921	chemicals	03/31		
FENWAL CONTROLS OF JAPAN LTD	6870	electrical	12/31		
FERROTEC CORP.	6890	elecrtrical	03/31		
FIRST CREDIT CORP.	8580	financials	03/31		
FOCUS SYSTEMS CORP.	4662	service	03/31		
FONTAINE CO. LTD	*7423	wholesale	02/28	TSE 2nd	1998/11/20
FORVAL CORP.	8275	wholesale	03/31		
FR CORP.	9822	retailsale	09/30		
FREUND INDUSTRIAL CO. LTD	6312	machinery	02/28		
F-TECH INC.	7212	trans eqp	03/31		
FUDO BUILDING RESERCH CO. LTD	1910	constructn	03/31		
FUJI CO. LTD	7471	retailsale	04/20		
FUJI CORP.	3515	textile	03/31		
RUJI ELECTRIC IND. CO. LTD	6654	electrical	01/31		
FUJI ELECTRONICS CO. LTD	9883	wholesale	02/28		
FUJI FOODS INC.	2913	foods	03/31		
FUJI GLASS CO. LTD	5212	glass/cera	03/31		
FUJI LATEX CO. LTD	5199	rubber	03/31		
FUJI MACHINERY CO. LTD	7252	trans eqp	03/31		
FUJI PHARMACEUTICAL CO. LTD	4554	pharmacy	09/30		
FUJI SEAL INC.	7864	other prot	03/31		
FUJI TECHNICA INC.	6476	machinery	03/31		
FUJI SANGYO CORP.	9906	wholesale	03/31		
FUJIKYU CORP.	9966	retailsale	06/30		
FUJIMI INC.	5384	glass/cera	03/31		
FUJIMORI KOGYO CO. LTD	7917	chemicals	03/31		
FUJITA ENGINEERING CO. LTD	1770	constructn	03/31		
FUKOKU CO. LTD	5185	rubber	03/31		
FUKUDA DENSHI CO. LTD	6960	electrical	03/31		
FUKUHARA CO. LTD	9965	retailsale	05/31		
FUKUI COMPUTER INC.	9790	service	03/31		
FUKUSHIMA FOODS CO. LTD	2921	foods	03/31		
FUKUYAMA CONSULTANTS CO. LTD	9608	service	06/30		
FUNABASHI YAKUHIN CO. LTD	7536	wholesale	03/31		
FUSO DENTSU CO. LTD	7505	wholesale	09/30		
GAKKEN CREDIT CORP.	8507	financials	03/31		
GAKKYUSHA CO. LTD	9769	service	03/31		
GAKUIKUSHA CORP.	9696	service	03/31		
GANTAN BEAUTY INDUSTRY CO. LTD	5935	metal pro	03/31		
GEOMATEC CO. LTD	6907	electrical	03/31		
GETZ BROS. CO. LTD	9839	wholesale	12/31		
GINZA RENOIR CO. LTD	9853	retailsale	03/31		
GINZA YAMAGATAYA CO. LTD	8215	retailsale	03/31		
GL SCIENCES INC.	7705	precision	03/31		

Name	SIC Code No.	Industry Name	Financial Year	Market	Date
GLOBAL FOOD CREATORS CO. LTD	7559	wholesale	03/31		
GOLDCREST CO. LTD	8871	real estat	03/31		
GOODMAN CO. LTD	7535	wholesale	06/30		
GOTO CO. LTD	9817	retailsale	08/20		
GOYO INTEX CO. LTD	7519	wholesale	03/31		
GRAPHIC PRODUCTS INC.	6886	electrical	12/31		
GREEN HOUSE CO. LTD	9689	service	03/31		
GULLIVER INTERNATIONAL CO. LTD	7599	wholesale	02/28		
GUNZE KOBUNSHI CORP.	4227	chemicals	03/31		
H.I.S. CO. LTD	9603	trans servs	10/31		
HACHI-BAN CO. LTD	9950	retailale	03/20		
HAGIWARA ELECTRIC CO. LTD	7467	wholesale	03/31		
HAKUSEISHA CO. LTD	9736	service	03/31		
HAKUSUI CHEMICAL IND. LTD	4079	chemicals	12/31		
HAKUTO CO. LTD	7433	wholesale	03/31		
HAMAI INDUSTRIES LTD	6497	machinery	12/31		
HAMAKATSU CO. LTD	7507	retailsale	02/28		
HAMAKYOREX CO. LTD	9037	land trans	03/31		
HANASHIMA ELECTRIC WIRE CO. LTD	5813	non-fer ml	03/31		
HAPPINET CORP.	*7552	wholesale	03/31	TSE 2nd	1998/12/17
HARADA INDUSTRY CO. LTD	6904	electrical	03/31		
HARIMA B·PSTEM CORP.	9780	service	03/31		
HARMONIC DRIVE SYSTEMS INC.	6324	machinery	03/31		
HARUYAMA CHAIN CO. LTD	7529	retailale	03/31		
HASHIMOTO SOGYO CO. LTD	7570	wholesale	03/31		
HATSUHO SHOUJI CO. LTD	7425	wholesale	12/31		
HIGASI NIHON HOUSER CO. LTD	1873	constructn	10/31		
HIKARI BUSINESS FORM CO. LTD	3948	pulp/paper	12/31		
HIKARI FURNITURE CO. LTD	8191	wholesale	03/31		
HIKARI TSUSHIN, INC.	9435	comunicton	08/31		
HIMARAYA CO. LTD	7514	retailsale	03/31		
HI-MART LTD	9881	retailsale	02/28		
HIMKO CO. LTD	9892	wholesale	03/31		
HINOKI REAL ESTATE CO. LTD	8862	real estat	03/31		
HIOKI E.E. CORP	6866	electrical	12/31		
HIRATA TECHNICAL CO. LTD	5989	metal pro	03/31		
HITACHI PLANT CONST & SERVICES CO. LTD	1751	constructn	03/31		
HOHRIN CO. LTD	9898	wholesale	03/31		
HOKKOKU CO. LTD	2906	foods	03/31		
HOKOKU SANGYO CO. LTD	3587	textile	03/31		
HOKUBU COMMUNICATION & IND. CO. LTD	6909	electrical	03/31		

Name	SIC Code No.	Industry Name	Financial Year	Market	Date
HOKURIKU DENWA KOUJI CO. LTD	1989	constructn	03/31		
HOKURIKU MISAWA HOMES CO. LTD	1763	constructn	03/31		
HOKUTO CORP.	1379	fishery/ag	03/31		
HONMA GOLF CO. LTD	7884	other prot	03/31		
HORAI CO. LTD	9679	service	09/30		
HORY CORP.	5927	metal pro	03/31		
HOSODA CORP.	1906	constructn	03/31		
HOSOYA FIREWORKS CO. LTD	4274	chemicals	03/31		
HOTEL NEW GRAND CO. LTD	9720	service	11/30		
HOUSE OF ROSE CO. LTD	7506	retailsale	03/31		
HUNET INC.	8836	real estat	03/31		
HURXLEY CORP.	7561	retailsale	03/31		
HUTECH NORIN CO. LTD	9056	land trans	03/31		
I.A. CORP.	7509	retailsale	03/31		
I.S. PRECISION MACHINERY INC.	7295	trans eqp	03/31		
ICHIMASA KAMABOKO CO. LTD	2904	foods	06/30		
ICHISHIN CO. LTD	4645	service	02/28		
ICHIYA CO. LTD	9968	retailsale	07/31		
IHARA SCIENCE CORP.	5999	metal pro	03/31		
IMAGINEER CO. LTD	4644	service	03/31		
IMASEN ELECTRIC INDUSTRIAL CO. LTD	7266	trans eqp	03/31		
IMI CO. LTD	7503	wholesale	12/31		
INABA SEISAKUSHO CO. LTD	3421	metal pro	07/31		
INFORMATION DEVELOPMENT CO. LTD	4709	service	03/31		
INNOTECH CORP.	9880	wholesale	03/31		
INSTITUTE OF GENERAL EDUCATION CO. LTD	9730	service	03/31		
INTERNATIONAL TELEVISION FILMS, INC.	9604	service	01/31		
I-O DATA DEVICE INC.	6916	electrical	06/30		
IRISO ELECTRONICS CO. LTD	6908	electrical	03/31		
ISB CORP.	9702	service	12/31		
ISEKI POLY-TECH INC.	6275	machinery	03/31		
ISHIGAKI FOODS CO. LTD	2901	foods	03/31		
ISHII TOOL & ENGINEERING CORP.	6314	machinery	03/31		
ISHIKAWAJIMA HANYOKI SERVICE CO. LTD	9781	service	03/31		
ITEC CORP.	9964	wholesale	03/31		
IUCHI SEIEIDO CO. LTD	7476	wholesale	03/31		
IUK INC.	7592	wholesale	12/31		
IVY COSMETICS CORP.	4918	chemicals	03/31		
IWABUCHI CORP.	5983	metal pro	03/31		

Name	Code No.	SIC Industry Name	Financial Year	Market	Date
IWATSUKA CONFECTIONERY CO. LTD	2221	foods	03/31		
IX CORP.	9659	service	03/31		
IZUMI INDUSTRIES LTD	7286	trans eqp	03/31		
JAFCO CO. LTD	8595	financials	03/31		
JALCO CO. LTD	6812	electrical	03/31		
JALECO LTD	7954	other prot	03/31		
JAMCO CORP.	*7408	trans eqp	03/31	TSE 2nd	1998/12/14
JAPAN AIR SYSTEM CO. LTD	9203	air trans	03/31		
JAPAN ASIA INVESTMENT CO. LTD	8518	financials	03/31		
JAPAN BUSINESS COMPUTER CO. LTD	9889	wholesale	03/31		
JAPAN CARE SERVICE CORP.	7566	wholesale	03/31		
JAPAN CBM CORP.	9920	wholesale	03/31		
JAPAN ELECTRONIC MATERIALS CORP.	6855	electrical	03/31		
JAPAN ENGINEERING CONSULTANTS CO. LTD	9626	service	06/30		
JAPAN IND. LAND DEVELOPMENT CO. LTD	1781	constructn	03/31		
JAPAN INDUSTRIAL TESTING CO. LTD	9784	service	03/31		
JAPAN KNOWLEDGE IND. CO. LTD	9753	service	09/30		
JAPAN LIFELINE CO. LTD	7575	wholesale	03/31		
JAPAN LOGISTIC SYSTEMS CORP.	9060	land trans	03/31		
JAPAN MARINE TECHNOLOGIES LTD	6348	machinery	12/31		
JAPAN MEDICAL DYNAMIC MARKETING, INC.	7600	wholesale	5/31		
JAPAN PROCESS DEVELOPMENT CO. LTD	9651	service	05/31		
JAPAN PUBLICATIONS TRADING CO. LTD	8072	wholesale	03/31		
JAPAN RELIANCE SERVICE CORP.	4664	service	03/31		
JAPAN SYSTEMS CO. LTD	9758	service	03/31		
JAPAN U-PICA CO. LTD	7891	chemicals	03/31		
JASTEC CO. LTD	9717	service	11/30		
JC FOODS CO. LTD	2876	foods	03/31		
J-COS CORP.	1977	constructn	03/31		
JEANS MATE CORP	7448	retailsale	02/20		
JOBAN KAIHATSU CO. LTD	1782	constructn	03/31		
JOINT CORP.	8874	real estat	03/31		
JOIS CO. LTD	8080	retailsale	03/31		
JONATHAN'S CO. LTD	8204	retailsale	12/31		
JUSPHOTO CO. LTD	4646	service	02/20		
JUSTSYSTEM CORP.	4686	service	03/31		
K.K. SEIYOKEN	9734	service	01/31		
KADOYA SESAME MILLS INC.	2612	foods	03/31		

Name	SIC Code No.	Industry Name	Financial Year	Market	Date
KAINOS LABORATORIES INC.	4556	pharmacy	03/31		
KAKIYASU HONTEN CO. LTD	2294	foods	09/30		
KAN DESIGN CO. LTD	4677	service	03/31		
KANDA CORP.	9059	land trans	03/31		
KANDA TSUSHINKI CO. LTD	1992	constructn	03/31		
KANEKO SEEDS CO. LTD	1376	fishery/ag	05/31		
KANEMORI CO. LTD	7571	retailsale	03/31		
KANEZAKI CO. LTD	2912	foods	02/28		
KAN-NANMARU CORP.	7585	retailsale	06/30		
KANSEKI CO. LTD	9903	retailsale	02/28		
KANTO BIOMEDICAL LABORATORY CO. LTD	9707	service	05/31		
KANTO SEINO TRANSPORTATION CO. LTD	9080	land trans	03/31		
KAPPA·CREATE CO. LTD	7421	retailsale	05/31		
KARAKAMI KANKOH CO. LTD	9794	service	03/31		
KASUMI CONVENIENCE NETWORKS CO. LTD	7454	retailsale	02/28		
KATSURAGAWA ELECTRIC CO. LTD	6416	machinery	03/31		
KAWACHIYA PAPER CO. LTD	9849	wholesale	03/31		
KAWADA CONSTRUCTION CO. LTD	1877	constructn	03/31		
KAWASAKI GEOLOGICAL ENGINEERING CO. LTD	4673	service	11/30		
KAWASAKE THERMAL ENGINEERING CO. LTD	6414	machinery	03/31		
KAWATA MFG. CO. LTD	6292	machinery	03/31		
KAWATETSU GALVANIZING CO. LTD	5696	iron/steel	03/31		
KAZOKUTEI CO. LTD	9931	retailsale	03/31		
KB CO. LTD	2920	foods	03/31		
KEL CORP.	6919	electrical	03/31		
KENKO MAYONNAISE CO. LTD	2915	foods	03/31		
KENSOH CO. LTD	7939	other prot	03/31		
KIKUCHI CO. LTD	5970	metal pro	09/30		
KIKUSUI ELECTRONICS CORP	6912	electrical	03/31		
KIMOTO CO. LTD	7908	chemicals	03/31		
KIMURA CO. LTD	7461	wholesale	03/31		
KING INDUSTRIAL CO. LTD	7986	other prot	12/31		
KING JIM CO. LTD	7962	other prot	06/20		
KITAC CORP.	4707	service	10/20		
KITAGAWA SEIKI CO. LTD	6327	machinery	06/30		
KITANOKAZOKU CO. LTD	9925	retailsale	06/30		
KITO CORP.	6409	machinery	03/31		
KOBADEN ELECTRONICS CORP.	9867	wholesale	03/31		

Name	Code No.	SIC Industry Name	Financial Year	Market	Date
KOBAYASHI YOKO CO. LTD	8742	sec/ commod	03/31		
KOGURE CORP.	9820	wholesale	08/31		
KOHA CO. LTD	6876	electrical	03/31		
KOHSOKU CORP.	7504	wholesale	03/31		
KOJITU CO. LTD	9905	retailsale	07/31		
KOKEN BORING MACHINE CO. LTD	6297	machinery	03/31		
KOKEN LTD	7963	other prot	12/31		
KOKUSAI DENSETU CO. LTD	1953	constructn	03/31		
KOKUSAI KANKO KAIKAN CO. LTD	9718	service	03/31		
KOKUSAI SYSTEM CO. LTD	9687	service	03/31		
KOMATSU STORE CO. LTD	8250	retailsale	03/31		
KOMATSU WALL INDUSTRY CO. LTD	7949	other prot	03/31		
KOSAIGOGEI CO. LTD	7878	other prot	01/31		
KOTOBUKI SEIKA CO. LTD	2222	foods	03/31		
KOURAKUEN CORP.	7554	retailsale	03/31		
KOZOSUSHI SO-HUNBU CO. LTD	9973	wholesale	12/31		
KRAFT INC.	7440	retailsale	03/31		
K'S DENKI CORP.	8282	retailsale	03/31		
KUNIMINE INDUSTRIES CO. LTD	5388	glass/cera	03/31		
KURAMOTO SEISAKUSHO CO. LTD	5216	glass/cera	12/31		
KUROGANEYA CO. LTD	9855	retailsale	05/15		
KUWAYAMA CORP.	7889	other prot	03/31		
KVK CORP.	6484	machinery	03/31		
KYODEN CO. LTD	6881	electrical	03/31		
KYODO COMPUTER CO. LTD	9685	service	03/31		
KYOEI CO. LTD	1830	constructn	03/31		
KYOGOKU UNYU SHOJI CO. LTD	9073	land trans	03/31		
KYORITSU AIR TECH INC.	5997	metal pro	12/31		
KYORITSU ELECTRIC CORP.	6874	electrical	06/30		
KYORITSU MAINTENANCE CO. LTD	9616	service	03/31		
KYOSAN CABLE, LTD	5814	non-fer ml	03/31		
KYOSEI RENTEMU CO. LTD	9680	service	03/31		
KYOSHIN ELECTRIC CO. LTD	7574	wholesale	03/31		
KYOWA ENGINEERING CONSULTANTS CO. LTD	9647	service	11/30		
KYOWAKENKO CO. LTD	1981	constructn	03/31		
KYOWAKOGYOSYI CO. LTD	5971	metal pro	04/30		
LAOX CO. LTD	8303	retailsale	03/31		
LASTERTEC CORP.	6920	electrical	06/30		
LEADER ELECTRONICS CORP.	6867	electrical	03/31		
LEO CO. LTD	7495	retailsale	02/28		
LEVI STRAUSS JAPAN K.K.	9836	wholesale	11/30		
LILYCOLOR CO. LTD	9827	wholesale	12/31		
LUCKLAND CO. LTD	9612	service	12/31		

Name	Code No.	SIC Industry Name	Financial Year	Market	Date
LUX CORP.	6811	electrical	3/20		
MAEDASEISAKUSHO CO. LTD	6281	machinery	03/31		
MAEZAWA KASEI INDUSTRIES CO. LTD	7925	chemicals	03/31		
MAKI MANUFACTURING CO. LTD	6304	machinery	03/31		
MAKIYA CO. LTD	9890	retailsale	03/31		
MAMMY MART CORP.	9823	retailsale	09/30		
MANDOM CORP.	4917	chemicals	03/31		
MARCHE CORP.	7524	retailsale	03/31		
MARKTEC CORP.	4954	chemicals	09/30		
MARUFURU CO. LTD	9877	retailsale	02/20		
MARUMITSU CO. LTD	8526	wholesale	03/20		
MARUWA CERAMIC CO. LTD	*5344	glass/cera	03/31	TSE 2nd	1998/12/2
MARUYAMA KOGYO CO. LTD	3588	textile	03/31		
MARUZEN CO. LTD	5982	metal pro	02/28		
MASARU CORP.	1795	constructn	03/31		
MASTERNET CO. LTD	4697	service	03/31		
MATSUDA SANGYO CO. LTD	7456	wholesale	03/31		
MATSUDO KOSAN CO. LTD	9676	service	03/31		
MATSUMOTO DENKI CO. LTD	9917	retailsale	03/31		
MATSUMOTO INC.	7901	other prot	04/30		
MATSUMOTO KENKO CO. LTD	1779	constructn	03/31		
MATSUMOTO YUSHI-SEIYAKU CO. LTD	4365	chemicals	3/31		
MATSUMOTOKIYOSHI CO. LTD	9875	retailsale	03/31		
MATSUYA CO. LTD	7452	retailsale	02/28		
MATSUYA FOODS CO. LTD	9887	retailsale	03/31		
MDI CORP.	8848	real estat	03/31		
MEDICAL & BIOLOGICAL LABORATORIES CO. LTD	4557	pharmacy	03/31		
MEFOS LTD	9779	service	03/31		
MEGACHIPS CORP.	6875	electrical	03/31		
MEGANE TOP CO. LTD	7541	retailsale	08/31		
MEIKO NETWORK JAPAN CO. LTD	4668	service	08/31		
MEIKO SHOKAI CO. LTD	9858	wholesale	05/20		
MEITO TRANSPORTATION CO. LTD	*9047	land trans	3/31	TSE 3nd	1998/12/25
MELTEX INC.	4105	chemicals	05/31		
MEMOREX TELEX JAPAN LTD	9862	wholesale	03/51		
MICRONICS JAPAN CO. LTD	6871	electrical	09/30		
MIKASA SEIYAKU CO. LTD	4542	pharmacy	03/31		
MILBON CO. LTD	4919	chemicals	12/20		
MINATO ELECTRONICS INC.	6862	electrical	03/31		
MITSUBOSHI CO. LTD	5820	non-fer ml	03/31		
MIYA CO. LTD	9901	retailsale	02/28		
MIYACHI TECHNOS CORP.	6885	electrical	09/30		

Name	Code No.	SIC Industry Name	Financial Year	Market	Date
MIYOTA CO. LTD	7770	precision	03/31		
MK SEIKO CO. LTD	5906	metal pro	03/20		
MONTECARLO CO. LTD	7569	retailsale	03/31		
MORINAGA DEVELOPMENT CO. LTD	8856	real estat	03/31		
MORISHITA CO. LTD	3594	textile	03/31		
MORITEX CORP.	7714	precision	03/31		
MORIYA CORP.	1798	constructn	03/31		
MOSHI MOSHI HOTLINE INC.	4708	service	03/31		
MR JOHN CO. LTD	7543	retailsale	02/20		
MURAKI CORP.	7477	wholesale	03/31		
MURO CORP.	7264	trans eqp	03/31		
MUSASHI CO. LTD	7521	wholesale	03/31		
MUSASHI SEIMITSU INDUSTRY CO. LTD	7220	trans eqp	03/31		
MUTO SEIKO CO.	7927	chemicals	03/31		
MYCAL HOKKAIDO CORP.	*7512	retailsale	02/28	TSE 2nd	1998/11/19
N.E. CHEMCAT CORP.	4106	chemicals	03/31		
N.I.C. CORP.	9652	service	03/31		
NADEX CO. LTD	7453	wholesale	04/30		
NAGAILEBEN CO. LTD	7447	wholesale	08/31		
NAGANO JAPAN RADIO CO. LTD	6878	electrical	03/31		
NAGANO KEIKI CO. LTD	7715	precision	03/31		
NAGANO TOKYU DEPARTMENT STORE CO. LTD	9829	retailsale	01/31		
NAGASE BROTHERS INC.	9733	service	03/31		
NAGAWA CO.LTD	9663	service	03/31		
NAKABOHTEC CORROSION PROTECTING CO. LTD	1787	constructn	03/31		
NAKANO REFRIGERATORS CO. LTD	6411	machinery	12/31		
NANBU PLASTICS CO. LTD	7880	chemicals	03/31		
NANNO CONSTRUCTION CO. LTD	1783	constructn	09/30		
NANSIN CO. LTD	7399	trans eqp	03/31		
NATOCO CO. LTD	4627	chemicals	10/31		
NAVITAS CO. LTD	6276	machinery	03/31		
NBC INDUSTRIES CO. LTD	3534	textile	03/31		
NET ONE SYSTEMS CO. LTD	7518	wholesale	03/31		
NEW COSMOS ELECTRIC CO. LTD	6824	electrical	03/31		
NEW JAPAN RADIO CO. LTD	6911	electrical	03/31		
NF CORP.	6864	electrical	03/31		
NHK PRECISION CO. LTD	7290	trans eqp	03/31		
NHK SALES CO. LTD	7563	wholesale	03/31		
NICE CLAUP CO. LTD	7598	retailsale	01/31		
NICHIDEN CORP.	9902	wholesale	03/31		
NICHII GAKKAN CO.	9792	service	03/31		
NICHIRYOKU CO. LTD	7578	retailsale	03/31		

Name	Code No.	SIC Industry Name	Financial Year	Market	Date
NICHIYU GIKEN KOGYO CO. LTD	4961	chemicals	03/31		
NIHON DENKEI CO. LTD	9908	wholesale	03/31		
NIHON FORM SERVICE CO. LTD	7869	other prot	09/30		
NIHON JUMBO CO. LTD	9677	service	09/30		
NIHON KAIHEIKI IND. CO. LTD	6943	electrical	03/31		
NIHON KOGYO CO. LTD	5279	glass/cera	03/31		
NIHON PLAST CO. LTD	7291	trans eqp	03/31		
NIHON SEIMITSU CO. LTD	7771	precision	03/31		
NIHON UNICOM CORP.	8744	sec/ commod	03/31		
NIKKATO CORP.	5367	glass/cera	03/31		
NIKKO SANSO CO. LTD	4101	chemicals	03/31		
NIKKODO CO. LTD	9841	wholesale	03/20		
NIPPAN RENTAL CO. LTD	4669	service	08/31		
NIPPI INC.	7932	other prot	03/31		
NIPPO LTD	9913	wholesale	03/31		
NIPPON ANTENNA CO. LTD	6930	electrical	03/31		
NIPPON COMPUTER SYSTEMS CORP.	9711	service	03/31		
NIPPON DOKEN CO. LTD	1998	constructn	06/30		
NIPPON FILING CO. LTD	7933	other prot	03/31		
NIPPON FURNACE KOGYO KAISHA LTD	6494	machinery	09/30		
NIPPON KATAN CO. LTD	5613	iron/steel	03/31		
NIPPON KODOSHI CORP.	3891	pulp/paper	03/31		
NIPPON KUCHO SERVICE CO. LTD	4658	service	03/31		
NIPPON LOGISTECH CORP.	9323	trans servs	03/31		
NIPPON MIC CO. LTD	9712	service	03/31		
NIPPON PALLET POOL CO. LTD	4690	service	03/31		
NIPPON SHIKIZAI INC.	4920	chemicals	02/28		
NIPPON STEEL SEMICONDUCTOR CORP.	6939	electrical	12/31		
NIPPON SYSTEMWARE CO. LTD	9739	service	03/31		
NIPPON ZENITH PIPE CO. LTD	5274	glass/cera	05/31		
NIRECO CORP.	6863	electrical	03/31		
NISCA CORP.	6415	machinery	03/31		
NISHIKAWA KEISOKU CO. LTD	7500	wholesale	06/30		
NISHIMATSUYA CHAIN CO. LTD	7545	retailsale	02/20		
NISSEI ASB MACHINE CO. LTD	6284	machinery	09/30		
NISSHIN ELECTRONICS SERVICE CO. LTD	4713	service	03/31		
NISSHO INTER LIFE CO. LTD	1986	constructn	02/20		
NISSO INDUSTRY CO. LTD	7881	other prot	03/31		
NITTOBEST CORP.	2877	foods	03/31		
NITTOH BION CO. LTD	4032	chemicals	06/30		
NITTOKU ENGINEERING CO. LTD	6145	machinery	03/31		

Name	Code No.	SIC Industry Name	Financial Year	Market	Date
NJK CORP.	9784	service	03/31		
NOEVIR CO. LTD	4916	chemicals	09/20		
NOJIMA CO. LTD	7419	retailsale	04/20		
NORITA OPTICAL CO. LTD	7742	precision	12/31		
NOVA CORP.	4655	service	03/31		
NS ENVIRONMENTAL SCIENCE CONSULTANT CORP.	4675	service	09/30		
OA SYSTEM PLAZA CO. LTD	7491	retailsale	09/30		
OBARA CORP.	6877	electrical	09/30		
ODAWARA ENGINEERING CO. LTD	6149	machinery	12/31		
ODELIC CO. LTD	6889	electrical	03/31		
OGURA CLUTCH CO. LTD	6408	machinery	03/31		
OHDE SANGYO CO. LTD	7900	other prot	03/31		
OHI SEISAKUSHO CO. LTD	7293	trans eqp	03/31		
OHKI CO. LTD	8120	wholesale	03/31		
OHMORIYA CO. LTD	2917	foods	09/30		
OHMOTO GUMI CO. LTD	1793	constructn	03/31		
OHMURA SHIGYO CO. LTD	3953	pulp/paper	03/31		
OI ELECTRIC CO. LTD	6822	electrical	03/31		
OK FOOD INDUSTRY CO. LTD	2905	foods	03/31		
OKATO SHOJI CO. LTD	8745	sec/ commod	03/31		
OKINAWA CELLULAR TELEPHONE CO.	9436	comunicton	03/31		
ONEX CORP.	5987	metal pro	06/30		
ONOKEN CO. LTD	7414	wholesale	03/31		
OPTEX CO. LTD	6914	electrical	12/31		
ORIGIN TOSHU CO. LTD	7579	retailsale	03/31		
ORII CORP.	6283	machinery	05/31		
OTA FLORICULTURE AUCTION CO. LTD	7555	wholesale	03/31		
OTAKE CORP.	7434	wholesale	05/31		
OTANI KOGYO CO. LTD	5939	metal pro	03/31		
OTSUKA KAGU LTD	8186	retailsale	12/31		
OZAKI FINE CHEMICAL CORP.	7899	chemicals	04/30		
OZU CORP.	7487	wholesale	05/31		
PALTAC CORP.	8283	wholesale	09/30		
PALTEK CORP.	7587	wholesale	12/31		
PARK24 CO. LTD	4666	service	10/31		
PARKER CORP.	9845	wholesale	03/31		
PASSPORT CO. LTD	7577	retailsale	02/28		
PCA CORP.	9629	service	03/31		
PEOPLE CO. LTD	4643	service	02/28		
PEOPLE CO. LTD	7865	other prot	03/20		
PETROLUB INTERNATIONAL CO. LTD	5015	oil/coal	03/31		

Name	Code No.	SIC Industry Name	Financial Year	Market	Date
PHOTRON LTD	6879	electrical	03/31		
PICOI CO. LTD	1769	constructn	01/31		
PLACO CO. LTD	6347	machinery	03/31		
PLAZA CREATE CO. LTD	7502	wholesale	03/31		
PLENUS CO. LTD	9945	retailsale	02/28		
POWDERTECH CO LTD	5695	iron/steel	03/31		
PREC INSTITUTE INC.	4701	service	03/31		
PULSTEC INDUSTRIAL CO. LTD	6894	electrical	03/31		
Q'SAI CO. LTD	2596	foods	02/28		
RALSE CO. LTD	9948	retailsale	02/28		
RECRUIT COSMOS CO. LTD	8844	real estat	03/31		
REGAL CORP.	7983	other prot	03/31		
RESORTTRUST INC.	4681	service	03/31		
RIGHT ON CO. LTD	7445	retailsale	08/20		
RIKENGREEN CO. LTD	9992	wholesale	03/31		
RION CO. LTD	6823	electrical	03/31		
RISO KAGAKU CORP.	6413	machinery	03/31		
RISO KYOIKU CO. LTD	4714	service	06/30		
ROKI TECHNO CO. LTD	6296	machinery	03/31		
RORZE CORP.	6323	machinery	02/28		
ROYAL ELECTRIC CO. LTD	6593	electrical	03/31		
RYOHIN KEIKAKU CO. LTD	*7453	retailsale	02/28	TSE 2nd	1998/12/14
RYOMO SYSTEMS CO. LTD	9691	service	03/31		
RYOYU KEISAN CO. LTD	4685	service	03/31		
S.E.S. CO. LTD	6290	machinery	09/30		
SACOS CORP.	9641	service	03/31		
SADO STEAM SHIP CO. LTD	9176	marn trans	12/31		
SAFTEC CO. LTD	7464	wholesale	03/31		
SAGAMI HAM CO. LTD	2298	foods	03/31		
SAINT MARC CO. LTD	7479	retailsale	03/31		
SAISON INFORMATION SYSTEMS CO. LTD	9640	service	03/31		
SAIZERIYA CO. LTD	7581	retailsale	08/31		
SAKAE ELECTRONICS CORP.	9567	wholesale	03/31		
SAKURAI LTD	7255	trans eqp	03/31		
SALOMON & TAYLOR MADE CO. LTD	7470	wholesale	12/31		
SAMPEI CONSTRUCTION CO. LTD	1908	constructn	03/31		
SANKO CO. LTD	6964	electrical	03/31		
SANKO GOSEI LTD	7888	chemicals	05/31		
SANKO JUNYAKU CO. LTD	8126	wholesale	03/31		
SANKO SANGYO CO. LTD	7922	other prot	03/31		
SANKYO FRONTIER CO. LTD	9639	service	03/31		
SANKYO RIKAGAKU CO. LTD	5383	glass/cera	03/31		
SAN-MIC CHIYODA CORP.	7439	wholesale	03/31		
SANRIN CO. LTD	7486	wholesale	03/31		

Name	Code No.	SIC Industry Name	Financial Year	Market	Date
SANRITSU CORP.	9366	trans servs	03/31		
SANSHIN CORP.	1984	constructn	03/31		
SANSO ELECTRIC CO. LTD	6518	electrical	03/31		
SANTO CO. LTD	1788	constructn	06/30		
SANWADO CORP.	7430	retailsale	02/20		
SANYEI CORP.	8119	wholesale	03/31		
SANYO DEP'T STORE CO. LTD	8257	retailsale	02/28		
SANYO KOGYO CO. LTD	8109	wholesale	03/31		
SANYO PAX CO. LTD	7876	chemicals	05/31		
SANYO CONSTRUCTION CO. LTD	1841	constructn	09/30		
SAPPORO CLINICAL LABORATORY INC.	9776	service	03/31		
SAPPORO FOOD CENTER CO. LTD	7465	retailsale	03/31		
SARI CORP.	9958	retailsale	03/31		
SATO FOODS INDUSTRIES CO. LTD	2814	foods	03/31		
SATOH & CO. LTD	9996	wholesale	03/31		
SATOHIDE CORP.	1874	constructn	03/31		
SAWAI PHARMACEUTICAL CO. LTD	4555	pharmacy	03/31		
SAWAKO CORP.	1784	constructn	07/31		
SAZABY INC.	7553	retailsale	03/31		
SDS BIOTECH K.K.	4952	chemicals	12/31		
SEED CO. LTD	7743	precision	03/31		
SEIJO CORP.	7429	retailsale	09/30		
SEIKAGAKU CORP.	4548	pharmacy	03/31		
SEIKO CHEMICAL INDUSTRIES CO. LTD	4964	chemicals	03/31		
SEIKO CORP.	6286	machinery	03/31		
SEIWA CORP.	7531	wholesale	12/31		
SEKI TECHNOTRON CORP.	7457	wholesale	03/31		
SEKICHU CO. LTD	9976	retailsale	02/20		
SEKIDO CO. LTD	9878	retailsale	02/20		
SEKIWA REAL, ESTATE LTD	8846	reat estat	01/31		
SEMBA TOHKA INDUSTRIES CO. LTD	2916	foods	03/31		
SENKON LOGISTICS CO. LTD	9051	land trans	03/31		
SETA CORP.	4670	service	05/31		
SHAKLEE JAPAN K.K.	8205	wholesale	03/31		
SHIBAURA ELECTRONICS CO. LTD	6957	electrical	03/31		
SHIBAZAKI SEISAKUSHO LTD	5904	metal pro	12/31		
SHIDAX FOOD SERVICE CORP.	9798	service	03/31		
SHIGEMATSU WORKS CO. LTD	7980	other prot	03/31		
SHIGI SHIPBUILDING CO. LTD	7052	trans eqp	09/30		
SHIMOJIMA CO. LTD	7482	wholesale	03/31		
SHINAGAWA SOKO TATEMONO CO. LTD	9314	trans servs	02/28		
SHINGAKUKAI CO. LTD	9760	service	03/31		

Name	Code No.	SIC Industry Name	Financial Year	Market	Date
SHIN-HOKOKU STEEL CORP.	5542	iron/steel	12/31		
SHINKI CO. LTD	8568	financials	03/31		
SHINKIGOSEI CO. LTD	7929	chemicals	03/31		
SHINKO SUGAR CO. LTD	2113	foods	03/31		
SHINKO TELECOM ENGINEERING CORP.	1758	constructn	03/31		
SHINMEI ELECTRIC CO. LTD	6956	electrical	01/31		
SHINNIHON GAS CORP.	9542	elec.pow/ gas	03/31		
SHIN-NIPPON M. & O. CONSULTANT CO. LTD	9768	service	03/31		
SHINPO CO. LTD	5903	metal pro	06/30		
SHINSEIDO CO. LTD	7415	retailsale	02/28		
SHINWA CO. LTD	6880	electrical	03/31		
SHINWA NAIKO KAIUN KAISHA LTD	9180	marn trans	03/31		
SHIZUOKA SUBARU MOTOR CO. LTD	7473	retailsale	03/31		
SHOBUNSHA PUBLICATIONS INC.	9475	other prot	03/31		
SHOEISHA CO. LTD	9478	other prot	03/31		
SHOKUBUN CO. LTD	9969	retailsale	03/31		
SHOWA INFORMATION SYSTEMS CO. LTD	6922	electrical	12/31		
SHUEI YOBIKO CO. LTD	4678	service	03/31		
SHUGAKUSHA CO. LTD	9634	service	03/31		
SIGMA KOKI CO. LTD	7713	precision	03/31		
SIGMA INC.	4712	service	03/31		
SK KAKEN CO. LTD	4628	chemicals	03/31		
SODA AROMATIC CO. LTD	4965	chemicals	03/31		
SOFTWARE RESEARCH ASSOCIATES INC.	9714	service	03/31		
SOKEN CO. LTD	7413	wholesale	03/31		
SONOCOM CO. LTD	7902	other prot	03/31		
SOPHIA SYSTEMS CO. LTD	6942	electrical	03/31		
SOSHIN ELECTRIC CO. LTD	6938	electrical	03/31		
SOTETSU KIGYO CO. LTD	9668	service	03/31		
SPACE CO. LTD	9622	service	12/31		
SPANCRETE CORP.	5277	glass/cera	03/31		
SPK CORP.	7466	wholesale	03/31		
SQUARE CO. LTD	9620	service	03/31		
STARTS CORP.	8850	real estat	03/31		
STEP CO. LTD	9795	service	09/30		
SUBARU CO. LTD	9778	service	02/28		
SUGAI ENTERTAINMENT CO. LTD	4650	service	03/31		
SUIDO KIKO KAISHA LTD.	6403	machinery	03/31		
SUKEGAWA ELECTRIC CO. LTD	7711	precision	09/30		
SUMIDA ELECTRIC CO. LTD	*6817	electrical	12/31	TSE 2nd	1998/12/03

Name	Code No.	SIC Industry Name	Financial Year	Market	Date
SUMISHO AUTO LEASING CORP.	4703	service	03/31		
SUMISHO ELECTRONICS CO. LTD	7556	wholesale	03/31		
SUMIYA CO. LTD	9939	retailsale	03/31		
SUN MESSE CO. LTD	7883	other prot	03/31		
SUN·LIFE CORP.	4656	service	03/31		
SUNDAY CO. LTD	7450	retailsale	02/20		
SUN-WA TECHNOS CORP.	8137	wholesale	03/31		
SUPER TOOL CO. LTD	5990	metal pro	03/15		
SURUGA CO. LTD	7874	chemicals	03/31		
SUZUDEN CORP.	7480	wholesale	03/31		
SUZUKI CONSTRUCTION CO. LTD	1995	constructn	03/31		
SUZUKI SHUTTER MANUFACTURING CO. LTD	5920	metal pro	03/31		
SYSTEMSOFT CORP.	7527	wholesale	03/31		
T&E SOFT INC.	9611	service	09/30		
T&K TOKA CO. LTD	4636	chemicals	03/31		
T.D.I. CO. LTD	9638	service	03/31		
T.HASEGAWA CO. LTD	4958	chemicals	09/30		
T.KAWABE & CO. LTD	8123	wholesale	03/31		
T.O. OGASAWARA CO. LTD	9812	wholesale	05/31		
TAIHO INDUSTRIES CO. LTD	4953	chemicals	03/31		
TAIRAYA CORP.	7520	retailsale	02/28		
TAISEI CO. LTD	4649	service	03/31		
TAISEI ONCHO CO. LTD	1904	constructn	03/31		
TAIYO BUSSAN KAISHA LTD	9941	wholesale	09/30		
TAIYO FIRE AND MARINE INS. CO. LTD	8764	insurance	03/31		
TAIYO INK MFG CO. LTD	4626	chemicals	03/31		
TAIYO KISOKOGYO CO. LTD	1758	constructn	01/31		
TAIYO KOGYO CO. LTD	7449	wholesale	09/30		
TAIYO WOOLEN SPINNING CO. LTD	3211	textile	09/30		
TAKACHIHO CO. LTD	8225	wholesale	03/31		
TAKAHASHI CURTAIN WALL CORP.	1994	constructn	12/31		
TAKAMISAWA CO. LTD	5283	glass/cera	06/30		
TAKAMISAWA CYBERNETICS CO. LTD	6424	machinery	03/31		
TAKARABUNE CO. LTD	8169	retailsale	08/31		
TAKASE CORP.	9087	land trans	03/31		
TAKASHO CO. LTD	7590	wholesale	01/20		
TAKEDA MACHINERY CO. LTD	6150	machinery	05/31		
TAKEFUJI CORP.	*8564	financials	03/31	TSE 1st	1998/12/02
TAKEI CO. LTD	5286	glass/cera	06/30		
TAKIZAWA HAM CO. LTD	2293	foods	03/31		
TAMA ELECTRIC CO. LTD	6940	electrical	03/31		
TAMRON CO. LTD	7740	precision	12/31		

Name	SIC Code No.	Industry Name	Financial Year	Market	Date
TANABE INDUSTRIES LTD	1828	constructn	03/31		
TANABE MANAGEMENT CONSULTING CO. LTD	9644	service	03/31		
TANAKA GALVANIZING CO. LTD	5980	metal pro	03/31		
TATSUMI CORP.	7268	trans eqp	03/31		
TAYA CO. LTD	4679	service	03/31		
TDC SOFTWARE ENGINEERING INC.	4687	service	03/31		
TECHNOL EIGHT CO. LTD	7288	trans eqp	03/31		
TECHNOL SEVEN CO. LTD	6852	electrical	03/31		
TECMO LTD	9650	service	03/31		
TEITO RUBBER LTD	5188	rubber	03/31		
TENNEX CORP.	7289	trans eqp	03/31		
TENOX CORP.	1905	constructn	03/31		
TENRYU SAW MFG CO. LTD	5945	metal pro	03/31		
TERASHIMA CO. LTD	7586	retailsale	02/28		
TESCO CO. LTD	4226	constructn	11/30		
THANKS JAPAN CORP.	7548	retailsale	02/20		
THE BANK OF JAPAN	8301	banks	03/31		
THE DAIEI PHOTO INC.	4702	service	02/28		
THE JAPAN CENTRAL REAL ESTATE CO. LTD	8805	real estat	12/31		
THE KAMOGAWA GRAND HOTEL LTD	9695	service	03/31		
THE OSAKA PORT DEVELOPMENT CO. LTD	8810	real estat	03/31		
THE TAIKO BANK LTD	8573	banks	03/31		
THE YONKYU CO. LTD	9955	wholesale	03/31		
THK CO. LTD	6481	machinery	03/31		
THREE F CO. LTD	7544	retailsale	02/28		
TIEMCO LTD	7501	wholesale	11/30		
TIETECH CO. LTD	6873	electrical	03/31		
TOA FENCE CO. LTD	7540	wholesale	03/31		
TOBA INC.	7472	wholesale	03/31		
TOCALO CO. LTD	5961	metal pro	03/31		
TOEI REEFER LINE LTD	9133	marn trans	03/31		
TOHO LAMAC CO. LTD	7422	wholesale	12/20		
TOHO PHARMACEUTICAL CO. LTD	8129	wholesale	03/31		
TOHOKEN SYSTEM ENGIN. CORP.	1990	constructn	03/31		
TOHOKU CHEMICAL CO. LTD	7446	wholesale	09/30		
TOHOKU ENTERPRISE CO. LTD	1772	constructn	03/31		
TOHOKU STEEL CO. LTD	5484	iron/steel	03/31		
TOIN CORP.	7923	other prot	03/31		
TOKAI ALUMINUM FOIL CO. LTD	5756	non-fer ml	03/31		
TOKAI SEINO TRANSPORTATION CO. LTD	9038	land trans	03/31		
TOKATSU FOODS CO. LTD	2909	foods	03/31		

Name	Code No.	SIC Industry Name	Financial Year	Market	Date
TOKEN CORP.	1766	constructn	06/30		
TOKKI CORP.	9813	wholesale	06/30		
TOKYO CATHODE LABORATORY CO. LTD	6868	electrical	03/31		
TOKYO DEN-ON CO. LTD	9847	wholesale	03/31		
TOKYO DERICA CO. LTD	9990	retailsale	03/31		
TOKYO KIHO CO. LTD	7597	wholesale	03/31		
TOKYO KOHTETSU CO. LTD	5448	iron/steel	03/31		
TOKYO KOZOSUSHI CO. LTD	9954	retailsale	03/31		
TOKYO LITHMATIC CORP.	7861	other prot	12/31		
TOKYO MISAWA HOMES CO., LTD	1915	constructn	03/31		
TOMEN ELECTRONICS CORP.	7558	wholesale	03/31		
TOMITA CO. LTD	8147	wholesale	03/31		
TOMITA ELECTRIC CO. LTD	6898	electrical	01/31		
TOMOE ENGINEERING CO. LTD	6309	machinery	10/31		
TOMY CO. LTD	7867	other prot	03/31		
TONE GEO TECH CO. LTD	1800	constructn	03/31		
TONICHI CABLE LTD	5818	non-fer ml	03/31		
TOSHIN HOUSING CO. LTD	1754	constructn	06/30		
TOTECH CORP.	9960	wholesale	03/31		
TOWA PHARMACEUTICAL CO. LTD	4553	pharmacy	03/31		
TOYO KOKEN K.K.	6352	machinery	03/31		
TOYO OFFICEMATION INC.	9970	wholesale	03/31		
TOYOKUNI ELECTRIC CABLE CO. LTD	5811	non-fer ml	03/31		
TRANCOM CO. LTD	9058	land trans	03/31		
TRAVELER CORP.	9838	retailsale	03/31		
TREND MICRO INC.	4704	service	12/31		
TSUCHIYA TWOBY HOME CO. LTD	1753	constructn	10/31		
TSURUHA CO. LTD	7573	retailsale	05/15		
TSUZUKU DENSAN CO. LTD	9884	wholesale	03/31		
TSUKUKI TSUSHIN GIJUTSU CO. LTD	1991	constructn	03/31		
UCHIDA ESCO CO. LTD	4699	service	07/20		
UEMATSU SHOKAI CO. LTD	9914	wholesale	03/20		
UEX LTD	9888	wholesale	03/31		
UHT CORP.	6148	machinery	04/30		
UNICO LEASING CO. LTD	8569	financials	12/31		
UNIDUX INC.	9897	wholesale	03/31		
UNIMAT OFFISCO CORP.	7560	retailsale	03/31		
UNION PAINT CO. LTD	4622	chemicals	03/31		
UNIPRES CORP.	5949	trans eqp	03/31		
UNIPULSE CORP.	6842	electrical	09/30		
UORIKI CO. LTD	7596	retailsale	03/31		
UP INC.	9630	service	03/31		
URBAN CORP.	8868	real estat	03/31		

Name	SIC Code No.	Industry Name	Financial Year	Market	Date
USC CORP.	9844	wholesale	03/31		
VENTURE LINK CO. LTD	9609	service	05/31		
VERTEX LINK CORP.	9816	wholesale	03/31		
VITEC CO. LTD	9957	wholesale	03/31		
WAKOU SHOKUHIN CO. LTD	2813	foods	12/31		
WARABEYA NICHIYO CO. LTD	2918	foods	02/28		
WATANABE GUMI CO. LTD	1807	constructn	03/31		
WATT MANN CO. LTD	9927	retailsale	03/31		
WEDS CO. LTD	7551	wholesale	03/31		
WILSON LEARNING WORLDWIDE INC.	9610	service	03/31		
WOODLAND CORP.	4652	service	03/31		
WORKMAN CO. LTD	7564	retailsale	03/31		
Y.A.C. CO. LTD	6298	machinery	03/31		
YACHIYO INDUSTRY CO. LTD	7298	trans eqp	03/31		
YAESU MUSEN CO. LTD	6821	electrical	03/31		
YAGI CORP.	3595	textile	03/20		
YAHOO JAPAN CORP.	4689	service	03/31		
YAMADA DENKI CO. LTD	9831	retailsale	03/31		
YAMADAI CORP.	7426	wholesale	03/31		
YAMAICHI ELECTRONICS CO. LTD	6941	electrical	03/31		
YAMAKA ELECTRIC CONSTRUCTION CO. LTD	1789	constructn	09/30		
YAMAKI CORP.	7418	retailsale	02/20		
YAMATO INDUSTRY CO. LTD	7886	chemicals	03/31		
YAMAU CO. LTD	5284	glass/cera	03/31		
YAMAX CORP.	5285	glass/cera	03/31		
YAMAYA CORP.	9994	retailsale	03/31		
YAMAZAKI CO. LTD	6147	machinery	03/31		
YAMAZAKI CONSTRUCTION CO. LTD	1902	constructn	03/31		
YAMAZAWA CO. LTD	9993	retailsale	03/31		
YOKOHAMA CHIKAGAI CO. LTD	8867	real estat	03/31		
YOKOHAMA GYORUI CO. LTD	7443	wholesale	03/31		
YOKOHAMA MARUUO CO. LTD	8045	wholesale	03/31		
YOKOHAMA STEEL CO. LTD	7410	wholesale	03/31		
YOSHICON CO. LTD	5280	glass/cera	03/31		
YOSHINOYA D&C CO. LTD	9861	retailsale	02/28		
YOSHITAKE INC.	6488	machinery	03/31		
YUSEN AIR & SEA SERVICE CO. LTD	9370	trans servs	03/31		
YUTAKA GIKEN CO. LTD	7229	trans eqp	03/31		
YUTAKA SHOJI CO. LTD	8747	sec/ commod	03/31		
ZAOH CO. LTD	9986	wholesale	03/31		
ZENSHO CO. LTD	7550	retailsale	03/31		
ZYPRO INC.	7511	wholesale	03/31		

Appendix 2
Companies visited

JASDAQ Companies – Direct Interviews List

19 November 1998 (Thursday)
People K.K.
Mrs Chizuko Kiribuchi
CEO

24 November 1998 (Tuesday)
ISB
Mr Moriyasu Wakao
Chairman
Mr Masaaki Komatsu
President

25 November 1998 (Wednesday)
TOMY
Mr Shigemi Sugaya
Executive Director & General Manager
Corporate Strategy

26 November 1998 (Thursday)
Cresco
Mr Masahiro Urasaki
President

27 November 1998 (Friday)
Hikari Tsushin
Mr Yasumitsu Shigeta
President & CEO

1 December 1998 (Tuesday)
Park 24
Mr Kiyoshi Nishikawa
President

2 December 1998 (Wednesday)
Shinwa
Mr Yoshifumi Naito
President & CEO

3 December 1998 (Thursday)
Green House
Mrs Chiaki Tanuma
President

4 December 1998 (Friday)
Tiemco
Mr Sadahiko Sakai
President

7 December 1998 (Monday)
ARUZE
Mr Sumio Manaka
Deputy Manager/Accounting Division

8 December 1998 (Tuesday)
Unipulse
Mr Takumi Yoshimoto
President

9 December 1998 (Wednesday)
Moritex
Mr Yuhkoh Morito
Chairman of the Board & CEO

14 December 1998 (Monday)
Paltek
Mr Tadahito Takahashi
President

14 December 1998 (Monday)
YAHOO! Japan
Masahiro Inoue
President & CEO

15 December 1998 (Tuesday)
PCA
Mr Masao Kawashima
President

17 December 1998 (Thursday)
Origin Tohshu
Mr Hideo Anzawa
President

18 December 1998 (Friday)
FANCL
Mr Kenji Ikemori
President

22 December 1998 (Tuesday)
Q'Sai
Mr Hiroaki Ohishi
Director/Corporate Administration
  Division

24 December 1998 (Thursday)
Altech
Mr Minoru Nakamura
President

24 December 1998 (Thursday)
Ferrotec
Mr Akira Yamamura
President & CEO

25 December 1998 (Friday)
Vitec
Mr Syunichi Shirai
President

29 December 1998 (Tuesday)
DAIOHS
Mr Shin-ichi Ohkubo
Chairman & CEO

19 January 1999 (Tuesday)
H.I.S.
Mr Hideki Kumon
Manager/President's Advisory Board

26 January 1999 (Tuesday)
Himiko
Mr Nobuyuki Susuki
Manager/Accounting Dept.

Appendix 3
Criteria of Selection of the
100 Samurai Companies

1. Past performance. To qualify Jasdaq companies had to show 3 consecutive years of sales growth of 5% or more; and also 3 years of growth of pre-tax profits (before extraordinary items) by 5% or more. The period considered was the most recent 3 years for which companies had reported. The Quick Information Sharing service (Nikkei's financial information vendor) and its CD-ROM (Nikkei Kaishajoho, Autumn 1998 Version) dated end September 1998 was used. Altogether 70 companies qualified. They are marked with ticks in the table.

2. Forecast earnings. To qualify Jasdaq companies had to have reported to the Japan Securities Dealers Association (JASDA) that they expected as follows:
- Sales to grow by 6% or more in the current year ending in 1999.
- Pre-tax profits (before extraordinary items) also to grow by over 6% in the same period.
- Pre-tax profits to be a record for the period.

Altogether 28 companies qualified under these forward-looking criteria. They are marked with circles in the table.

3. Exceptional cases. Originally, the first criterion provided us with 72 companies. Two pulled out of our list by mutual agreement, due to business difficulties. We filled the 2 empty slots with Shinwa, which failed to qualify due to exceptional management problems (which had been put right), and Sazaby, whose exclusion appeared anomalous given the success of the company in marketing in Tokyo.

Criteria List

	check	code	name				code	name
1	○	4700	Accès		17	✓	9698	Creo
2	✓	7918	Akatsuki Printing		18	✓	4674	Cresco
3	○	4641	Altech		19	○	9926	Daika
4	○	8047	AM Japan		20	○	4653	Daiohs
5	○	7562	Anrakutei		21	✓	6884	Digital Electronics
6	✓	7595	Argo Graphics		22	○	4921	Fancl
7	✓	7873	Arrk		23	○	6890	Ferrotec
8	○	6425	Aruze		24	✓	4662	Focus Systems
9	○	9799	Asahi Intelligence Service		25	○	7471	Fuji
10	✓	9669	Aucnet		26	○	7864	Fuji Seal
11	✓	7546	Bamiyan		27	✓	5384	Fujimi
12	✓	7588	C Two-Network		28	○	8871	Gold Crest
13	✓	6892	Citizen Electronics		29	✓	6886	Graphic Products
14	✓	2224	Como		30	○	9689	Green House
15	✓	6905	Cosel		31	✓	9603	H.I.S.
16	✓	5187	Create Medic		32	✓	9435	Hikari Tsushin
					33	✓	9892	Himiko

34	✓	1379 Hokuto		70	✓	7502 Plaza Create
35	○	9702 ISB		71	✓	2596 Q'Sai
36	✓	6314 Ishii Tool & Engineering		72	✓	9948 Ralse
37	✓	7476 Iuchi Seieido		73	○	7445 Right On
38	○	7408 Jamco		74	✓	7453 Ryohin Keikaku
39	✓	9889 Japan Business Computer		75	✓	9691 Ryomo Systems
40	✓	7575 Japan Lifeline		76	✓	7479 Saint Marc
41	✓	9651 Japan Process Development		77	○	7581 Saizeriya
42	✓	8204 Jonathan's		78	✓	1784 Sawako
43	✓	1376 Kaneko Seeds		79		7553 Sazaby
44	✓	6919 Kel		80	✓	8568 Shinki
45	✓	4643 KK People		81		6880 Shinwa
46	✓	7554 Kourakuen		82	✓	9795 Step
47	✓	6881 Kyoden		83	✓	8137 Sun-Wa Technos
48	✓	6874 Kyoritsu Electric		84	✓	7520 Tairaya
49	✓	7524 Marche		85	✓	4626 Taiyo Ink Mfg.
50	✓	9875 Matsumotokiyoshi		86	○	4687 TDC Software Engineering
51	○	9887 Matsuya Foods		87	○	7586 Terashima
52	✓	6875 Megachips		88	✓	7501 Tiemco
53	✓	7714 Moritex		89	✓	5961 Tocalo
54	✓	9652 N.I.C.		90	✓	7861 Tokyo Lithmatic
55	✓	7435 Nadex		91	✓	7867 Tomy
56	✓	6878 Nagano Japan Radio		92	✓	9838 Traveler
57	✓	7518 Net One Systems		93	○	4704 Trend Micro
58	✓	9792 Nichii Gakkan		94	✓	1753 Tsuchiya Twoby Home
59	✓	9739 Nippon Systemware		95	✓	7573 Tsuruha
60	✓	7545 Nishimatsuya Chain		96	✓	6148 UHT
61	○	9436 Okinawa Cellular Telephone		97	✓	6842 Unipulse
62	✓	6914 Optex		98	✓	9957 Vitec
63	○	7579 Origin Toshu		99	○	4689 Yahoo Japan
64	✓	8186 Otsuka Kagu		100	○	7550 Zensho
65	○	7587 Paltek				
66	✓	4666 Park24			✓	70
67	○	7577 Passport			○	28
68	✓	9629 PCA				2
69	✓	7865 People KK